THE MILD
MURDERER

By the Same Author

THE MILD
MURDERER

The True Story
of the
Dr. Crippen Case

TOM CULLEN

Illustrated with Photographs

BOSTON
HOUGHTON MIFFLIN COMPANY
1977

TO JOHN HILL, OF WILDY'S,
WITHOUT WHOSE HELP THIS BOOK
COULD NOT HAVE BEEN WRITTEN

Library of Congress Cataloging in Publication Data

Cullen, Tom A   The mild murderer.

1. Crippen, Hawley Harvey, 1862–1910. 2. Crime and
criminals — England — London — Biography. 3. Murder —
England — London — Cast studies. I. Title.
HV6248.C687C84   364.1'523'0924   77-24440
ISBN 0-395-25776-X

Printed in the United States of America

V 10 9 8 7 6 5 4 3 2 1

CONTENTS

'I have no natural empathy with men who dissect their wives' bodies and bury their remains in the cellar, but . . . I cannot help wishing that Crippen had been able to slip away, to start a new life somewhere with his devoted Ethel . . . He must have had something that was not so much meat for the hangman.'

—J. B. Priestley, *The Edwardians*

AUTHOR'S NOTE

The protagonist of this book (the word 'hero' almost slipped out) was christened Hawley Harvey Crippen; but he was known to some, notably to his wife and her friends, as 'Peter' Crippen, the wife being of the opinion that 'Hawley' sounded faintly ridiculous. But then Mrs Crippen was no respecter of names. In her own case she rang the changes from Kunigunde to Cunagunda, from Cora to Corrinne, before settling on 'Belle Elmore' as her stage name and the name by which she wished to be known to her friends.

To avoid confusion I shall stick to 'Hawley' and to 'Belle' whenever christian names are used. More often than not, however, the protagonist will be referred to in these pages as just plain 'Crippen', the honorific prefix 'Dr' being dropped. In this the author is following the practice of Polk's *Medical and Surgical Register of the United States*, then the *vade mecum* of the American medical profession, which after 1900 scrubs Crippen from its pages. The unadorned 'Crippen' has also seemed preferable to the practice followed by *The Times* of putting the 'Dr' in front of Crippen's name in quotation marks. In point of fact, Crippen after 1894 ceased to practice as a medical doctor, but became a quack of the more flagrant variety, operating chiefly as the promoter of patent medicines.

Anyone writing a book about Crippen is bound to be indebted to *The Trial of Hawley Harvey Crippen* in the Notable Trials Series edited and with an excellent introduction by Filson Young. (Young's introduction was later reprinted as a separate essay in the Penguin Series, *Famous Trials I*.) To avoid treading on that familiar ground the present author has concentrated less on the trial and more on the man himself. Here the competition is less keen. Hawley Crippen is remembered chiefly for his capture at sea by means of wireless telegraphy, and as such rates a chapter in many a crime collection, but, surprisingly, there has been no full-length study of him to date that makes use of original research.

In the present study I am indebted for its first-hand account to *I Caught Crippen* by Walter Dew, the ex-Scotland Yard Chief

Inspector who captured Crippen. Of other printed sources the author found most helpful the short autobiographical sketch by Ethel LeNeve, which first appeared in *Lloyd's Weekly News*; the newspaper articles by Adeline Harrison, who was a close friend of the Crippens; and finally Crippen's letters to Ethel LeNeve, which were reprinted in J. C. Ellis's *Black Fame*.

Of individuals who have been most helpful I should single out first the book's dedicatee, John Hill; Fred Ingalls, a friend of forty years' standing, who dug into the files of Los Angeles newspapers; Tom and Elizabeth Van Dycke, who read the book in manuscript; Richard Whittington-Egan, who has been helpful in various ways, not least in the discovery of Crippen's letters. I should also like to take this means of thanking publicly novelist Ursula Bloom, and Cynric Mytton-Davies, who gave most generously of their recollections.

I am especially grateful to Wolf Mankowitz and to Monty Norman, authors respectively of the book and of the lyrics of the musical 'Belle or the Ballad of Doctor Crippen', for permission to quote from some of the excellent songs of this 'Music Hall Musical', which was first produced at the Strand Theatre in London in May, 1961.

Of others who have given advice or aid of one kind or another I should mention Juliet Simpkins, press officer of Madame Tussaud's; Eric Barton, bookseller; B. Beesley, information officer for Canadian Pacific; Mrs Eve Bonham, of Bonham's, the auctioneers; Hester Ferris; Pat Frank, librarian at Scotland Yard; Mrs B. Hance, company historian at GEC-Marconi Electronics, Ltd; Ray Mackender; George Musk; H. G. Pearson, departmental records officer at the Home Office; Bert Ross, historian, British Music Hall Society; Hazel Timm, librarian at Coldwater, Michigan; Penelope Wallace; and Estolv Ward.

The numbers in the text refer to sources used, which are given at the end of the book.

I

THE CURSE
OF HILLDROP
CRESCENT

BALLAD SINGER
'Here's a little story,
A touching tale of woe.
Happened here in London
'Bout fifty years ago.
CHORUS
'Fifty years ago, fifty years ago.
BALLAD SINGER
'A little Yankee doctor
Created quite a din,
All because he gave his
Dear wife a Mickey-Finn

Funny little fellow,
Crippen was his name,
See him for a six-pence
In the hall of fame'.

—*from 'Belle or the Ballad
of Doctor Crippen'*.[1]

[1]

After every murder of a sensational nature legends spring up which partake of the supernatural. If the murderer is not caught his victim comes back crying for vengeance; but even if the killer is apprehended the victim is said to haunt the scene, perhaps out of envy for the living, perhaps out of chagrin for a life untimely snuffed out. Sometimes it is the killer himself who returns troubled in spirit, desirous of expiating his crime, or again, bent upon revenging himself on those who have betrayed him. These restless shades usually foregather at the scene of the crime which, if it is a house, is then said to be haunted, and the landlord has difficulty in persuading new tenants to move in.

No. 39 Hilldrop Crescent in Holloway, North London, where the Crippens lived, is no longer standing, it having suffered a direct hit from a bomb during the 1939–45 war; but it certainly had the reputation of being haunted. After the tragic events of 1910, No. 39 became a Jonah among haunted houses, and the owner was glad to lease it for a peppercorn rent to a Scottish comedian named Sandy McNab, who planned to turn it into theatrical digs. But McNab forgot that stage folk are notoriously superstitious, and that nothing would induce a member of the acting profession to spend a night in a so-called 'jinx' house, so the comedian ended up with a huge python, which he had bought from a dealer in Tottenham Court Road, as the sole occupant of the front parlour. When McNab then tried to turn No. 39 into a Crippen museum, the neighbours protested; and as a result, the landlord revoked the lease.*

So No. 39 remained empty, slowly falling to pieces during the inter-war years, until the Luftwaffe finally put it out of its misery. Empty, but not silent, according to local inhabitants whom the author talked to in The Brecknock, the big Edwardian-type pub just around the corner from Hilldrop Crescent (in Crippen's time it was known as The Brecknock Arms). On winter nights shrieks

* The author is indebted to Bert Ross, historian of the British Music Hall Society, for this information.

could be heard emanating from the upper floors of the three-storey house where the bedrooms were — the shrieks of a woman *in extremis*, the older pub-goers will tell you. Others the author talked to claimed that on winter nights a scraping noise could be heard coming from the direction of the cellar at No. 39, the kind of noise made by a trowel as it scrapes the excess mortar from between bricks.

Whether the residents of Margaret Bonfield House,* the block of council flats which has risen on the ashes of No. 39, have their sleep disturbed by these noises is not known, but they are real enough to those who remember things as they were. There may be no such thing as 'The Curse of Hilldrop Crescent', but one would be hard put to convince the regulars at The Brecknock that this is so.

*   *   *

In reality, Hilldrop Crescent's pretensions to middle-class gentility had been shattered long before the Crippens moved into this tree-lined scimitar off the Camden Road. They were wrecked by the construction nearby, first of the City House of Correction, later known as the Holloway Prison for Women, then of the Caledonian Cattle Market (was it entirely fortuitous, one wonders, that both of these fortresses were designed by the same architect?). So that by 1905 when the Crippens took up residence in the crescent the neighbourhood had suffered a general lowering of tone. Mrs Crippen, for example, was soon complaining that the bellowing of the terrified cattle being led to slaughter at the nearby market kept her awake at night.

By 1905 Hilldrop Crescent had in fact become Pooter heartland, as immortalised in that classic of lower middle-class mores, *The Diary of a Nobody*. For it was in Holloway — at 'The Laurels' in Brickfield Terrace, to be precise — that the Pooters organised their little soirees, Lupin and his friends in the amateur dramatic society known as the 'Holloway Comedians' being regaled with bubbly (Jackson Frères, 3/6 a bottle). 'We have a little front garden', Pooter writes in his diary, 'and there is a flight of ten steps up to the front door, which, by-the-by, we keep locked with the chain up.'

* Named after Britain's first woman Cabinet member.

[14]

No. 39 Hilldrop Crescent too was approached by a flight of ten steps, beneath which was the cellar that was to give the house such an evil repute. Like the Pooters, the Crippens kept their front door on the latch except when they 'received', preferring to use the side, or tradesmen's, entrance. The front parlour likewise was closed off unless there was company, its blinds being drawn in the daytime for fear that the sun would fade the carpet.

The neighbours on either side frequently saw American-born Dr Hawley Harvey Crippen in his backyard in shirt-sleeves pruning plants, or raking leaves into a pile and burning them. He was a small man in his mid-forties, with a fresh complexion, light brown hair which he brushed carefully over a bald spot, and a straggly, sandy moustache above a receding chin. His grey eyes, which were magnified slightly by gold-rimmed spectacles, were undoubtedly his most remarkable feature, but they were in no wise as bulgy as later writers, in their efforts to paint Crippen as some sort of monster, would have one believe. Thus the London *Daily Mail* was to describe Crippen as having 'the glassy protruding eyes of some deep-sea creature', while his friend Seymour Hicks, the actor-manager, professed that 'in looking at him I was by no means sure I was not talking to a bream or a mullet'.[2] Hawley Crippen suffered from many disabilities during his lifetime, but ophthalmic goitre was not among them.

Sometimes Mrs Crippen would join her husband in the backyard, and then it was, 'Peter, do this', and 'Peter, do that', and 'Peter, the irises want watering', and 'Peter, the rose bushes need pruning'. Crippen was not only a gardener, but he was handy at carpentry and bricklaying. He had constructed a low brick wall to separate his backyard from his neighbour's, and he had carried out other improvements as well, such as the erection of a small greenhouse, and the installation of a fresh-water aquarium. At his wife's behest, he had then constructed a cage in which two female cats — a white Persian and a black one of uncertain origin — could take the air without menacing the goldfish in the aquarium or, in turn, being menaced by 'the shafts of illicit love', as one neighbour expressed it.

The neighbours knew that Mrs Crippen was a music hall artist of sorts, a serio-comic singer who went by the stage name of Belle Elmore; but, without passing judgment on her voice, they judged that she was too short and dumpy to have enjoyed much success.

Belle's figure was the very opposite of that of the 'Gibson Girl', the Circe with the eighteen-inch waist as drawn by the American artist Charles Dana Gibson, and as personified by actress Camille Clifford, who was then all the vogue.

Belle also acquired the reputation among her neighbours of being a penny-pincher. 'I have seen her go out shopping for her own green groceries with a little cloth bag slung on one of her fingers containing hundreds of pounds worth of diamonds and other jewels,' writes Mrs Adeline Harrison, who was a close friend and neighbour of the Crippens. At the Caledonian Market Belle bought only the cheapest chickens, while in Brecknock Road she would haggle with the butcher over the price of a chop for her husband's dinner. 'One morning she would have for lunch a cup of coffee and a piece of bread and butter,' Mrs Harrison observes, 'and the same evening, attired in a Parisian gown, she would be holding a lavish dinner party at the Savoy or the Trocadero.'[3]

Never a top-liner herself, Belle worked her passage to friendship with top-liners by plugging their favourite charities. She sold programmes at charity matinees. She became treasurer of the Music Hall Ladies' Guild. No rout sponsored by the Variety Artistes' Federation, no river outing organised by the Grand Order of Water Rats, was held without Belle selling more tickets than anyone else. She moved in a world peopled by serio-comics, acrobats, tap-dancers and contortionists, where the White-Eyed Kaffir was king, and Datas, the Memory Man (he had willed his brain to a London hospital for £3,000, according to his publicity hand-outs) his jester. Into the tinselly world of the music hall Belle dragged a reluctant husband. 'Dr Crippen was the typical quiet, unassuming American, who gave his wife all the running socially,' Mrs Harrison observed. 'His devotion to her was remarkable.' What made it all the more remarkable was that Belle treated him openly with contempt, preferring the company of almost any other male to that of her husband.

*　　*　　*

The shrieks of a woman in distress were not the only sounds emanating from No. 39 according to one old-timer I talked to in The Brecknock. This senior citizen claimed that music — the tinkling of a piano — and ghostly laughter could be heard coming from the front parlour on a wintry night. Then in the early hours of the morning there would be the sound of voices on the front steps, ghostly voices as the hosts took leave of their guests, followed by the slam of cab doors, and the clip-clop of horses' hooves, gradually receding until the crescent was once more silent. This phenomenon, the author was told, continued long after horse carriages had disappeared and Hilldrop Crescent itself had become lined with Morris Minors and Hillman Minxes.

It is true that the Crippens did entertain a great deal. Belle was always organising little dinner parties at which she would show off her latest acquisitions from the auction salerooms. For after moving to No. 39 Belle took to haunting auctions, at which she picked up odds and ends of furniture and trumpery *objets d'art*. Belle had decorated the parlour in blushing pink, which she considered to be her lucky colour. ('Gee, you've got a real hoodoo there,' Belle told her friend Mrs Harrison when, horrified, she discovered that the latter had chosen green wallpaper for her drawingroom.) Belle's preference for blushing pink was evident not only in the wallpaper, but in the shades of the bracket lamps that flanked the china dogs on the mantelpiece. She had even tied pink velvet bows at the corners of the small oil and water colour paintings that dotted the walls.

After the ladies had been taken on a tour of the house to admire Belle's knick-knacks they would be rejoined by the men, and the company would then settle down to whist or bezique, or perhaps Belle could entertain at the upright ebony piano, singing 'Sister Mary Ann', or one of her other serio-comic songs that had failed to fire music hall audiences.

On Sunday nights the Crippens had a standing engagement to play whist either with Paul and Clara Martinetti (he was a famous mime artist), or with the Nashes (she was Lil Hawthorne, of the Hawthorne Sisters, and married to her manager John Nash). This breach of the Sabbath scandalised the more pious of the Crippens' neighbours, who no doubt were unaware that Sunday night was the only night that most entertainers had free.

There would have been no 'Curse of Hilldrop Crescent' had not Crippen late in January, 1910 suggested a slight deviation in the weekly routine. Instead of coming to dinner on Sunday night, Crippen proposed that the Martinettis should come on Monday night, January 31st. In fact, the doctor did more than propose —

he practically insisted that the Martinettis should dine, overruling their objections. Dinner was followed by the usual whist game, and at 1.30 the Crippens bade their guests good-night. The temperature had fallen to just above freezing, and Clara Martinetti after kissing Belle, urged her, 'Don't come down, Belle, you'll catch your death.' Belle obeyed her friend's injunction. After one last wave of the hand at the departing cab, she went inside, shut and bolted the door, and was never seen again by the Martinettis or by any of her other friends. That night Belle caught her death all right, but not from cold.

*   *   *

The changes which took place at No. 39 after that last night in January, 1910, were so gradual and subtle as to be almost imperceptible. True, Crippen a day or two later trotted round to the newsagent to cancel Belle's subscription to *The Stage* and *Era*, the two theatrical weeklies that were her bible; but then he explained that his wife had gone to America and would not be returning until some months hence.

So far as the neighbours on either side were concerned, life at No. 39 went on much as before. The goldfish darted about, their aquarium world protected from the sudden intrusion of a furry paw. The cats in their cage basked in the wintery sun, protected from the advances of amorous toms. Only the raucous voice of Belle Elmore, calling to 'Peter' to do this and to do that, was heard no more. Nor was her buxom self to be seen in the garden directing operations. Instead, a new woman had appeared, a woman who was young enough to be Crippen's daughter. Indeed, the rumour quickly spread that Ethel LeNeve, the woman in question, was Crippen's niece, come to keep house for him during his wife's absence in America. Then it was noticed that the two left for work at the same hour each morning.

Ethel Clara LeNeve was no beauty, but she had the kind of face that made a married woman clutch her husband's arm a little tighter when Ethel was around. Her mouth, which turned down at the corners, could be interpreted either as tragic, or as an invitation to sensuality. She had light brown hair, which she wore piled on her head, a long, straight nose, grey eyes, and a way of looking up intently into the face of her interlocutor when in conversation.

[18]

Ethel's position in the Crippen household became a little clearer when around June, 1910, a French *au pair* girl named 'Valentine' appeared at No. 39 and was to be seen hanging out the washing in the backyard instead of Ethel. Valentine could not have been more than sixteen, and apparently she spoke not a word of English, for she always replied to Ethel, whom she addressed as 'Madame', in French.

Another incident occurred at about this time which an inquisitive neighbour, whose house overlooked the Crippens' backyard, was to remember long afterwards. One evening the neighbour happened to look across to No. 39, and was surprised to see Ethel in an upper room trying on dresses which the neighbour had previously seen on Mrs Crippen. 'They were handed to her by Crippen from a large luggage basket such as is used by theatrical people on tour,' the neighbour later told a London *Evening News* reporter. 'He also helped her to fit them on.'[4] The neighbour added that the couple appeared to live almost entirely in the kitchen, whose window overlooked the back garden. The blind of this window was never pulled down.

*   *   *

Into the quiet, leafy, cosy world of Hilldrop Crescent one morning in July the unfamiliar intruded in the form of two burly strangers. The neighbours, peering from behind lace curtains, might have guessed they were either bailiffs, detectives, or plain-clothes police, not only by their dress (both wore dark overcoats with velvet collars, bowlers with narrow, curling brims) but by their bearing, by the self-assured manner in which they brushed past Valentine when the little *au pair* answered the door at No. 39. The taller of the two men who had a wedge of black moustache under his nose was in fact Chief Inspector Walter Dew of Scotland Yard's CID, and he was accompanied by Detective-Sergeant Arthur Mitchell.

Some time later the two men appeared in the backyard in shirt-sleeves and armed with spades, and to the horror of the neighbours on either side proceeded to dig up the garden. Working intermittently over the next few days they dug up all the rose bushes, which were then in full flower. They also destroyed the dahlia beds, turning up the bulbs to rot in the sun. They even went so far as to move the greenhouse in order to dig beneath its foundations.

Valentine appeared in the backyard only once, and then she looked distressed, her eyes reddened, as though she had been weeping. Soon afterwards she was seen trudging up the crescent to Camden Road with a cheap suitcase in her hand. As for Dr Crippen, he was nowhere to be seen. Nor was there any sign of the youthful companion who lately had replaced Mrs Crippen. The neighbours had no way of knowing, but the pair had been missing for several days. They had in fact fled in what appeared to have been a state of utter panic.

Meanwhile, inside No. 39, the detectives had been thorough in their search. The house was a three-storey semi-detached consisting of nine rooms. Beneath the front steps and running the full length of the house was a sub-basement divided into a breakfast-room, kitchen and coal cellar, all of which were on a level with the back garden. On the ground floor were the two parlours where the Crippens did most of their entertaining. On the first floor were a master bedroom, a smaller, locked bedroom, which Belle had used to store her theatrical costumes, a bathroom and a lavatory. On the top floor were three small bedrooms, one of which Valentine had occupied, the other two being filled with rolled carpets and furniture packed as though for removal.

Inspector Dew had even stood on a chair and run his hands along the rafters, but he had turned up nothing of interest, nothing, that is, except a six-chambered revolver found in one of the dressing-table drawers. The inspector, however, attached little importance to this firearm. His inquiries indicated that the Crippens had kept a quantity of expensive jewelry—diamond rings, brooches and earrings—on the premises, and in these circumstances it seemed only natural that they should take precautions against burglary. Besides, Americans had a penchant for weapons of this sort, as was well known. It had to do with their right to bear arms as guaranteed by the American Constitution, and harked back to the insecurity of life on the American frontier.

*　　*　　*

'There was one place in the house which had a peculiar fascination for me,' writes Inspector Dew. 'This was the coal cellar . . . Even in bed, what little I got of it during those hectic days, I couldn't keep my mind from wandering back to the cellar.'

The cellar, which measured no more than 9 ft by 6 ft, was at the bottom of a short, dark passage leading from the kitchen to the back door. Dew had been over it several times without discovering anything to arouse his interest, for it contained nothing but a small quantity of coal, and some kindling which looked as though it had been pruned from the garden trees. Indeed, after two days of fruitless search he was about to abandon the whole of No. 39 as a bad job, when on the third day, Wednesday, July 13th, he decided to have another go at the cellar which haunted his dreams. This time he was armed with a poker when he entered the cellar, and dropping to his knees he began to probe its brick floor.

What happened next Dew records in his autobiography.[5] 'Presently a thrill of excitement went through me,' he writes. 'The sharp point of the poker had found its way between two of the bricks, and one of them showed signs of lifting.' 'I toiled away hopefully,' he continues, 'all sense of fatigue vanishing in the excitement of hope. The brick came out. Then another and another.' Sergeant Mitchell, who had been helping, ran to get the spade with which the two men had been digging up the garden. With this the detective removed the clay that was immediately underneath the bricks, digging down to a depth of about five inches. 'Then came evidence nauseatingly unmistakable.'

The stench that filled the cellar drove both men into the garden gasping for air. 'When we had sufficiently recovered we resumed our task,' he comments laconically; 'and this time we stuck the putrefied atmosphere long enough to unearth a large piece of what I easily recognised to be human remains. Again we had to fly, and before re-entering the cellar a third time Mitchell and I were fortified with a long drink of brandy.' Dew then dispatched Mitchell to telephone the news to Sir Melville Macnaghten, head of the CID, Scotland Yard, who arrived on the scene soon afterwards. 'Before leaving,' Macnaghten writes, 'I put a handful of cigars into my pocket; I thought they might be needed by the officers — and they were.'[6]

What the detectives had uncovered were parts of a human torso wrapped in a man's pyjama top which bore the label 'Jones

Brothers, Shirtmakers, Holloway'. Missing were both arms and legs, as well as the head, which had been severed so as to leave $2\frac{1}{2}$ inches of windpipe exposed. Obliterated were the genital organs and all other indications of sex, and, most gruesome of all, the remains had been carefully filleted so as to remove all bones. It was more the work of a master charcutier than of a surgeon of human anatomy.

Upon analysis later the remains were found to contain traces of hyoscine hydrobromide, a poison derived from henbane, of the deadly nightshade family.* Buried with the remains was a woman's cotton undervest whose lace armlets and collar were heavily encrusted with a cement-like material which, upon examination, proved to be lime.

Found in the shallow grave was an artefact which caused thousands of women in Britain to shudder. It was a metal hair curler of the type that these same thousands used commonly, subjecting themselves to its nightly torture in an effort to make themselves beautiful. Coiled round the curler was a tuft of hair six inches long which graduated in colour from dark brown at the roots to a straw-like blonde at the ends. Reading about this find, her neighbours in Hilldrop Crescent suddenly remembered that Mrs Crippen peroxided her hair and that she was not always careful to touch up its roots.

The newspapers were in fact full of what was headlined as the 'North London Cellar Murder'. And not only the newspapers — every police station in the United Kingdom was circularised with a full description of Dr Crippen and his paramour Miss LeNeve as the hue and cry got underway. A watch was kept on seaports in particular in case the missing pair decided to bolt abroad. Police on the Continent and in America were asked to be on the look-out for the fugitives among passengers disembarking from vessels coming from Britain. Meanwhile, handbills with the words 'WANTED FOR MURDER AND MUTILATION' in bold type, and giving descriptions of the missing couple and samples of their handwriting, were posted in public places.

From the descriptions the piquant detail emerged that Ethel LeNeve in all likelihood had cut off her hair and was fleeing disguised as a boy, a complete outfit of boy's clothing having been

* So far as I have been able to discover this is the first case of murder by hyoscine in British legal history.

purchased for her on Saturday, July 9th, the day the couple decided to cut and run.

*   *   *

More nonsense has been written about Hawley Harvey Crippen than about any other murderer with the possible exception of Jack the Ripper. Crippen was 'one of the most dangerous and remarkable men who have lived in this century', according to Frederick Edwin Smith, the barrister who was briefed to defend Ethel LeNeve. Smith goes on to describe Crippen as 'a compelling and masterful personality' who 'feared neither God nor man'.[7] That he was the very opposite is the verdict of others who knew him. 'He was as docile as a kitten . . . He was quite incapable of murdering his wife' (Professor Munyon, the patent medicine manufacturer, who employed Crippen off and on for nearly twenty years);[8] 'A more humble unassuming little man I have never met, and to me it seems unthinkable that he would have committed so dastardly a crime' (Dr Gilbert W. Rylance, Crippen's partner in a dental practice);[9] 'A kindly, gentle man . . . most people felt sorry for him being married to Belle Elmore' (music hall star Gertie Gitana's opinion, as relayed to the author by her husband Don Ross);[10] 'To look at him you would not have believed he could kill a mouse' (W. E. Henchy, managing clerk to the solicitor who defended Crippen).[11] One of the key prosecution witnesses at Crippen's trial, Ethel LeNeve's landlady Mrs Emily Jackson, went so far as to pronounce Crippen 'one of the nicest men I ever met'.

Humble . . . unassuming . . . kindly . . . gentle . . . docile as a kitten — these are the adjectives employed by those who had contact with Crippen. One and all they found it incredible that he could have committed murder. Alongside these judgments Douglas Browne's verdict that Crippen was 'one of the most methodical and deliberate of murderers' seems singularly inappropriate.[12] Crippen was anything but methodical. He was the pink panther among killers just as Inspector Clouseau (as portrayed brilliantly on the screen by Peter Sellers) is the pink panther among detectives. The murder of Belle Elmore was a series of blunders from beginning to end. In fact, it could provide the subject for black comedy as well as for tragedy: the comedy of a little man who sets out to commit the perfect crime, but for whom everything goes wrong, so much so that in disgust he ends by giving himself up to the police. (Charlie Chaplin used this as the theme of *Monsieur Verdoux*, to cite another cinematic parallel.) Crippen never gave himself up. He made the police chase him and Miss LeNeve disguised as his son three thousand miles across the Atlantic before surrendering, but the comic analogy holds good.

Take such a simple matter as the destruction of the remains, which Crippen was so foolish as to leave buried in a shallow grave beneath the cellar floor. For this purpose Crippen employed what he thought was quicklime, sprinkling it liberally over the pieces of flesh he buried. Now Crippen had paid his way through the University of Michigan's School of Homoeopathy by working as an assistant in the school's chemical laboratory. Later, as general manager of Munyon's Homoeopathic Remedies, he had acted not only as the firm's advisory physician, but had been in charge of its chemical laboratory as well. However, his knowledge of chemistry apparently did not enable him to distinguish slaked lime, which preserves human flesh, from quicklime, which destroys it. By mistaking the former for the latter, Crippen made certain that most of Belle Elmore's organs, notably the heart, were in an excellent state of preservation when eventually they were dug up.

But, as Raymond Chandler points out, 'I cannot see why a man who would go to the enormous labour of de-boning and de-sexing and de-heading an entire corpse would not take the rather slight extra labour of disposing of the flesh in the same way, rather than bury it at all . . . Here was a man who apparently had the means and opportunity and even the temperament for the perfect crime, and he made all sorts of mistakes . . .'[13]

What saves the Crippen story from becoming comedy of the blackest hue was his love for Ethel LeNeve, which none can doubt was genuine. 'Hawley Harvey Crippen . . . was one of the world's great lovers,' writes his biographer Max Constantine-Quinn, who would have the reader believe that beneath the mild exterior of this Caspar Milquetoast beat the heart of a Romeo, a Paolo, an Abelard. 'That such a fine and generous quality could not rescue its possessor from the darkness which engulfed him was in itself a tragedy,' the biographer adds.[14]

The regulars of The Brecknock would perhaps not agree. To them Crippen was simply the hen-pecked husband who rose in revolt against a shrewish wife (one wonders how many of those who take refuge in this pub are themselves fugitives from domestic dramas). As such, Crippen is deserving of sympathy, if not applause, these drinkers will tell you. Incidentally, those who knock back the pints at The Brecknock might be disappointed to learn that their hero was a life-long teetotaller. 'He was unable to smoke; it made him ill,' Mrs Adeline Harrison claims. 'He refrained from the consumption of alcoholic liquor in the form of wine and spirits, as it affected his heart and digestion . . . No man had ever known him to join in a convivial bout; he was always back to time and never came with a meaningless grin on his face at two o'clock in the morning attended by pals from a neighbouring club.'[15]

Great lover then, and at the same time a henpecked, not to mention abstemious, husband — the contradictions are not so glaring as they seem at first glance. The truth is that Crippen possessed nearly all the characteristics ascribed to him to a greater or lesser degree. In a paradoxical way, his crime brought out the best in Crippen, as well as the worst. As Filson Young points out, 'There are two sides of the story — the physical, which is sordid, dreadful, and revolting, and the spiritual, which is good and heroic . . .'[16]

II

BELLE

CRIPPEN (singing):
'Way down in Coldwater Michigan,
Coldwater Michigan,
That's where I was born,
Where my life began.
And every day how I wish again
That I was on my way
To Coldwater Michigan
U.S.A.'.

—from 'Belle or the Ballad
of Doctor Crippen'.[1]

[2]

Playwright John Van Druten considers the Crippen murder to be the classic crime; moreover, one that has withstood the test of time — 'the years that have passed since it took place have diminished its quality not at all,' he writes.[2] In analysing wherein the fascination of this particular crime lies, Van Druten thinks that it is in 'the intrusion of the totally unfamiliar into the totally normal', an intrusion which in turn begets true terror. It is the spine-tingling terror which a man experiences in walking down a dark street on a windy night when a newspaper suddenly blows against his legs. It is the terror which the neighbours in Hilldrop Crescent felt when Scotland Yard detectives arrived on the scene and began digging up the backyard of No. 39.

'I would have no interest in reading of a murder which took place in a ruined castle in Transylvania,' Van Druten continues. 'There is no background there with which I am familiar . . . But a murder in a small suburban villa at Putney, with the "Stag at Bay" hanging over the mantelpiece and a geyser in the bathroom, is what calls to my attention. I want my murderers to be, outwardly, the most ordinary of men, the men who read cheap popular novels, do fretwork and carpentry as a pastime, and eat potted shrimps for supper.'[3] These sentiments are echoed by Filson Young. 'Most of the interest and part of the terror of great crime,' Young writes, 'are due not to what is abnormal, but to what is normal in it; what we have in common with the criminal, rather than that subtle insanity which differentiates him from us . . .'[4] Certainly this was true of the Crippen murder.

Putney is south of the Thames, and was less fashionable at that time, but there was not all that much difference between it and Holloway. There is certain to have been a 'Stag at Bay' which Belle had picked up at auction hanging somewhere at No. 39. As for Hawley Crippen himself, he may not have done fretwork, but he was a dab hand at carpentry and bricklaying, as has been seen, and he also played the violin, albeit indifferently.

Another who is fascinated by the terror that resides in the

everyday is Alfred Hitchcock, who acknowledged that the Crippen murder was his inspiration for the film *Rear Window*, starring James Stewart and Grace Kelly. In so acknowledging, no doubt Hitchcock had in mind the claustrophobic atmosphere of No. 39, and in particular that kitchen in which the Crippens did most of their living, according to the neighbours, washing, dressing and eating there in plain view of all. The white Persian, too, seems to have been a victim of the claustrophobia, for Mrs Harrison pictures the cat 'scratching wildly at a window in a vain attempt to attract the attention of a passing Don Juan'.

It would have been difficult to have found a more ordinary man to all outward appearances. Like Van Druten's hypothetical killer Crippen was a devourer of popular novels, books with titles like *Nebo the Nailer*, but he read books with an uplift message as well, like G. H. Lorrimer's *Letters of a Self-Merchant to His Son*. Crippen was the living embodiment of Babbitt, the backbone of lower middle-class, middle-town American philistinism. Had he remained in his native Coldwater, Michigan, Crippen might well have become its leading, if not its only family doctor, and have earned the gratitude of Coldwater's 4,320 inhabitants. He might in time have risen to become the leading light of its Rotary and Kiwanis clubs. But an early restlessness of spirit set Crippen's feet wandering, until eventually he met Belle; then all was changed.

* * *

Not that Crippen was without his private daimons. 'The devil took up residence in our household when I was a child, and never left it,' Crippen was to tell his business partner, G. W. Rylance, later in life. Born in Coldwater, where his grandfather Philo Crippen had been a pioneer, Hawley Harvey Crippen was brought up in the harsh, self-denying religion of his grandparents and parents. Hard work and fear of the devil were the twin tenets upon which that religion was based. In response to the first imperative, Philo had opened a dry goods store soon after his arrival in Coldwater. In those days Coldwater was little more than a handful of log cabins at the confluence of the Chicago Turnpike (now U.S. Highway 112) and the Coldwater River. Then, as the fur trappers and loggers passed through on their way to the northern woods,

Philo had fitted them out. By the time Hawley's father, Myron Augustus Crippen, had inherited the business, it was prosperous enough for him to marry Andresse Skinner, a local girl, who became Hawley's mother. By 1862, when Hawley was born, the Crippen house, at the corner of Grand and Monroe streets where the Branch County Savings Bank now stands, was easily the most imposing in Coldwater.

An only child, Hawley was spoilt by parents and grandparents alike, as a result grew up to be opinionated and self-important. From an early age he determined to follow in the footsteps of his Uncle Bradley, who was Coldwater's family doctor; and in the games of hospital which he played Hawley persuaded the other children to be the nurses and patients while he pre-empted the role of physician. On Sunday, when he was old enough, Hawley accompanied his parents and his grandfather to chapel, where they occupied a front pew.

Here it was that Hawley learned for the first time that the devil was a woman. Her name, he learned, was 'Mystery, Babylon the Great, the mother of harlots', and she was seated upon a scarlet coloured beast, 'full of names of blasphemy', having seven heads and ten horns, and she drank from a golden cup 'full of abominations and filthiness'. Young Crippen would return home, his head reeling with these wonders, only to have it crammed further with Old Testament readings which his father or grandfather chose in amplification of the theme. Sometimes it was Proverbs ('The lips of a strange woman drop honey . . . But her latter end is bitter as wormwood.')

Or, again, it might be the Book of Isaiah, which was Hawley's favourite. ('Because the daughters of Zion are haughty, and walk with stretched forth necks and wanton eyes . . . therefore the Lord will smite with a scab the crown of the head of the daughters of Zion, and the Lord will discover their secret parts.') Hawley would picture to himself the scab which made these daughters bald, and wonder why it was that the Lord had not discovered their secret parts before, since He knew all things. ('In that day the Lord will take away the bravery of their tinkling ornaments about their feet, . . . the bonnets, and the ornaments of the legs, and the headbands, and the tablets, and the earrings, the rings, and nose jewels . . . the mantles, and the wimples, and the crisping pins, the glasses, and the fine linen, and the hoods and the veils, and it shall come to pass, that instead of a sweet smell there shall be stink.') It was all very graphic, the way his father or his grandfather read the passage, lingering over each detail; but instead of imparting fear in the breast of the youthful Crippen, it aroused his curiosity.

Hawley delayed satisfying that curiosity until after he had completed his studies at the University of Michigan, had taken his M.D. at the Homoeopathic Hospital College in Cleveland, Ohio and had set up to practice as a homoeopathic physician. He then was twenty-five, and it was his misfortune that the first fruit he plucked should be green and insipid to the taste. Charlotte Jane Bell who was born in Dublin, was a student nurse at the Hahnemann Hospital in Manhattan, where Dr Crippen, who had just qualified as an eye and ear specialist, was serving his internship. Convent-bred Charlotte had emigrated to America late in life, and spoke with a thick Irish brogue, which Crippen found charming. She had also brought with her all the dark lore and superstitions of that priest-ridden land. Crippen being Protestant, they had had to get a special dispensation to marry—Charlotte insisted upon that. Then, instead of being wedded to a woman whose lips dripped honey Crippen found himself married to a moody colleen who never made love without rushing off to a priest afterwards. He felt cheated.

Charlotte bore him a son, Otto Hawley Crippen, and was within two or three days of giving birth to another child when in Salt Lake City in January, 1892, she died suddenly of apoplexy. Crippen lost no time in mourning this wife who had proved to be such a bitter disappointment. He left his son with the boy's grandparents, who had moved from Coldwater to San Jose, California, and he himself headed for New York. It was six months later that he met Belle.

*   *   *

Whether Belle wore tinkling ornaments on her feet that day in July, 1892, when she came mincing into the Brooklyn surgery where Dr Crippen was locum, whether she wore crisping pins in her hair and nose jewels is unimportant. What matters is that Crippen recognised her instantly for the real article, Mystery, the Mother of Babylon, the forbidden thing that had been denied him until that moment. Even at nineteen Belle, whose real name was Kunigunde Mackamotzki, but who was then known as Cora

Turner, was mature for her age. The daughter of a Polish grocer named Joe Mackamotzki, who kept a fruit stand in Brooklyn, and of a German mother whose maiden name was Wolff, Belle betrayed this racial mixture only too obviously in her looks. The merry black eyes, the rounded face with its high cheek bones and re-troussé nose, bespoke the father's Polish origins, while the deter-mined set of Belle's jaw was purely her mother's. 'She would never give in to anything,' was the posthumous tribute which Crippen was to pay to Belle from the witness-box. Belle's was not just a baby-doll face then, such as one finds painted on those wooden babushka dolls that fit inside one another. It had character and determination.

At the moment Crippen met her Belle had her heart set on succeeding as a singer, and she was not too particular how she went about it. She was being kept by a Brooklyn stove manufacturer, a married man named Lincoln, who had not only installed her in a flat of her own, but who was paying for her singing lessons. Belle was also being treated for some sort of female complaint by Dr Jeffery, whose assistant Crippen was. 'I believe she had had a miscarriage, or something of that kind,' Crippen later explained.[5]

Crippen's age advantage was such as to make him, a widower at thirty, feel protective toward this nineteen-year-old. As for Belle, she had the second generation American's respect for those who were in the professions. To become a doctor, a lawyer, or a professor—the children of immigrants had it engrained into them that this was the way to succeed in America. Did she not herself aspire to a career as a singer? And had she not aimed at the very top—grand opera, no less?

Belle was a mythomaniac of the first order. It all had to do with being born in a Brooklyn slum, and with not getting enough love as a child. Belle's father had died when she was only two years old, after which her mother had re-married; and although her step-father, Fritz Mersinger, had raised Belle as his own daughter she had had to compete with five half-brothers and half-sisters for a share of the mother's love. It had to do, too, with Belle's friends telling her what a pleasing voice she had, and why didn't she have it properly trained? Belle's high-pitched soprano was good enough for solos with the parish church choir (like Crippen's first wife Belle was a Catholic) if a trifle thin and uncertain in the upper registers. Belle's stepfather taught her to play the zither and other

[33]

musical instruments; then, as a birthday treat, he had taken her to hear opera, and suddenly the whole of Belle's life had been transformed.

It was the age of the great divas—the age when Adelina Patti could demand and get $5,000 a performance at the Metropolitan Opera House, where her contracts stipulated the size her name was to appear on the posters; the age when Emma Calve, when she sang *La Traviata*, was gowned by Patou, and her jewels came from Cartier's. From the 'peanut gallery' where she and her stepfather had seats, Belle could gaze down at the Golden Horseshoe where the Vanderbilts, the Morgans and the Goulds had their boxes, and she could catch the fire of the jewels worn by their ladies. From below and from all sides came the dry crackle of applause, which greeted the singers as they took their curtain calls. For a teenage mythomaniac such as Kunigunde Mackamotzki it was heady stuff indeed. There and then she determined that she would be an opera star.

*   *   *

To get Dr Crippen to propose had been easy. 'One day Belle told me Mr Lincoln (the stove manufacturer) wanted her to go away with him,' Crippen was to tell Inspector Dew. 'I told her I could not stand that, and would marry her right away.' They were married by a Catholic priest, Father William Eakins, at St Paul's Church, Jersey City, on September 1, 1892.

Crippen had been swept off his feet. No doubt the prospect of acting as Belle's patron as well as her protector, of helping her to realise a musical career, appealed to Crippen's ego. But then he was under her spell, so much so that he believed Belle when she told him that in reality her father had been a Polish nobleman, the Baron Mackamotzki, whose vast estates in Poland she hoped one day to reclaim.* There was no sign of vast estates when Belle took Hawley home after their marriage to meet her mother and stepfather. A group photograph taken upon that occasion looks

---

* Crippen was to get milage out of this myth when, in 1908, he marketed a preparation called 'Ohrsorb' as the wonder deafness cure of 'Baron Mackamotzki', otherwise identified as a German scientist. Upon analysis the cure proved as fraudulent as the baron himself, consisting largely of scented vaseline.

like a study of poverty row, with Belle's stepfather stooped like an old man, and her mother looking worn-out from child-bearing, surrounded by Belle's ragged half brothers and sisters. In contrast, the newly-weds look prosperous. Crippen wore a spade beard in those days which, aside from concealing a want of chin, gave him a distinguished air.

The marriage might have succeeded, might even have been a happy one, had there been children. But Belle had not been long married before it became necessary to remove her ovaries (was this a complication, one wonders, of the female trouble for which she was being treated by Dr Jeffery when Crippen met her?). It was to affect her married life profoundly. Even if they had adopted a child it might have made a difference, but they appeared set against this course. 'There was only one little shadow in their lives of which I was aware,' their friend Mrs Harrison was to write later. 'They both were passionately fond of children, and she was childless.'[6] Belle's half-sister, Mrs Louise Mills, agreed. 'Sister craved motherhood,' Mrs Mills was to tell a reporter. 'When I visited them four years ago they appeared to be perfectly happy except at times Belle would bemoan the fact that she had no child. I fear that in the latter part of her married life she became more and more lonesome.'[7]

Also, in the first two years of her married life Belle saw her plans for a career go awry. There was no money for singing lessons nor for any of the other things on which she had set her heart. These were the years of the great depression which began with Grover Cleveland's second administration as President of the United States. They were the years when America protested with its feet —when Coxey led a tattered army in a march on Washington, Pullman workers went out on strike in Chicago, and men everywhere shuffled in breadlines, or did solo jigs on street corners out of desperation waiting for someone to drop pennies in their up-turned hats. During the winter of 1893-94 in New York City alone 20,000 vagrants slept rough on park benches or wrapped in newspapers against the cold huddled on the pavements beneath the Third Avenue 'El'.

So far as Crippen was concerned, they were the years when doctors' bills went unpaid. In particular, he saw the bubble burst for homoeopathic medicine, until diplomas from homoeopathic colleges such as the one he kept framed on his wall were scarcely worth the parchment they were written on.

Homoeopathy was the brain child of Dr Hahnemann, an eighteenth century German naturalist, who, after experimenting with the curative qualities of chinchona bark from which quinine is extracted, had enunciated the doctrine of *similia similibus curentur* ('like cures like'). Briefly, Hahnemann held that disease could be cured by minute dosages of drugs which induced symptoms similar to those of the disease under treatment, a principle enshrined in modern serum therapy. In the 1880s homoeopathy had swept America, enjoying all the prestige which today attaches to certain forms of alternative medicine—acupuncture, for example. In 1882 the fad was at its height when Crippen had enrolled as a student at the University of Michigan's School of Homoeopathic Medicine, which had been established despite earlier objections from the university's regents.* Crippen left the university in 1883 without graduating, opting instead to spend a year in London, where he pursued his medical studies. This included a course of lectures on mental disorders at London's Royal Bethlehem Hospital, whose name in the sixteenth century had been corrupted to 'bedlam'. Returning to America, he had taken his MD in Cleveland in 1884. By the time Crippen married Belle, homoeopathy was already on the wane, and he had been forced to acquire new skills as an eye and ear specialist. Pickings were so slim that for a while the Crippens had been forced to move in with Belle's family, the already crowded Mersinger menage. 'About two years after their marriage they came to live with me, staying about ten weeks,' Fritz Mersinger was to tell a reporter. 'Business had been against the doctor,' he explained, adding that 'it was his wife's ability that gave him a place and pushed him ahead.'[8]

* * *

Belle was quick to perceive that if Dr Crippen was to get on in the world he would have to forget all about the Hippocratic oath

* The regents clearly regarded homoeopathy as the work of the devil. Thus in 1851, in rejecting a demand that a homoeopathic professor be added to the faculty, they had fired off this salvo at the Michigan State Legislature: 'Shall the accumulated results of three thousand years of experience be laid aside because there has arisen a sect in the world which by engrafting a medical dogma upon a spurious theology, has built up a system, so called, and baptized it homoeopathy?'

and become a quack. In the depressed nineties this was where the money was. No longer able to afford doctors, the sick had taken to doctoring themselves with patent medicines. Americans were in fact spending $75 million a year for the privilege of 'swallowing huge quantities of alcohol, an appalling amount of opiates and narcotics, a wide assortment of varied drugs ranging from powerful and dangerous heart depressants to insidious liver stimulants.'* These lethal palliatives were recommended to the gullible by various renegade medicos. Belle proposed that her husband should join their ranks. Not that Dr Crippen probably needed much persuasion to scuttle his medical ethics for a mess of pink pills. In the event he went to work early in 1894 for Munyon's Homoeopathic Remedies, which had just opened offices on East 14th near Sixth Avenue. Belle helped out as cashier, and the couple were so hard up at first that they slept in a room above the office.

Professor Munyon was by no means the worst of the nostrum vendors, whose number included the manufacturers of Grandma's Secret, Mother's Treasure, and Kopp's Baby Friend, all of which contained enough opiates to put baby under, sometimes permanently. Nor did the professor traffic in such concoctions as Peruna's Catarrh Cure, whose high (28%) alcoholic content gave rise to what was known as a 'Peruna jag'. No, the chief ingredient in Munyon's patent remedies was fraud. The professor, who combined piety with quackery, himself figured prominently in full-page newspaper advertisements abjuring readers to 'Heed the Sign of the Cross', while at the same time keeping 'regular'. Photographs of the grim-visaged Munyon, his arm upraised, his index finger pointing heavenwards, for all the world like some frock-coated Moses about to hand down a new Decalogue, became familiar to millions of Americans, as did Munyon's Pile Cure. Indeed, that extended index finger when combined with the advertising copy for the pile cure ('cures Piles, Blind or Bleeding, Protruding or Internal, Stops Itching . . . heals Fissures, Ulcerations, Cracks') gave rise to many ribald jokes. But Professor Munyon, when Crippen went to work for him, was one of America's

* Samuel Hopkins Adams, whose series of articles entitled 'The Great American Fraud', appearing in Colliers Magazine in 1905, did much to secure passage the following year of the U.S. Pure Food and Drugs Act, thereby ending many patent medicine abuses.

most successful patent medicine kings.

The professor took a liking to Crippen from the start. 'He was one of the most intelligent men I ever knew,' Munyon told a *New York Times* correspondent later, adding that Crippen 'was so proficient that I gave him a position readily, nor have I ever regretted it'. Indeed, Crippen's advancement was so rapid that by mid-1895 he had been called to Munyon's head office in Philadelphia and had been made general manager. 'In that capacity I acted as advisory physician and had charge of the chemical laboratory besides,' Crippen later explained. When it was a question of opening a Canadian branch of the firm, Crippen was selected for this important assignment, remaining in Toronto six months until Munyon's was firmly on its feet and he could return to Philadelphia. Crippen's reputation was high with the Toronto business community, which found him to be 'of excellent education, a rapid and persuasive talker . . . and a keen business man,' according to the *Montreal Star*.

Crippen had left Belle behind while he was in Toronto, an arrangement which did not displease her. With promotion Crippen could now afford to hire the best teachers of *bel canto* to give Belle lessons. The couple put nothing aside in the way of savings, but began at this time to invest their surplus cash in diamonds, about which Crippen now became an expert. He could talk knowledgeably about the intricacies of cleavage and refractivity in diamonds, knew the difference between table-cut, rose-cut, and brilliant-cut stones, could appreciate the subtle beauties of the pinks and sapphire blues. As for Belle, diamonds became an obsession with her. 'She was like a child with new toys,' her friend Mrs Harrison was later to remark. 'She would babble to her diamonds and kiss them.'[9] It was a mania not uncommon among actresses.*

---

* In her autobiography Beatrice Lillie tells how she and Fanny Brice, the American comedienne, used to gloat over the latter's collection of gems. 'Up in the boudoir, I'd say, "Come on, get the jewels out. Let's see them",' Bea Lillie writes. 'She'd disappear from the room then come back in with her hands full of bracelets and necklaces, rings and tiaras, oozing emeralds and diamonds and pearls. "Put them on, Fanny," I'd say. She'd dress up with as much as she could carry and hang the rest on me.' See *Every Other Inch a Lady*, by Beatrice Lillie, London, W. H. Allen, 1973.

When Crippen first introduced Belle to Professor Munyon the latter was not favourably impressed. It was not only that the professor saw at once through Belle's flimsy pretension of being the daughter of a Polish nobleman, but he sensed that she was a flirt, or as he expressed it, 'a giddy woman who worried her husband a great deal'. 'Some years after he started with me I saw he was distressed,' Munyon told a London reporter later. 'I attributed it to the annoyance of his wife,' the professor went on, adding, 'He had reason to be jealous of her.' The professor's son Duke Munyon was even more explicit when interviewed by the *New York Tribune*. 'She liked men other than her husband, which worried the doctor greatly,' Duke declared, 'he never struck her or anything of the kind, but I believe that if he thought he had cause for jealousy his rage could not be governed.'

Belle flirting with other men? Crippen jealous, liable to fly into an ungovernable rage? And all of this happening within a few years of their marriage? Part of the trouble arose from separation. Not only were the couple apart for the six months that Crippen spent in Toronto, but when he returned to Philadelphia Belle left almost immediately for Manhattan, pleading that Manhattan was a showcase for a musical talent such as hers. When Crippen visited her some time later he was distressed to learn that Belle had decided to abandon the operatic stage for vaudeville. She had it in mind to appear in a brief operatic sketch which would give 'scope to both her dramatic and musical talents', as Belle expressed it. Not only was she neglecting the expensive singing lessons for which he had paid, but she was splurging on new finery with which to dazzle the men—managers, small-time vaudevillians, talent scouts—'who could help her in her career', so she said.

To add to Crippen's torment, Professor Munyon early in 1897 asked him to go to England to open a London branch of the firm. In one respect it was a leg-up in the world, for it meant that Munyon reposed almost unlimited confidence in Crippen. Besides, the position of London manager carried with it a salary equivalent to $10,000 a year, which was considerable in those days. On the other hand, it meant separation from Belle: Hawley would not be able to send for her for months, and in the meanwhile he would be exposed to all of the tortures of a jealous husband in wondering who was squiring her in his absence. Too late Hawley remembered that a strange woman whose lips dripped honey was apt to be as bitter as wormwood at the other end. 'Her feet go down to death, Her steps take hold on Sheol,' as the Scriptures have it.

[3]

Hugh Jay Didcott (he shed an unpronounceable Russian name when the train on which he was travelling happened to be passing through Didcot junction, according to stage gossip) was in the habit of dropping in at the Bedford Theatre in Camden Town to watch the new turns audition. A spotter of talent, 'Diddy', as he was known, had found it in such unlikely places as pub sing-songs, end-of-pier pierrot shows, provincial music halls. Diddy had watched a trained dog act on this particular afternoon, and stood chatting with Harry Goodson, the stage manager, at the back of the stalls when into the lemon-coloured spotlight stepped a short, stocky blonde of buxom proportions. Her make-up was too heavy, she wore too many jewels, and the pelts of too many small, furry creatures were strung together round her neck. No sooner had her mascaraed eyes adjusted to the spotlight's glare than she began to sing a sentimental ballad entitled 'Down Lover's Walk' in a high, but uncertain soprano. The accent was unmistakably American.

American entertainers were then all the rage in London—so much so that perfectly good turns from Yorkshire and Lancashire changed their accents and billed themselves as 'the Knickerbocker Kut-ups' or 'the Madcaps from Manhattan'. 'You have to be pretty bad to get the bird if you're a Yank,' was a byword in the profession. The Yank auditioning at the Bedford was pretty bad.

Diddy was noted for his sharp tongue. Of a well-known serio-comic he had booked he once remarked, 'She will spend a hundred guineas on a gown, but you can't get her to wash her neck.' But this time he merely stared in disbelief. 'Good heavens!' the agent finally exclaimed as the blonde finished her number, 'how perfectly dreadful!' 'Yes, isn't she?' a voice from somewhere nearby in the velvety darkness agreed. 'She's my wife.'

The story is apocryphal. Belle Elmore was never that bad. Diddy, if indeed he saw her act, had caught it when Belle was past her prime, had put on weight, and had taken to peroxiding her hair. 'She wasn't a top-rank artist, but, in her way not bad,' concedes Clarkson Rose, who saw Belle at the Dudley Empire when George Formby, Sr topped the bill.[1] Rose goes on to describe Belle as a 'blowsy, florid type of serio,' which is not as damning as it sounds—Dudley's foundry workers were partial to blowsy, florid types.*

Playing to foundry workers was a far cry from Belle's dreams and ambitions when she first arrived in London in August, 1897. Then she was confident that she would take the West End's theatre-land by storm, according to Mrs Adeline Harrison, lyricist and sketch writer, who became Belle's close friend. Mrs Harrison had been called in to doctor a one-act operetta which Belle had written for her London debut 'She showed me a few feeble lines of dialogue, and asked me if I could add something to it, "to lengthen it". I suggested that a little plot might improve matters'. They met for the first time in Munyon's luxurious offices in Shaftesbury Avenue opposite the Palace. 'Presently the green draperies parted and there entered a woman who suggested to me a brilliant, chattering bird of gorgeous plumage,' Mrs Harrison recalls. 'She seemed to overflow the room with her personality. Her bright, dark eyes were twinkling with the joy of life. Her vivacious rounded face was radiant with smiles. She showed her teeth and there was a gleam of gold.'[2]

'Come, sit down here,' Belle invited, patting the cushions of the green settee with a plump, bejewelled hand. 'I guess we'll have a little chat right away. You know,' she confided, 'I'm going to make my debut at the Empire, Leicester Square.' (In those days the Empire was to music hall what La Scala was to opera.)

It was Mrs Harrison's introduction to a *folie de grandeur* that never ceased to amaze. For Belle fancied that she bore a strong resemblance to Marie Lloyd, whose star quality Belle confused with the gorgeous gowns Miss Lloyd wore.† But Marie Lloyd was

---

* A contrary view of Belle's talent is expressed in a letter to the author from Don Ross, whose wife, the late Gertie Gitana, knew Belle slightly, as Belle appeared once or twice on bills which Gertie topped. 'I know very few people had any admiration for Miss Elmore's work,' Ross writes. 'She had very little talent, but apparently immense confidence and nerve, which got her odds and ends of work.'

† According to one version, Belle copied her stage name from Marie

much more than a 'dress act'; she had a touch of genius, as critics as divergent as James Agate and T. S. Eliot were quick to recognise. It was no good slashing your skirt, so as to show off diamond garters if you were short both on talent and in the legs, as Belle was to discover.

Not the Empire in Leicester Square, but the Old Marylebone Music Hall was the scene of Belle's London debut in 'The Unknown Quantity', the mini-operetta which Mrs Harrison had cobbled together from Belle's scanty notes. On the programme Belle was billed as 'Cora Motzki', an unfortunate contraction of 'Mackamotzki', and she was partnered by an Italian tenor named Sandro Vio. The operetta, itself,was a feeble affair about blackmail with overtones of 'Manon Lescaut'.* The Old Marylebone audiences were not rowdy like those of the Varieties in Hoxton, for example; nor were they stuffy like those who patronised the Palace, where the attendants wore knee breeches and powdered their hair. When spectators at the Old Marylebone disliked a number they simply sat on their hands, which was what happened on Belle's opening night. She was given the run of the week, but at the end of it her contract was not renewed.

Her response to this fiasco was to rush out and buy herself more expensive gowns, then to hurry round to Hana, the theatrical photographer, and to have herself photographed in various artistic poses. Armed with these bits of pasteboard Belle made the rounds at that end of Waterloo Road known as 'Poverty Corner', where the agents had their offices. In time she got engagements as a 'middle of the bill' at the Grand in Clapham, the Camberwell Music Hall, and the Holborn. But for a long time she smarted under the humiliation of her initial flop at the Old Marylebone, for which she blamed her husband. Crippen had always been opposed to her going on the music hall stage, she told friends; indeed, he had sabotaged her career step by step, she claimed. She repeated it so many times that in the end she believed it. It was the beginning of many bitter recriminations.

At this distance one wonders if there was any truth in Belle's

Lloyd, who first appeared on the halls as 'Bella Delmare'.

* At its climax Belle was required to fling a sheaf of £5 notes at her lover's feet, while hitting high C. In her search for realism she insisted that the money be genuine bank notes, with the result that on opening night when the curtain was rung down there was a frantic scramble to

accusation. The Coldwater, Michigan, of Crippen's youth would have considered a career in opera as perfectly respectable (after all, Coldwater did have an 'opera house', even though it was only used for the occasional Chatauqua lecture). But Crippen's parents had regarded as agents of the devil all 'carney folk', in which category they lumped both actors and circus performers. It may be that some of this innate puritanism had rubbed off onto their son. Significantly, in explaining why Dr Crippen had given his son Otto for adoption by the boy's grand-parents, Myron Crippen told a Los Angeles reporter, 'His [Dr Crippen's] second wife was an actress, and he believed that the boy would receive better training with us than with her.'[3] All of which was not very complimentary to Belle. More significantly still, when his partner in later life, Dr Rylance, talked about permitting Mrs Rylance to go on the stage, Crippen sought to discourage him, saying, 'I do not think there could be a chaste woman in the profession'.

That Crippen may have practised a subtle form of sabotage at Belle's expense may be deduced from the fact that when she first came to London he had insisted that his wife use 'Cora Motzki' as her billing instead of the 'Belle Elmore' which she would have preferred. 'Motzki' combined with Belle's plump figure inevitably had led to her being dubbed 'the Brooklyn Matzos Ball'.

On the other hand, it can be argued that Crippen had been neglecting his own work in order to further Belle's career, a fact which came to light when in November, 1899, he was suddenly recalled to Philadelphia. Professor Munyon's attention had been drawn to a theatre handbill in which Crippen's name appeared as business manager for 'Vio and Motzki's Bright Lights Company, Fresh from its Broadway Triumph'. The professor was suitably horrified. For Munyon's homoeopathic remedies to be associated with the entertainment business in so intimate a fashion smacked too much of the Wild West medicine show for the professor's liking. The heavenward-pointing finger descended to point accusingly at Dr Crippen while its owner barked 'You're fired!' To Crippen it was a shattering blow.

*　　　*　　　*

recover the notes, Crippen himself joining in the paper chase. After that stage money was used.

But worse was in store for Crippen upon his return to London. He came back to find that he had been cuckolded in his absence by an ex-prize fighter from Chicago named Bruce Miller. Not only that, but his seven-year marriage was in danger of going onto the rocks. There had been warning signs before. As far back as August, 1897, when Belle had first joined him in London in a flat he had rented in South Crescent, Crippen had noticed a change in attitude, a cooling-off in her affection for him. 'She had cultivated a most ungovernable temper, and seemed to think I was not good enough for her,' Crippen complained. 'She boasted of the men of good position travelling on the boat who had made a fuss of her, and, indeed, some of these visited her at South Crescent . . .'⁴ But these were only shipboard flirtations.

Bruce Miller was a serious threat. He was to Crippen what Blazes Boylan was to Leopold Bloom in *Ulysses*, the arch cuckolder. A flashy dresser, Miller had abandoned the prize ring for vaudeville, and was appearing in London in a 'one-man band' act in which he played several instruments — banjo, harmonica and drum — simultaneously. Belle had met him at a party given by her music teacher in Torrington Square, and had immediately succumbed to his raffish charm. It made no difference to Belle that the ex-pugilist had a wife and children back in Chicago, to whom he intended to return one day. All that mattered to her was that Miller was big and handsome in a battered way, and that he knew how to pay pretty compliments to a woman. Nor did she have any intention of giving Miller up. 'She told me then,' Crippen later recalled, 'that she had got very fond of him, and that she did not care for me any more. She was always finding fault with me,' he added, 'and every night she took some opportunity of quarrelling with me, so that we went to bed in rather a temper with each other.'⁵

Now that the moment of decision had arrived what would Crippen do? Seek a showdown with his wife's lover? Order Belle to pack, or himself quit their flat leaving Miller to foot her bills? Crippen did none of these things.

In endeavouring to understand why he chose to play the complaisant husband it is as well to understand the peculiar state of sexual bondage to Belle in which he existed, a bondage which only she could break off. There was a curious reversal of gender roles so far as these two were concerned. Filson Young touches upon this reversal when he writes: 'His [Crippen's] attitude to women was peculiar. He was not the type of man that likes to dominate women; he was of the type that loves to be dominated by them; and in his love for showering presents upon his wife in public, and in spending a quite ridiculous proportion of his income in the adorning of her plump little person, he exhibited the symptoms of the psychopathic type to which undoubtedly he belonged.'[6] The type Young refers to is the masochist.

'He was not a man's man,' Mrs Adeline Harrison agrees. Mrs Harrison recalls how 'just for fun' Crippen on one occasion dressed up as a woman, covering his moustache with wig paste in order to hide it. 'His slight figure carried out the illusion to perfection,' she adds.[7] Crippen in fact was so hen-pecked that he even let Belle choose his suits. 'She would discuss the colour of his trousers with the tailor, while he stood aside looking on, without venturing an opinion,' Mrs Harrison records.

'Fear of losing the companion and the desire to keep him (or her) always content, amiable, and inclined to sexual intercouse' — these are the elements that cause a weak-willed individual to subject himself to the tyranny of another, according to sexologist Richard von Krafft-Ebing, who adds, 'Among married men, hen-pecked husbands belong to this category . . .'[8]

Concerning Bruce Miller's affair with Belle, not the least astonishing aspect is that the two rivals never met. 'I never saw Bruce Miller,' Crippen told Inspector Dew, 'but he used to call when I was out, and used to take her out in the evenings.' Crippen told the detective that he had, however, seen letters from Miller to Belle which ended 'With love and kisses to Brown Eyes'. Miller, when it came his turn, denied that he had ever tried to avoid Crippen, adding that on several occasions when he had called on Belle 'I had reason to believe Dr Crippen was in the house'.[9]

*   *   *

But to return to the period when he first discovered that he had been cuckolded by Miller, this blow, combined with loss of his $10,000 a year position with Munyon's, left Crippen floundering, and it was many months before he again found his feet. First he went to work for a rival concern, the Sovereign Remedy Company, but this firm was under-capitalised and failed after eight months.

Then he tried marketing a nerve tonic called 'Amorette', bottled from his own recipe. Meanwhile, he and Belle had moved to a cheaper flat in Store Street, near the British Museum.

Crippen's experience with Munyon's had made him a specialist in the mail order cure business. Thanks to Munyon's he knew how to prepare advertising copy, and where to place the ads (usually it was in popular weeklies like *Tit-Bits* or *Comic Cuts*) so that they would catch the eyes of the semi-literate who suffered from real or imaginary illnesses. He brought all of this expertise to bear to promote 'Amorette', but the nerve tonic failed to get off the ground. Finally in desperation Crippen hung a shingle outside the door of the Store Street flat reading 'Belle Elmore, Miniature Painter'. Belle did not paint the miniatures herself; the work was farmed out to others on a piece-rate basis.

Then towards the end of 1901 the Drouet Institute for the Deaf advertised for a 'consulting physician'. Crippen applied, and was accepted. Thus began his descent into the lower depths of quackery. For quackery, like Dante's conception of hell, had its upper and its nether regions.*

Mention was made earlier of the nostrum vendors who under such names as Grandma's Secret and Mother's Treasure, peddled opiates to soothe baby. Even lower than these dope peddlers were those who advertised 'sure cures' for diseases that were incurable. 'Every man who trades in this market, whether he pockets the profits of the maker, the purveyor, or the advertiser, takes toll of blood,' writes Samuel Hopkins Adams, adding 'Here the patent medicine business is nakedest, most cold-hearted.'[10] Dropsy, epilepsy, tuberculosis and cancer were diseases for which 'sure cures' were advertised in the popular press. Typical of these cures was Tuberculozyne, a morphine concoction brewed by a horse doctor in Kalamazoo, Michigan, whose net effect was to hasten the progress of tuberculosis.

The lowest of the low were the drug habit specialists. 'They are the scavengers,' Adams writes, 'delving amid the carrion of the fraudulent nostrum business for their profits. The human wrecks

---

* It is noteworthy that Dante in his ten circles of hell places the Falsifiers, who include quacks, next to the bottom rung. They are stricken with hideous diseases; the trench in which they lie being 'a running sore of gangrened limbs'. Only the traitors — Cain, Judas, Cassius — are placed lower.

made by the opium and cocaine laden secret patent medicines come to them for cure, and are wrung dry of the last drop of blood . . . They have discovered a money-making villainy worse than murder.'

In a limbo midway between the upper and the lower regions of this noisome pit of charlatanry dangled the Drouet Institute for the Deaf. The London branch of a French swindle, Drouet's had sumptuous offices first at 72 Regent's Park Road, then at Marble Arch. From these premises the institute dispensed what purported to be the secret discoveries of Dr Drouet, described as a 'distinguished man of science' but in reality a drunkard from the tough Belleville quarter of Paris. Shortly before his death from alcoholism, Dr Drouet had allowed his name to be used in exploiting a so-called deaf cure, consisting of little plasters that the patient was directed to stick behind his ears and that were supposed to have wonderful penetrating powers. Other Drouet remedies included drops, gargles and anti-catarrhal snuff.

'A disgraceful institution carried on for unworthy objects by discreditable means,' is the way Lord Chief Justice Mathew stigmatised the Drouet Institute. Evan Yellon, the editor of *The Albion Magazine*, which was devoted to protecting the interests of the deaf, agreed that it was 'one of the biggest and most ambitious frauds on the deaf ever engineered in this country'. An estimated one in ten of the deaf in the United Kingdom poured money at one time or another into this racket, which spent between £20,000 and £30,000 a year on full-page advertisements featuring testimonials secured from the ignorant and the gullible.[11] In addition Drouet's name was also writ large on the sides of London's horse-drawn omnibuses.

Nearly all of Drouet's business was conducted by mail, the deaf persons who answered its ads being sent a questionnaire to fill in, on the basis of which a diagnosis would be made. In reality Crippen, by means of a lightly pencilled mark in the corner of the questionnaire, would indicate which of several form letters was to be sent. The letter would then be typed out for his signature. The 'diagnosis' made use of such medical terms as 'Post Otorrhea and Tinnitus' or 'Rhinitis Chronica Rhino Pharyngitis Eustachian Salpingitis', and prescribed the anti-catarrhal plasters or gargle plus nasal spray plus anti-catarrhal powders, as the case might be.

Patients were not encouraged to present themselves at Drouet's offices at Marble Arch, the institute preferring to hold them at arm's length by means of His Majesty's postal service. However, Yellon, who was stone deaf, decided to see for himself what went on behind the scenes at Drouet's, made an appointment accordingly. Rewarded with a private consultation with Crippen, the magazine editor was not favourably impressed. 'His [Crippen's] face and eyes told the story of a life miserably misspent,' Yellon records.

But first Yellon was ushered into an ante-chamber whose furnishings were designed to impress ("The carpet was fine, really fine, and the chairs were good specimens of modern Chippendale . . . the various china knick-knacks were chosen and placed with good taste.') In contrast Crippen's consulting room was anything but imposing. 'Upon the walls were large and very ugly coloured pictures of anatomical subjects; there was a large operating chair, and by it a queer instrument very much like a hand fire-extinguisher in appearance.'

And what of Crippen himself? 'The man facing me was got up in a very fantastic fashion for a member of a learned and sober profession and an aural specialist,' writes Yellon. 'His frock-coat was orthodox enough,' he continues; 'but he wore with it a shirt of startling hue, adorning the front of which was a "diamond" as big as a marble; and the jaunty butterfly tie vied in hue with the shirt. His patent leather shoes were a trifle cracked, and his face a warning to all observant beholders. The flabby gills, the shifty eyes, and the man's appearance generally, would effectually have prevented me from being taken in . . .'[12]

The lack of antisepsis appears to have alarmed Yellon almost as much as Crippen's unusual get-up. For after asking one or two routine questions 'he [Crippen] picked up one of those filthy specula, and, without in any way disinfecting it, put it into my ear! He looked for about two minutes, then he bade me turn my head and put the same speculum, still uncleansed, into the other ear; having "examined" that, he did just what I had anticipated, dropped the speculum back among the other instruments with never a bath in an antiseptic at all!' Altogether the examination lasted five minutes. At its conclusion Crippen said, 'I cannot promise anything, but if you will try the treatment I will do my utmost for you.' Yellon, in turn, lost no time in warning his readers against the Drouet racket.

*   *   *

The full exposure of that racket as a menace not only to hearing but to life itself had to wait until 1912 when a House of Commons Select Committee on Patent Medicines sat at Westminster. P. Macleod Yearsley, a Fellow of the Royal College of Surgeons, told the Committee how the Drouet Institute had prescribed drops, plasters and snuff for a thirty-year-old man who had been suffering from an ear discharge since infancy. 'I found the ear full of polypi,' Yearsley declared. 'He presented symptoms which any aural surgeon would have recognised as indicating dangerous complications.' Yearsley also cited the case of a servant girl who had been diagnosed by a Drouet 'specialist' (Crippen or another?) as having 'middle ear disease' when in reality the nerve apparatus of both ears had been destroyed owing to congenital syphilis, and she had a discharge in one ear. Drouet's had already wrung £12.12s, or nearly a year's wages, from the servant girl, by promising her a complete cure. 'I found that she had caries of the temporal bones,' the aural specialist concluded, adding that after two operations he had her taught lip-reading.

Meanwhile, Drouet's downfall had come about with the death of a Staffordshire locksmith named Johnson from an ear abscess while under treatment by the institute. At the inquest Dr Percival Tildesley told a coroner's jury how he had found Johnson unconscious and dying when he called to attend the locksmith, and how he was shown plasters from Drouet's which the man had been using. In his post-mortem examination Dr Tildesley found that the right lobe of the brain had abscessed as a result of middle-ear disease, and that the lobe was in contact with skull bone that was so diseased that one could have passed a knitting needle from the ear into the brain. 'The treatment Johnson had been receiving was quite useless in my opinion,' Dr Tildesley told the jury. 'If the plasters contained a powerful irritant, it is quite possible that the inflammatory trouble would have been aggravated by their use.'

Drouet's did not long survive the bad publicity attracted to it by the Staffordshire inquest. But Crippen's employment there was to change his life profoundly. It was at Drouet's that he at last found love.

*　　*　　*

A popinjay Crippen, with his flashy clothes, may have appeared to a muck-raking magazine editor, but to at least one person at the

Drouet Institute he was a god. Ethel Clara LeNeve would not have been put off by the cracks in those patent leather shoes, nor would she have questioned whether the diamond stud was real. It would certainly never have occurred to her that the doctor had flabby gills, nor to detect that his eyes shifted when he talked, and this for the simple reason that Ethel Clara LeNeve had conceived a crush for Dr Crippen almost as soon as she laid eyes upon him.

Fresh from Pitman's school, Ethel at the age of seventeen had gone to work for Drouet's as a shorthand typist, her younger sister Nina having preceded her at the institute. Crippen liked the two sisters from the start, and invited them to take their tea with him in his office in the afternoon. He even visited them at their home in Hampstead. When in July, 1903, Nina left Drouet's to get married, Ethel succeeded her as head of the ladies' department, which brought Ethel into closer contact with Crippen. At first she looked upon Crippen as a father substitute, her own father being a drunken brute, but gradually her feelings towards her employer became more tender.

'Large grey or blue eyes, good teeth, nice looking, rather long straight nose (good shape), medium build, pleasant, lady-like appearance. Quiet subdued manner . . .' Thus reads the police description of Ethel which would one day circulate on two continents. Like most such descriptions it is deceptive. The eyes were large and grey and attractive, it is true; but that lady-like appearance was somewhat belied by a mouth that was frankly sensual. Beneath that quiet, subdued manner lurked a highly-spirited woman.

Ethel herself is the authority for the statement that as a child she lived the life of a tomboy, climbing trees, playing marbles, shooting with a catapult, 'dressing up' as a boy. 'For dolls or other girlish toys I had no longing,' she confesses in her autobiography. Instead she went on train-spotting expeditions with an uncle who worked for the railway. 'Nothing delighted him more than to take me to see the trains,' she goes on, 'and even to this day there are few things that interest me more than an engine.'[13] The brief memoir is notable in that while full of praise for the railway-enthusiast uncle it makes no mention whatsoever of Ethel's father, Walter Neave. (Ethel changed her name to 'LeNeve' partly because it sounded more romantic, partly as a gesture of rebellion against her father.)

Ethel's hatred of her father is not hard to trace. One of six children, Ethel was born in Diss, Norfolk with a deformity known as 'frog foot'. 'The doctors at the Jenny Lind Hospital near our home,' writes Walter Neave, 'were . . . anxious to perform an operation. But I was opposed to it; and that my judgment was sound is proved by the fact that the deformity has now entirely disappeared, and Ethel has as fine a carriage as one could wish to see in any girl.'[14] The father makes no mention of the agonies Ethel suffered in learning to walk straight, thanks to his rejection of medical advice. This suffering explains much of her strength of character.

Walter Neave, too, at one time had worked for the railways, not as a chief agent for the Great Eastern Railway, as he gave out in the four-ale bars he frequented, but in the much humbler capacity of 'railway clerk', the occupation entered on Ethel's birth certificate. He also boasted that he had once sung at the choir festival in St Andrew's Hall, Norwich, and had even been featured as a soloist in Norwich Cathedral. But by the time Ethel went to work for Drouet's, her father, who made a scrappy living as a coal canvasser, was being thrown out of pubs for bawling ribald ditties at the top of his lungs while drunk. He was also arrested on at least one occasion for battering his own children when in his cups, but Mrs Neave's tearful pleas got him off the charge.

To add to her troubles, there was a strong sibling rivalry between Ethel and her sister, who was the younger by eleven months. 'Nina got the upper hand always,' their mother, Mrs Charlotte Neave, declares. 'She was stronger and perhaps cleverer, and at school they always thought she was much older than her sister, instead of the other way around.'[15] The father confirms this impression. 'Of the two sisters,' he writes, 'Nina, although younger, was the cleverer, and she enjoyed better health than Ethel, who was constantly catching cold.' 'Catching cold' was Ethel's way of diverting attention from the sibling rival. That, and throwing tantrums, for Ethel had a temper, according to her father. 'She was, generally speaking, retiring and shy in disposition,' the father writes, 'but there were times when she would break out into a passion, and then, child as she was, everybody within reach would receive the full benefit of her little tongue.'

By the time Ethel went to work for Drouet's she had become a confirmed hypochondriac, complaining of catarrh and of neuralgic pains in her head—complaints which earned her the nickname 'Not Very Well, Thank You', Ethel's invariable reply when anyone asked after her health. Then came the miracle cure—for miracle seems hardly too strong a word to apply to the results which Crippen obtained when he started treating Ethel. One may be certain that Crippen prescribed none of the quack remedies he had been accustomed to peddling, such as Munyon's Special Catarrh Cure ('cures the most aggravated cases of hawking and spitting . . . dryness or scabs in the nose, gloomy, dull spirits . . .'). No, instead of placebos, Crippen offered the kindness and understanding of which Ethel had been starved by her own father. Thanks to this treatment, 'Not Very Well, Thank You' no longer grumbled, but actually smiled when she arrived at work in the mornings. As Ethel herself records, 'It was entirely to him [Dr Crippen] that I owed my cure. I had reason to feel under an obligation.'

Crippen, like many another married employer whose secretary has a crush on him, was not adverse to passing as a bachelor for as long as this pose could be maintained. A propos, Ethel's recollection of an early encounter with Crippen at Drouet's is revealing. 'I quickly discovered that Dr Crippen was leading a somewhat isolated life,' she writes. 'I did not know whether he was married or not. Certainly he never spoke of his wife. But one day a friend of his called at the office. My sister and I were taking tea with the doctor . . . When the friend had gone my sister asked the doctor whether he was really married. "It would take the lawyers all their time to find out," was the mysterious reply. That was all he said.'[16] Ethel must have been struck by the reply, for she told Mrs Jackson, her landlady, that 'Dr Crippen did not know if it [his marriage to Belle] was legal or not.'[17] From which it may be inferred that Crippen deliberately sought to mystify.

Ethel's doubts concerning Crippen's marital status were soon resolved when Belle burst into the office one day. 'Her coming was of a somewhat stormy character,' Ethel recalls. 'I was leaving the office for lunch when I saw a woman come out of the doctor's room and bang the door behind her. She was obviously very angry about something.

' "Who is that?" I said in a whisper to Mr Long.

' "Don't you know?" he said. "That's Mrs Crippen" . . . After that I quickly realised Dr Crippen's reluctance to speak about his wife. He was obviously not happy at home. In fact, he told me he was not.'

More amazing still was Belle's next visit to the office, which occurred when Ethel was taking dictation from Dr Crippen. 'There were more angry words,' Ethel writes, 'and just before she [Belle] left I saw the doctor suddenly fall off his chair. I ran up to him. He was very ill, and I believed that he had taken poison.' Why, one wonders, did Ethel leap to this melodramatic conclusion? Why could not Crippen have blacked out in a momentary fainting fit? Why did Ethel's mind immediately turn to poison? The whole tragi-comic episode has an air of unreality about it. 'He told me that he could bear the ill-treatment of his wife no longer. However, I managed to pull him round with the aid of brandy, and we did our best to forget the painful incident.'[18]

What was Dr Crippen's reaction, one wonders, when he came to and found those sorrowful grey eyes gazing down into his? He must have been struck by the ambiguity of the situation, for again there was a curious reversal of roles. By right, the healer's role, that of the restorer, belonged to him—had he not cured Ethel of her catarrh, thereby earning her undying gratitude? But the knight-errant had fallen from his horse, and there he lay while the erst-while damsel in distress succoured him with brandy. Crippen, accustomed to being nagged by an unloving wife, must have been struck by the novelty of the situation, to say the least.

[4]

Starting in 1905 Belle Elmore, by virtue of being a good mixer socially, found herself increasingly in the company of ladies who were top-liners on the music hall stage—artistes like Marie Lloyd, Lottie Albert and Lil Hawthorne of the Hawthorne Sisters—who foregathered once a week to talk shop over teacups. Not all of the company were artistes in their own right—some were married to men who topped the bill in variety, entertainers like Eugene Stratton, who had taught London to sing 'Little Dolly Daydream' and 'Lily of Laguna'; Paul Martinetti, the prince of mimes; and Fred Ginnett, whose equestrian act, 'Dick Turpin's Ride to York', still thrilled audiences up and down the land.

Out of these parties grew the Music Hall Ladies' Guild. The guild was born of nostalgia as much as anything else, of a fond recollection of the bad old days, for these ladies, most of them, had arrived the hard way. All knew what it was like to play to half-empty houses in the sticks, to be stranded without the railway fare back to London. All had endured the horrors of bug-infested digs. Time, however, had blunted the edges of these hardships, and made them appear in retrospect as amusing if not exciting adventures. Nevertheless, as these ladies reminisced about hard times over their teacups, it was perhaps natural that their thoughts should turn to the less fortunate in the profession, to helping artistes like Flora Lington, for example, who had been forced to enter a tubercular sanatorium leaving a blind husband at home to look after their two children.

Sympathy for the under-dog came naturally to Marie Lloyd, the guild's first president. The daughter of a pothouse waiter, Marie could never see a child playing barefoot in the street without ordering her carriage to stop, then scooping up the urchin, and delivering him or her to the nearest bootmaker to be fitted out with shoes. 'It was part of Marie's religion,' writes a chronicler of the music halls. 'It was also linked with her intense class consciousness—a fierce upholding of the less lucky among those who had been born into her own world.'[1]

Belle Elmore herself was not particularly class-conscious, though she had come up from the Brooklyn slums. But having failed to make a grand entrance into the music hall world by the front door, she tried a side entrance, found that there was a need for her talents as a fund-raiser. Belle in truth was not afraid to tackle anyone to get money for the Music Hall Ladies' Guild. Some of the guild ladies pretended to be shocked by her methods —the way she flirted with everyone from stage doormen to actor-managers. But of course it was all in a good cause. It bought layettes for expectant mothers, and toys for sick children at Christmas.

It was a measure of Belle's popularity that even though she turned blackleg during the music hall strike of January, 1907, the ladies forgave her. 'Belle, stay out and help your own people,' Millie Payne had pleaded as Belle crossed the picket-line at the Bedford Music Hall in Camden Town. 'Don't be daft,' countered Marie Lloyd. 'Let her in, and she'll empty the house!' Belle outlived her reputation as a blackleg to become the guild's honorary treasurer. As such in July, 1908, she shared a platform with the Bishop of Southwark and actresses Phyllis Broughton and Irene Vanbrugh, and had the satisfaction of hearing the Actors' Church Union vote unanimously to admit as members variety artistes, whom it had formerly sneered at as 'people who walk slack wires and perform with trained monkeys'. Still later at the guild's annual banquet Belle was presented with a silver slave bracelet inscribed 'To The Hustler' in recognition of 'her excellent work on behalf of the charity', according to *The Performer*.

*   *   *

The guild ladies' admiration for Belle did not extend to her husband. 'That little shrimp!—what can Belle possibly see in him?' one of the ladies mused aloud upon meeting Crippen for the first time. Crippen was such an odd one—always fussing around Belle, making her little presents in public, then looking around for the company's approval. He was not manly like their own husbands and men friends, the ladies decided. They thought to discern in Crippen another trait which was anathema to variety performers—they thought he was a sponger. It was Marie Lloyd who nicknamed Crippen 'The Half-Crown King', according to

Naomi Jacob. 'He was fond of asking people to have a drink with him,' Miss Jacob writes; '. . . then the "fumbling" began. Finally, he would giggle nervously, and say: "I'm afraid that I've—stupidly—come out without any money. Could you lend me half a crown?" ' As this was in the days when champagne sold on draught at sixpence a glass Crippen usually pocketed a considerable amount of change. 'When Crippen asks you to have a drink —pay for your own, it's a damn sight cheaper,' Marie Lloyd is quoted as saying.[2]

However, this story, like many others told of Crippen, has the ring of counterfeit coinage. Certainly he was generous as far as Belle was concerned. For example, he did not hesitate to buy her an ermine and guipure wrap to wear at the guild's annual banquet, at a time when he was overdrawn at the bank.

Crippen liked the guild ladies no more than they liked him. 'His role in the social life was that of a spectator,' Filson Young writes. 'He was the silent member of the gay little companies . . .'[3] For 'silent' read 'disapproving'. Crippen could not help but contrast Belle's shallow existence given over to pleasure with the deprived life Ethel was forced to lead. In the midst of some glittering charity ball at the Café Monica or the Trocadero to which his wife had insisted upon going Crippen's thoughts would stray to the little typist in her drab Hampstead lodgings. How was she spending her evening, he would wonder. Crippen had no illusions as to the sincerity of Belle's friends. He knew that they ridiculed him the moment his back was turned. He was glad to escape from their company to Ethel. The deep sympathy and fellow-feeling that had been aroused when Ethel had rescued her knight-errant had gradually ripened into mutual love.

*   *   *

'I see ourselves in those days of courtship,' Hawley was to remind Ethel later, 'having our dinner together after our day of work together was done, or sitting sometimes in our favourite corner in Frascati's by the stairway, all the evening listening to the music . . .' What a contrast these *tête-à-têtes* with Ethel made to the garish balls Belle dragged him to, and how he looked forward to those tranquil evenings spent listening to the strains of Frascati's palm court orchestra. In their favourite corner by the stairs,

[57]

chosen no doubt in hopes that it screened them from recognition by Belle's friends, the lovers could hold hands beneath the
napery. 'Ah! how even in those days,' Crippen recalled, 'we
began to realise how near and dear we were to become to each
other.'

'One Sunday, how early I came to see you—six years ago last
summer it was—and we had a whole day together, which meant
so much to us then. A rainy day indeed, but how happy we were
together, with all sunshine in our hearts.'*

In the summer of 1903 then—the date is carefully pin-pointed—
a whole day together savoured of the rare and beautiful. 'Courtship'—how curious is Crippen's use of this word, so closely
associated with marriage—was still a matter of a few golden hours
snatched from domesticity. How, one wonders, did they spend
that rainy Sunday? In the British Museum among the embattled
amazons and centaurs of the Elgin Marbles? At the National Gallery admiring the Italian Renaissance? At the Regent's Park Zoo?
Or did they tramp the streets of London, ducking into doorways
when it showered? It is tempting to think that they spent that
Sunday at some hotel with a 'Do Not Disturb' sign hung on the
door. But such was not the case. It was not until seven years after
Ethel and Hawley had first set eyes upon one another that their
love was physically consummated.

The picture of continence contrasts sharply with that of Crippen
the seducer of innocence, which was later given to the world by
popular journalists. 'She passively accepted his love at first and
was clay in his hands . . .', claims one such writer. 'Although he
was middle aged, it was impossible for her to resist him: he
focused on her all the force of his starved affections and his
thwarted passions.' Again, 'His appearance was no barrier, for
beneath it there was an inflexible will and nerves of steel. She was
unhappy and ductile, the very type of woman to yearn for complete
possession by a man.'[4]

For one supposedly versed in the arts of seduction the man of
'inflexible will and nerves of steel' was singularly ineffective in
persuading Ethel to his bed. Those 'starved affections' and that
'thwarted passion' were to be kept bottled up for seven years while
Ethel, this highly 'ductile' young lady who yearned for 'complete

* For full text see Appendix.

[58]

possession by a man', made up her mind.

What was the stumbling block? Why did they remain chaste, these lovers who were said to have been straining at the leash? Religious scruples? Regard for Belle and the by now shop-soiled marriage vows Hawley had exchanged with her? Any guilt feelings Ethel may have entertained about taking Hawley away from his wife were eased when 'by sheer accident — the expression is Ethel's — she saw some letters Bruce Miller had written to Belle. 'This, I need hardly say, relieved me somewhat of any misgivings I had with regard to my relations with her husband,' Ethel writes. 'He [Hawley] told me often that she was his wife only in name, and that I was everything to him.'[5]

No, it was for none of these reasons. Crippen's ardour foundered on the hard rock of Ethel's lower middle-class morality. For even more than she longed to be possessed by her lover Ethel yearned for Respectability. She was holding out for marriage lines and a home of her own, an 'Acacia Villa' in that row of suburban 'Chez Nous' and 'Bide-a-wee' and 'Mon Repos' villas that stretches to infinity. Early in their 'courtship' Crippen had dangled in front of Ethel the prospect of marriage. Belle was on the point of leaving him for Bruce Miller, after which a divorce would be arranged, he told Ethel. When this prospect failed to materialise Ethel's resolve to hold out for marriage, far from being weakened, was strengthened. She had waited this long without surrendering to Crippen, now she would wait a bit longer.

Curiously, Crippen was not Ethel's first suitor. Before going to work at Drouet's Ethel had had a boy friend her own age, according to her father. 'My daughter used to receive letters from someone regularly, and she refused to tell us the name of her correspondent,' Walter Neave writes. 'I have little doubt that these were love letters.' Ethel used to sneak out of the house at night to go dancing with this same boy friend, her father claims. 'I forbade my daughter to go to dances, but I have since learned that she often set my orders at defiance. She kept her dancing pumps under lock and key . . . it was years before I found out.'[6] One can imagine the perverse delight Ethel would have taken in defying her father's orders.

Neave is also the authority for the statement that Ethel was attracted to older men. He quotes her as saying, 'I think if I ever marry it will be with an old man — a man much older than myself.'

Why this preference? 'Because all the young men I see seem to be foppish, and to have nothing in their heads but thoughts of dress and amusement.'[7] Crippen at forty-one, when these two first started to keep company, was hardly an old man; and although he was something of a fop, with his fancy waistcoats and diamond stickpins, he certainly had more on his mind than amusement and clothes.

*　　*　　*

In April, 1904, Bruce Miller suddenly remembered that he had a wife and children in Chicago, and, with a show of reluctance, took his leave of Belle. Belle, in turn, dabbed at her eyes with a chiffon handkerchief as she had seen it done in the Lyceum melo-dramas. Significantly, she did not remove the many photographs of Miller with their affectionate inscriptions that held pride of place in the parlour. Far from leading to any reconciliation between the Crippens, Bruce Miller's departure only served to make Belle more irritable, and she found fault with Hawley upon every occasion.

Crippen, in turn, was under increasing pressure from Ethel to do something about a legal separation from Belle. It was the great sorrow of Ethel's life that Crippen continued to live under the same roof as Belle; indeed, to share Belle's bed, for their flat in Store Street had only one bedroom. It was not enough that Hawley should assure Ethel that 'she [Belle] was his wife only in name, and that I was everything to him'. Ethel demanded further proofs. Thus it was the need to have separate bedrooms as much as any-thing else that dictated the Crippens' removal to No. 39 Hilldrop Crescent, Holloway, in September, 1905, Hawley renting the semi-detached on a three-year lease at £52 10s per annum.

Belle immediately threw herself into the redecoration of the house, dispensing her lucky shade of pink with a lavish hand. Now that she had more spacious living quarters, Belle also took to entertaining the Music Hall Ladies' Guild to tea, and to giving small supper parties. So as to be able to splurge on her guests, Belle practised all sorts of economies at Crippen's expense, in particular skimping on the table.

As Belle had a horror of domestic servants, she refused to have a cook or maid living in, but relied upon the services of a 'daily'. Even then she was impatient: a neighbour later recalled seeing Belle snatch a broom from the daily, who was slow in beating a carpet in the backyard, and, although she was dressed for town, finish the job herself.

In spite of Belle's parsimony Crippen (was it because he had found love at last?) put on weight. 'He . . . chuckled with delight when he told us his clothes were becoming too small for him,' according to Mrs Harrison, who found him 'quite jolly and lively'. Crippen also allowed Belle to take the credit for his conversion to Catholicism, which took place at about this time. 'One Sunday morning they both called early, after Mass,' Mrs Harrison relates, 'and it was then the doctor informed us that his wife had made him a Catholic. He always appeared subservient to her wishes,' she adds.

Belle's religion—and she remained a practising Catholic all her life—was as much a matter of superstition as it was of anything. She would no more miss Mass on a Sunday if she could help it than she would tolerate the colour green in her home decoration. She was superstitious to the point where the mere sound of someone whistling backstage in any theatre in which she worked was enough to make her ill. Belle never let her religious convictions interfere with her life style, however. In particular, she regarded the Seventh Commandment as a dead letter.

*   *   *

Paradoxically, it was Ethel who gave the alarm about the parlous state of Crippen's finances. The paradox arose from the fact that Crippen, on the surface at least, appeared to be doing well. Far from being hurt by the Drouet debacle, Crippen had, if anything, profited from it; for he had been able to buy up the Drouet assets, including its mailing lists, 'very cheap', according to the editor of *Truth*, who comments: 'He [Crippen] thus became the last depository of the epoch-making discoveries of the immortal Drouet, out of which various rascals . . . have drawn a magnificent revenue . . .'[8]

These epoch-making discoveries, plasters, anti-catarrhal snuff and all, now reappeared under the label of the Aural Remedies Company, with a convenience address at Craven House, Kingsway, London. Those who answered the Aural Remedies ads were invited to fill in an 'Analytical Form' and return it to 'H. H. Crippen, M.D. (U.S.A.)', who promised to make 'an exhaustive study' of the symptoms described and to recommend treatment. Enclosed with the 'Analytical Form' was a copy of a fake 'Otological Gazette', complete with drawings of the inner ear, which assured the prospective customer that a simple head cold could lead to deafness, which in turn could entrain other disastrous consequences, 'the eyes being weakened ... the brain being affected ... even paralysis has been known', ending with an abscess 'eating its way into the brain'. All of this could be avoided by Dr Crippen's Simple Home Treatment ('No matter how many disappointments ... no matter how severe, obstinate or chronic the form of deafness ... this method has made it possible for patients to effect a positive and permanent cure by treating themselves in their own home.')

Ethel, however, by virtue of the fact that she kept the books, was able to see that Crippen, far from putting anything by, was in danger of plunging into the red. Thanks to Belle's extravagances, which were on a rising scale, there was a gap between income and expenses. If he were to avoid bankruptcy, Crippen would have to develop new sidelines. It was at this point that Ethel brought her influence to bear on Crippen to abandon the patent medicine racket entirely. Ethel had watched with apprehension the collapse of the Drouet Institute, which had shown her how vulnerable were the quacks who diagnosed by mail. Overnight they could be ruined by bad publicity. Not only that, but they laid themselves open to prosecution on charges ranging from fraud to manslaughter.

Above all, Ethel feared Crippen's involvement with a character named Eddie Marr, who was the financial backer of the Aural Remedies Company. Marr remains a somewhat shadowy figure in Crippen's background.* He was named as Crippen's 'angel' by William E. Scott, a New York advertising man, who knew both men well through handling their patent medicine ads. Scott told a

---

* Marr peddled patent medicines under such aliases as Professor Keith-Harvey, Elmer Shirley, and W. S. Hamilton, 'obesity expert'. But it was as a bucket shop operator dealing in bogus mining shares under the name of 'Arnold and Butler' (telegraphic address 'Lucrative') that Marr came to the notice of Scotland Yard's fraud squad. 'Arnold and Butler', in the words of *John Bull*, were 'cover snatchers, fraudulent stock and share dealers, sham bankers, bogus financial experts and pests of society.'

New York Tribune reporter that without Marr's aid 'Crippen would never have gained the material success he attained'.[9] He went on to hint that blackmail lay at the bottom of the partnership, claiming that 'the two men have holds on each other'. 'Dr Crippen,' Scott concluded, 'was never the financial power behind the ventures which were supposedly his. He handled these affairs and seemed to be the man in absolute charge, but when it came to the actual settling of accounts and other matters where the purse was in demand Dr Crippen made a pilgrimage to Marr's office to secure the money.'*

Ethel's advice was not entirely disinterested. Ethel had a scheme in the back of her head whereby Crippen could not only assure himself of a steady income, but free himself from Marr's influence once and for all. In thumbing through the pages of *The Stage* and *Era*, the theatrical weeklies which cluttered up Crippen's office by virtue of his wife's interests, Ethel had noticed a number of advertisements for 'American Painless Dentistry' and 'American Crown Bar and Bridge Work'. It suddenly struck her that there was a very good living to be made in catering to the dental requirements of the theatrical profession. Often a performer's chief asset was a dazzling smile revealing flawless teeth, and Ethel knew from remarks made by Crippen how much time Belle's friends spent with their dentists, and how they were always on the look-out for the very latest in dental techniques. (One American dentist, a Dr Goldberg, with offices in the Strand, actually listed in his advertisements the music hall artistes who were his clients.) What better than that Hawley should cash in on this vogue by taking an American dentist as partner and exploiting him as a 'painless wonder' using the advertising techniques he had perfected when working for Munyon's? Ethel even thought of a name to bestow upon such a partnership — 'The Yale Tooth Specialists'.

Once more Crippen could not help but contrast Ethel's selfless attitude with the selfishness of Belle, whose reaction at the first hint of financial difficulties was to rush out and buy herself a new wardrobe. 'Ethel LeNeve has loved me as few women love men,' Crippen was to write later, adding that such a love 'may not be

---

* When Crippen was first being sought by police Marr scurried around to Craven House, where the Aural Remedies Company had a convenience office, and scraped Crippen's name from the office door.

denounced by men who have not been so happy as I have been, and by women whose hearts are not big enough for such devotion.'[10]

Belle, of course, was aware of his ripening love for Ethel, but appeared not to care. Hawley, in turn, emboldened by Belle's indifference, made no secret of his true feelings. The Crippens had in fact arrived at a *modus vivendi*. 'I never interfered with her movements in any way,' Crippen was to tell Inspector Dew later. 'She went in and out just as she liked, and did what she liked; it was of no interest to me.'

For the benefit of Belle's friends the Crippens continued to play Happy Families long after the game had lost its point. Thus Mrs Harrison tells of calling on the Crippens one day to find them sitting on the sofa, 'he with his arm round her waist, with the sweetest domestic intimacy. In fact, no one ever knew them to be otherwise than lovable and affectionate to each other.'[11] The felicity was only apparent, however, according to Hawley; beneath the surface other emotions were in play. 'Although we apparently lived very happily together,' Crippen declared, 'as a matter of fact there were very frequent occasions when she got into most violent tempers, and often threatened she would leave me, saying she had a man she could go to, and she would end it all.'[12]

In retrospect, a strange apathy appears to have overtaken all three characters in this triangular drama. All three seemed determined to renounce freedom of choice, and to allow circumstances to dictate the course of their lives. Why did not Hawley leave Belle and live openly with Ethel? He could have done so at any time. Why did Ethel consent to what to her must have been an intolerable arrangement, as Crippen continued to live under the same roof as his wife? And Belle, if she found her husband such a ridiculous figure, why did she not try going it alone, or pick up with another man? It was as though they were paralysed, and could only look on helplessly as alternative courses of action dwindled away.

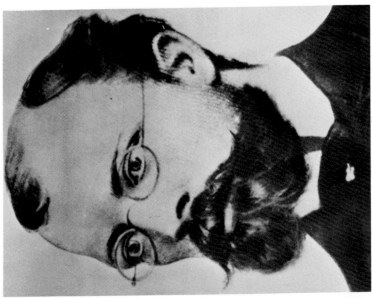

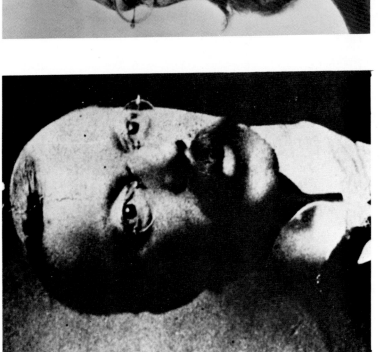

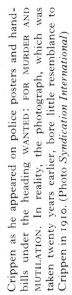

Crippen as he appeared on police posters and hand-bills under the heading WANTED: FOR MURDER AND MUTILATION. In reality, the photograph, which was taken twenty years earlier, bore little resemblance to Crippen in 1910. (Photo *Syndication International*)

Highly romanticised version of Crippen with a beard drawn by a police artist as an aid to identifying the doctor, who was then on the run from police. In July, 1910 the real Crippen was forty-eight, had sandy hair, and had shaved off his moustache to foil the police.

Belle Elmore as she appeared during her brief and unsuccessful career in music hall. Her plumpness, shortness of stature and lack of grace were not to the taste of Edwardian audiences, besides which she had no talent for singing.
(Photo *Syndication International*)

The historic wireless message sent by Captain Kendall notifying Crippen's presence on board with Ethel LeNeve disguised as his son. This marconigram, together with others pertaining to Crippen's capture, fetched £1,600 at auction in July, 1974. (Courtesy Bonham's)

Inset: Captain Henry Kendall of the liner *Montrose*. It was Kendall's suspicions which resulted in a Scotland Yard detective chasing Crippen 3,000 miles across the Atlantic to arrest him in Quebec waters. (Photo *Syndication International*)

Treatment of the Crippen story by one London newspaper at the height of the hue and cry. The *Weekly Despatch* devoted its entire front page on Sunday, 31st July, 1910 to telling its readers how Crippen and his paramour Ethel LeNeve spent their time at sea aboard the *SS Montrose*. (Photo courtesy of The Marconi Company Limited)

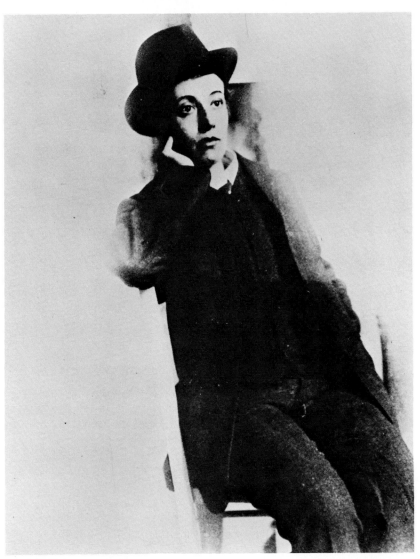

Above: Ethel LeNeve, Crippen's mistress, in the boyish disguise in which she tried to pass herself off as Crippen's son. The trousers were so tight that they split up the back and had to be held together with safety pins, which tipped off Captain Kendall that there was something suspicious about 'Master Robinson'. (Photo *Syndication International*)

Left: Crippen and Ethel LeNeve snapped by one of the *Montrose*'s crew while strolling along the deck of the liner. It is clear that Ethel did not make a very convincing boy. (Photo courtesy of The Marconi Company Limited)

Above: Crippen in handcuffs being led down the gangplank of the *Megantic* at Liverpool by Chief Inspector Walter Dew. Crippen is wearing Dew's ulster with the collar turned up in an effort to hide his face from the mob milling on the quayside. (Photo *Syndication International*)

Below: Crippen and Ethel LeNeve in the dock at the Bow Street Police Court, where they were committed for trial in September, 1910. Ethel, whose hat is heavily veiled to shield her from the public gaze, heard the charge against her reduced from murder to one of being an accessory after the fact. (Photo *Syndication International*)

The wax effigy of Crippen in Madame Tussaud's Chamber of Horrors. The features were modelled by Jack Tussaud, the great-great-grandson of the waxworks' founder, who attended Crippen's trial and took a photograph of him with a camera hidden in a bowler hat. (Photo courtesy of Madame Tussaud's)

Poster for 'Belle, or the Ballad of Dr Crippen', a musical by Wolf Mankowitz and Monty Norman. Presented in May, 1961, the critics found it to be in 'bad taste', and it closed after six weeks.

III

INSPECTOR
DEW

'It seems doubtful whether any murderer
of the past century, excepting Palmer
and Jack the Ripper, will be so long
remembered as Crippen.'

—DOUGLAS G. BROWNE[1]

'. . . no case has ever fascinated the
British public, and, indeed, engaged the
attention of the whole world, in quite
the same way that the case of Dr Crippen
did . . .'

—SIR MELVILLE MACNAGHTEN[2]

[5]

It was suggested earlier that it is Hawley Crippen's ordinariness, his capacity to embody *l'homme moyen sensuel*, that makes him a fascinating if not unique study in the annals of great crime. In a sense the same could be said for Chief Inspector Walter Dew, who in July, 1910, suddenly found himself in charge of 'the biggest murder mystery of the century', as he describes it. Dew, who when last glimpsed was standing aghast over the remains his spade had turned up in the cellar at No. 39 Hilldrop Crescent, was ordinary both in appearance and habits to the point of being nondescript, which perhaps is not a bad quality in a detective. Actually, Crippen and Dew had much in common, which explains why the two men hit it off so well together later.

Born in 1863 at Far Cotton, Northampton, one of eleven children, Dew came from just such a humble family background as Crippen, his father having been a railway guard on the London & Northwestern. With so many mouths in the family to feed, not much time was wasted on the children's education. Besides, Dew was not an apt pupil. 'I detested school, and was an absolute dud there, and promptly left when I attained the ripe age of thirteen,' he writes.[3] Dew's first job was as a dogsbody to a solicitor in Chancery Lane, which made him familiar with the law courts, and which may have encouraged him to join the Metropolitan Police at the age of nineteen. The raw recruit brought to police work physical robustness, courage and a phenomenal memory. Of this latter gift he writes, 'I made notes, of course . . . but it was rarely indeed that I made use of my notebook when giving evidence.'

Assigned to Paddington Green station, Dew volunteered to track down the sheep-stealers who were making nightly raids on flocks in the Harrow and Sudbury areas. 'We patrolled in couples,' he recalls, 'armed only with small wooden truncheons as against the sharp butchers' knives which the raiders carried.'

Dew got his detective badge in 1887 in time to join in the hunt for the master butcher of them all—Jack the Ripper. It was in Whitechapel also that he acquired the nickname of 'Blue Serge', in denigration of his habit of wearing his Sunday best suit when on duty. Promoted to the rank of inspector, Dew was in charge first of the Hammersmith division, then of the Bow Street CID, before being selected for the Criminal Investigation Department at Scotland Yard with the rank of chief inspector.

In retrospect it is evident that Dew was never really happy in the detective role. On the one hand, he had too much sympathy for the poor wretches his work at Scotland Yard brought him up against—he was that rarity among detectives, a genuinely compassionate man. On the other hand, he loathed the paper work, despised the routine checking and re-checking that makes up so large a part of modern detection. He was more of a thief-taker than an executive type.

Unfortunately for him, Dew's work, at the beginning of the cellar murder at least, consisted largely of checking out the reports which came flooding into Scotland Yard that Crippen had been sighted in various parts of Britain—and not only Britain, for the hue and cry spread to the other side of the Atlantic as well. The manhunt for Crippen, which forms an exciting chapter in the history of modern crime detection, was really a tale of three cities, London, New York and Los Angeles, California.

*   *   *

On Friday, July 15th, the sun came up over the Manhattan sky-line red as a boil, threatening to send the temperature soaring once again into the nineties. New York was in the grip of a heat wave which had melted the asphalt in the streets, sent tenement dwellers with their mattresses onto the fire escapes at night gasping for air.

On Pier 56 at the foot of West 14th Street, where the big Cunarder *Lusitania* was due to dock at eight thirty, the stevedores took refuge in the shade of the corrugated iron sheds. It was too hot to argue why the Highlanders, as the New York team was known, had slid into third place in the American League, or to discuss that other febrile topic of the hour, Jack Johnson's knock-out victory over Jeffries in the fifteenth round, a victory which was sparking off race riots elsewhere in the United States. Instead, the dockers squatted listlessly against the shed walls, waiting as the huge transatlantic liner was nudged towards her berth in the North River.

The more alert among the stevedores might have been mildly curious concerning Mme Isabel Ginnett (the 'Mme' dated from her circus days, when she was always billed as such) who, flanked by two obvious plainclothes detectives, stood where the gangplank was due to be run up the ship's side. They would have been even more curious had they known that this pert little woman with a gold watch pinned to her starched shirtwaist was an ex-circus bareback rider. Most probably they would have scratched their heads with astonishment and have forgotten the heat momentarily had they heard her speak with her Cockney accent. Mme Ginnett, who had succeeded Marie Lloyd as president of the Music Hall Ladies' Guild, happened to be in New York when the news that Belle had been found murdered broke. This accounted for her presence on the Cunard pier so early on the Friday morning.

As the gap between the liner and the dock narrowed, Mme Ginnett scanned the passengers who lined its decks. 'I would know Dr Crippen anywhere,' she assured the detectives at her side. 'I would recognise him no matter what his disguise.' Why was she so certain that Crippen would cut and run for America? Mme Ginnett was asked by reporters. Because he had spoken to her often and nostalgically about his early life in the States, she replied. Had she not often heard him talk of selling up his London practice in order to buy a fruit farm in California? The suggestion, she added, had met with a dim response on the part of Belle.

The *Lusitania* failed to yield any sign of Crippen, disguised or otherwise; but Mme Ginnett was not discouraged. After the last of the *Lusitania*'s cabin passengers had landed, Mme Ginnett boarded the liner where she subjected remaining passengers, stewards and stokers alike to her piercing gaze. Still not satisfied, with the two detectives in tow, she took the ferry to Ellis Island, where she gave the once-over to the *Lusitania*'s steerage passengers. Not even the roughest of these immigrants who returned her gaze coolly could intimidate the little woman, who was accustomed to breaking in horses for her husband's act.

In the days that followed Mme Ginnett made special trips to the docks to meet the *Lorraine* arriving from Le Havre, the *St Paul* docking from Southampton, the *Cedric* from Liverpool. Some days she reinforced in her vigil by Belle's sister, Mrs Theresa Hunn, and by Belle's step-sister, Mrs Louisa Mills; other days she took up her stand alone. On Monday, July 18th, Mme Ginnett wrote to Melinda May, secretary of the Music Hall Ladies' Guild: 'Up till today we have met, and searched every passenger of five boats from England and France ... May we soon catch him!' The Furies were noted for their persistence. They did not give in until they had driven the object of their vengeance mad and then sucked his blood.

* * *

At the moment Mme Ginnett began her waterfront vigil, people in Los Angeles three thousand miles away were awakening to discover that in the Crippen case they had a murder on their doorstep. 'LOS ANGELES CENTER OF LONDON MURDER MYSTERY' screamed a headline in the *Los Angeles Examiner* for Friday, July 15th. 'WANT TO QUESTION L.A. MAN ABOUT A MURDER' the *Record*, not to be outdone, replied. The headlines referred to the fact that both Crippen's father and Crippen's son Otto were living in Los Angeles, where Crippen's mother had died only the previous year.

Reporters found the father, Myron A. Crippen, aged 83, living in a run-down boarding-house at Third and Flower Streets. Myron was even smaller than his son Hawley, judging from the photograph of him which appeared in the *Examiner*. His body appears shrunken, the cheeks gaunt and weathered by age. The stoop of his shoulders signals defeat.

Crippen senior seemed utterly bewildered by the turn of events which had made his son the world's most sought after criminal. But his belief in Hawley's innocence was absolute. Obviously Hawley could have had nothing to do with Belle Elmore's death; murder would have been utterly alien to his gentle nature. Reporters who tried to interview Otto H. Crippen got shorter shrift. Otto, who worked as a telephone linesman, had not long been married and was living in Hollywood at the home of his father-in-law, J. C. Herwick. A Hearst representative who knocked at the Herwick door found himself looking down the muzzle of a Winchester rifle while the father-in-law ordered him off the premises. 'If you don't git I'll use this,' Herwick threatened. The Hearst reporter, 'git'.

* * *

Meanwhile, in Britain the hue and cry had reached a feverish peak. 'The newspapers were full of the case,' as Inspector Dew writes in his autobiography. 'It was the one big topic of conversation. On the trains and buses one heard members of the public speculating and theorising as to where they [the fugitives] were likely to be.' If only the talk in the train compartments and on the bus tops had confined itself to theories and speculation. Unfortunately, otherwise sane members of the public fancied they saw the fugitives on every street corner.

One of the earliest sightings came from Waltham Abbey, Essex, where a Mr J. Johnson claimed that he had spotted Crippen. 'I noticed him particularly because he was a small man and was carrying a large brown Gladstone bag,' Johnson told detectives. (The Gladstone bag was an all-too-familiar artefact to Dew; such pieces of luggage had been strewn along the garden path of that most elusive of killers, Jack the Ripper.) 'He looked haggard, as if he had walked a long way,' Johnson added. That same day a Liverpool barber remembered having shaved off Crippen's moustache, while a Ramsgate beach attendant swore that he had rented a deck chair to the missing doctor, who likewise was seen travelling to Folkestone on the cross-Channel boat train ('He is said to have taken a ticket for the harbour, but to have alighted hastily at the Central Station'). As Crippen was usually reported as being 'seen' alone, the press began to speculate that his companion, Miss LeNeve, might have met a fate similar to that meted out to Belle Elmore, for by now it was assumed that the little American-born doctor was a killer.

But Crippen was not always alone when 'sighted', as the following report from *The Times* of July 22, 1910, makes clear: 'A remarkable scene took place at Stonebridge (Willesden) yesterday. A middle-aged man wearing spectacles and accompanied by a young lady, called at a number of houses, stating that he had just come up from the country and desired lodging for himself and his daughter. A rumour quickly spread that they were "Dr" Crippen and Miss LeNeve, and a hostile crowd of several hundred people quickly gathered round the man and woman. The police were called, and with some difficulty the couple were got to the police station, where they proved beyond doubt that they were not the persons who were wanted.' One wonders whether this suspect is the one Inspector Dew refers to when he writes: 'On two occasions a gentleman who was unfortunate enough to resemble Crippen facially was brought to Scotland Yard ... On the first occasion he took the experience in good part, but when the same thing happened a second time he was highly indignant, and said it was getting to be a habit.'[4]

* * *

On Monday, July 18th, Inspector Dew had the distinction, reserved for but few men, of hearing himself described as a genius when Coroner Danford Thomas opened the inquest on the cellar remains. 'Many a man might have gone into that cellar and made no discovery,' the coroner pointed out. 'It remained for a detective with a genius for his work to go a step further . . .' Dew needed all the praise he could muster, for just at that moment he was being hammered from all sides for letting Crippen slip through his grasp. That very morning the *Daily Mail*, in an editorial headed 'Scotland Yard and Dr Crippen', had observed that the police had taken 'a half-hearted course'. 'They did not entirely believe Dr Crippen,' the editorial pursued. 'On the contrary, they made such pressing inquiries that he presently bolted . . . But while they were making these inquiries they kept no close watch upon him.' Not only that but William Thorne, Labour Member of Parliament for West Ham, had tabled a question in the House of Commons directed to Winston Churchill, the Home Secretary: 'Will the Right Honourable Member state who is responsible for allowing Dr Crippen to get out of the hands of the police when it was known by the Chief of Police, Scotland Yard, that Crippen had made several false statements about the murdered woman?'

However, on the morning the inquest opened the beleaguered Dew was to redeem himself once more when, during a recess in the proceedings, he overheard an important conversation. 'I was standing idly outside the court close to a group of women who were discussing the case,' he writes. 'One of the women was Mrs Paul Martinetti, who had been a close friend of Belle Elmore, and I pricked up my ears when I overheard her say something about Belle having undergone a serious operation. I called Mrs Martinetti to one side and asked her if I had heard aright.

' "Oh yes," she replied. "Belle had an operation years ago in America. She had quite a big scar on the lower part of her body. I have seen it." '

'Here was something really vital,' Dew concludes. 'If that scar could be found on those gruesome remnants of human flesh lying in the Islington Mortuary it might provide the missing link in the chain of evidence of identification.'[5]

* * *

Meanwhile, as the watch kept of transatlantic liners docking in New York proved negative, Inspector Dew inclined more strongly to the view that the fugitives were probably hiding out on the Continent. He had made inquiries and discovered that Crippen and Ethel had spent most of their holidays in Normandy, at Calais, Boulogne and Dieppe. Crippen had learnt French at school and had retained enough of it to make his wants known. He could thus mingle with the holiday-makers then thronging these seaside resorts without attracting attention to himself or to his companion, Dew reasoned.

It was a view subscribed to by Ethel's father. 'I am practically certain that Ethel is somewhere in France,' Neave told a *Daily Mail* reporter. The father added that in France the couple 'generally stayed in quiet little hotels a little way off the usual track of tourists. Crippen has often told me how fond he is of these secluded retreats . . .' Neave said that it would not surprise him if Crippen were disguised as a woman. 'His gait, his effeminate mannerisms and his gentle manner all combine to make such a make-up easy for him.'

Earlier M. Roussel, a train guard, claimed that he had seen the fugitives travelling on the Dieppe–Paris Express. They were in a second-class compartment, and the man spoke with an American accent, M. Roussel declared. If so, they were swallowed up on their arrival in the French capital, Dew concluded, for there the trail petered out. In desperation on Tuesday, July 19th, Scotland Yard offered a reward of £250 for information leading to the arrest of the couple, and the following day Crippen was reported to have been seen at Vernet-les-Bains in the Pyrenees near the Spanish border, where he had registered at a hotel as 'Henri Tarbot', rentier from Narbonne. He had spent the weekend at this thermal resort, then left on Monday morning by private motor car, possibly for Spain. The man had worn a straw hat, alpaca jacket, and grey-striped trousers, 'and was obviously worried and uneasy', according to the newspaper accounts. The fact that he had been seen alone again increased anxiety for Ethel's safety.

Finally, a Delaware minister was arrested as Crippen when the Red Star liner *Kroonland* docked in Manhattan on Wednesday, July 20th. He was the Reverend William H. Laird, rector of the Episcopal Church of Birmingham, Delaware, who had the misfortune to resemble Crippen in stature and in general appearance, according to the *New York Tribune*. 'They should have asked my advice,' the irrepressible Mme Ginnett commented. 'The reverend gentleman looked about as much like Crippen as I do,' she added scathingly.

A whole week had gone by without news of the fugitives. 'I began to get a little anxious,' Dew confesses in his autobiography. 'Every day that passed increased the chances of the runaways.' The second week had almost run its course when on Friday, July 22nd, came the news the detective inspector had hardly dared hope for. 'It was eight o'clock in the evening,' Dew recalls. 'Almost completely worn out with the strain of work, I was chatting with a confrere in my office at the Yard when a telegram was handed to me. As I read its contents a wave of optimism swept over me. My fatigue instantly vanished.'

The telegram was from Liverpool police, who, in turn, were relaying to Dew a wireless message they had received from Captain Henry Kendall, of the *S.S. Montrose*, bound from Antwerp to Quebec, and then somewhere in the Atlantic.

IV

ETHEL

'Dr Crippen's love for the girl, for
whom he had risked so much, was the
biggest thing in his life . . . He
never seemed to care so much what
happened to himself, so long as her
innocence was established.'

—CHIEF INSPECTOR WALTER DEW[1]

[6]

The strange apathy in which Belle, Hawley and Ethel appeared content to renounce freedom of choice and simply to drift with events, was broken early in October, 1906, by a trivial-seeming incident. An announcement appeared in the small ads section of the *Daily Telegraph* to the effect that No. 39 Hilldrop Crescent welcomed paying guests, who would find: 'Pleasant surroundings . . . convenient to central London . . . suitable young businessman/ student.' The idea was Belle's (Mrs Harrison calls it 'Belle's little harmless whim'), and Hawley had encouraged it simply in order to get Belle off his back.

For ever since Bruce Miller's precipitate return to Chicago Belle had been restless, bored. At first the redecoration of the house had absorbed her energies. It was at this period that she began to haunt the salerooms and to pick up knick-knacks and furniture. But Belle soon tired of dusting the occasional tables she had acquired as bargains. She was lonely. It gave her 'the willies' to be in the empty house all day long with no one to talk to, Belle complained. She craved company, the stimulus of conversation. So it was partly at least to calm her discontent that Crippen consented to Belle advertising for paying guests.

The first to answer Belle's ad in the *Daily Telegraph* was Richard Ehrlich, a personable young student from Heidelberg, who had come to London to perfect his English, and who was delighted to learn that his plump little hostess spoke his native tongue (Belle's mother, it will be recalled, was German). Ehrlich was soon joined by three other German students, so that life at No. 39 took on the aspect of an amateur production of *The Student Prince*. Crippen would return from work in the evening to find that the front parlour had been preempted by youths in tasselled caps who smoked meerschaum pipes and swilled beer from tankards, and who were always ready to burst into song. At the centre of the group would be Belle, who, seated at the ebony upright, would oblige with 'Sister Mary Ann' and 'She Never Went Further Than That', songs which she had introduced with less success on the halls. Crippen was made to feel an outsider.

Thanks to the paying guests, Crippen's day now began at 6 am, when he rose, brought up the coal, laid the fires and took tea to Belle in bed. Coming down again, the doctor would lay the table for breakfast in the kitchen, then climb to the second floor where the students had left their boots outside their doors for him to clean. This was the most onerous task of all. As he scraped the mud from the boots, Crippen had time to reflect on the bondage to Belle which had brought him to this abject state.

Sundays were the worst days of all. Early morning Mass, according to Mrs Harrison, was followed by 'breakfast to be prepared [for the boarders], . . . boots to clean, beds to make, crockery to wash, dinner for midday to be cooked and served, and all this to be done without domestic assistance'. Even after the dinner dishes had been dried the Crippens were not free to do as they pleased. 'After dinner they played cards with their boarders, gave them tea at five o'clock and supper at nine.' 'It was a trying time, and quite unnecessary exertion for both,' Mrs Harrison comments, with masterful under-statement. She adds that Belle 'annexed the extra money from the boarders for personal adornment, and he [Crippen] continued to pay the household bills.'[2]

*   *   *

Richard Ehrlich was Belle's particular favourite. She had engaged to give him English lessons, but in no time at all the lessons were forgotten as their relationship moved onto a more personal plane. To the young Heidelberger Belle poured out her heart, telling of her hopes, her disappointments, the emptiness of her present life. She might have been another Marie Lloyd, or another Vesta Tilley, Belle gave Ehrlich to understand. (One has only to compare the plump figure of Belle dressed for her song 'The Major' in frogged tunic, striped trousers, and with a swagger stick under her arm, with that of the svelte Miss Tilley to appreciate the depths of the former's self-deception.) It was her husband who had ruined her career, Belle asserted. Dr Crippen had been jealous of her success, and had made her abandon the music hall just as her stage career looked most promising. She blamed him bitterly for all of her present woes.

It was at this point that Crippen reached the nadir of his degradation. For Belle took to reviling him in front of the paying guests, usually after she had had too much brandy. 'She often lost her temper,' Ehrlich told a reporter from *Le Petit Parisien.* 'There were frequent bickerings and open quarrels.' Curiously, in view of the way the triangle was to evolve, Ehrlich comes down firmly on Crippen's side. 'The doctor,' he declared, 'never lost his temper though his wife's reproaches were frequently unjustified. He always answered her in a gentle tone, and was never rude to her.' The French newspaper then went on to quote Ehrlich as saying that 'the husband must have possessed an extraordinary amount of self-control to endure his wife's stinging sarcasms for so long.'[3]

Self-control? Or was Crippen merely biding his time?

The scene now changes to a mid-morning late in November, 1906. Crippen returns home unexpectedly, and lets himself in by the side door, as is his habit. Is it true that he has forgotten the Analytical Forms that the Aural Remedies Company sends out to all prospective customers? Has he really forgotten those copies of that *Otological Gazette* he intended to mail out? Or are these mere pretexts for returning home in mid-morning? There is no sign of Belle in the kitchen—only a table littered with unwashed breakfast dishes, the egg hardened on some of them. Can it be that Belle is lying in bed with a hangover, having had too much cognac the night before? Crippen calls her name, but not too loudly. Then he starts up the stairs, but noiselessly, avoiding the steps that creak. Is it wholly out of consideration for Belle? Is he being careful not to disturb her sleep? Just as noiselessly he turns the handle on the bedroom door. Does he not know what awaits him on the other side? Belle in bed with the German lodger.

Crippen did not make a scene. After all, this was not the first time that Belle had been unfaithful to him, though it was possibly the first time that he had caught her in bed. No, he shut the door firmly so as to let the couple on the other side know. Then he went downstairs. No doubt there was a look of grim satisfaction on his face at this final proof of Belle's fecklessness. Such lingering affection as he might have felt for her, harking back to the early days of their married life, now gave way to a deep and abiding loathing.

*   *   *

It would be difficult to over-estimate the effect this final perfidy of Belle's had upon all their lives, its repercussions being felt long after the German students had been sent packing (Ehrlich claimed that he left No. 39 because 'he did not get enough practice in English', but he showed a reporter from *Le Petit Parisien* some of the letters he received from Belle after his departure, including one in which she cautions him not to get 'too fond of the girls'). For Crippen and Ethel at least, it was as though they had suddenly been released from an evil spell. What it meant was that henceforth Crippen would regard Ethel as his real wife, and Belle as the usurper.

Fairy tales are full of such metamorphoses. (Interestingly, the fairy tale model is one that Crippen chose to express the relationship of Ethel and himself to external reality, writing, 'We were like two children in the great unkind world, who clung to one another and gave each other courage.')[4] In the traditional fairy tale it is not uncommon for the wicked witch to substitute herself between the sheets of the king's bed, having first got rid of the rightful queen by hurling her out of the window. The simpleton of a king upon his return from the hunt suspects nothing when he retires, for the witch orders him 'upon your life' to keep the curtains drawn. The tale of course ends happily when the witch's spell is broken and the legitimate queen is restored in full health and vigour. The old crone is then stripped naked, put into a barrel which is studded inside with sharp nails, and rolled down a hill.

Those 'poor children in life,' as Hawley in another context described Ethel and himself, did not roll the wicked witch cum stepmother cum counterfeit wife down a hill in a nail-studded barrel, but they did the next best thing. They celebrated their liberation from her evil enchantment by becoming lovers in the physical as well as the spiritual sense of the word. For the first time since they had met at Drouet's seven years earlier they became one in flesh, this latter-day Heloïse and her Abelard.

'It is good to think, darling wifie, that even in those early days before our wedding came that we were always in perfect harmony with each other.'* This is Hawley writing to Ethel four years afterwards; by which time both of their lives had been shattered, and all hope of finding happiness together doomed. The words 'wifie'

---

* For full text of letter see Appendix.

and 'wedding' spring to the eyes. How strange they sound in this context, for at the time referred to Belle was still very much alive and passing in the world as 'Mrs Crippen'.

'Then came those days,' the letter continues, 'when hub felt, and wifie too so earnestly felt, it was impossible to live on and not be all in all to each other, and from our wedding day all has been a perfect honeymoon of four years to Dec. 6 next.' Thus Crippen has carefully pinpointed the date of their 'wedding' as December 6, 1906, which should remove any doubt as to whether Hawley and Ethel were lovers in the physical sense before that date. (It will be noted that the date coincides with the exodus of the German students from No. 39.) There is more than a hint here that the hymen celebrated, this becoming 'all in all', was something more than the fulfilment of the flesh. Lovers do not ordinarily refer to the first time they go to bed together as their 'wedding', and thereafter refer to each other as 'hub' and 'wifie'. One can only conclude that the union of Hawley and Ethel was solemnised by some secret ritual they had elaborated, perhaps involving the exchange of vows as well as of talismanic gifts. Whatever it involved, both looked upon the union as binding. 'We are to each other, truly husband and wife, sacredly so,' Hawley reminds Ethel in one of his last letters to her, adding that 'no more sacred relations . . . could ever exist.'

In his 'farewell letter to the world' Crippen reiterates these sentiments. 'We were as man and wife together, with an absolute communion of spirit,' he writes. He declares that 'this love was not of a debased and degraded character.' 'It was,' he concludes, 'if I may say so to people who will not, perhaps, understand or believe, a good love. She comforted me in my melancholy condition. Her mind was beautiful to me. Her loyalty and courage and self-sacrifice were of a high character.'

*   *   *

Nearly two decades later an Ilford housewife was to be hanged at Holloway Prison because she made the same mistake in confusing her lover with her lawful spouse, and regarding the latter as a usurper. Referring to her husband, Edith Thompson wrote to her lover Frederick Bywaters in September, 1923, 'he has the right by law to all that you have the right to by nature and love.'

In asking a jury to reject this doctrine as 'disgusting', the trial judge proceeded to twist these words out of all recognition, holding them to mean that 'the love of a husband for his wife is something improper . . . and that the love of a woman for her lover, illicit and clandestine, is something great and noble.' The judge ended in a plea for 'commonsense' that was to send Mrs Thompson to the gallows.

Because the Thompson-Bywaters case affords interesting parallels with the Crippen case it is worth recalling the circumstances of the former. Edith and her husband Percy Thompson were on their way home from a West London theatre on the night of October 3, 1922, when the latter was set upon by Bywaters and stabbed to death. Edith, who had been heard to cry out 'Don't, oh, don't!' when the fracas occurred, was tried for the murder jointly with Bywaters and convicted, the two of them being hanged on the same day in January, 1923. 'At no time was it suggested that she played a physical part,' Edgar Lustgarten writes in his analysis of the case; 'the Crown acknowledged that she did not lift a finger. Their case was that she urged murder on her lover; that the latter in her presence carried out the wicked deed; and that these two factors taken in conjunction made her under English law a principal in the crime.'[5]

Frederick Bywaters, who was eight years Edith Thompson's junior, was a steward aboard the P & O liner *Morea*, which meant that Edith spent most of her spare time writing to him. Unfortunately for her, Bywaters saved sixty-five of her letters, each of which was to help to convict Edith, for the letters, in one vast stream-of-consciousness outpouring, revealed not only her adulterous thoughts, but her longings to be rid of her husband.

Ethel LeNeve left no letters, which is a pity, for they might, like Edith's, have shed more light on her character.* On the other hand, they might have imperilled her life, as was the case with Mrs Thompson. Actually, the two women had much in common. Both were the same age (twenty-seven) when tragedy overtook them. Neither was a beauty in the conventional sense of the word. There was something wistful, troubled-looking about Ethel, for example,

* The few letters Ethel wrote to Crippen while he was in Pentonville prison were, at his request, buried with him, together with Ethel's photograph, in an unmarked grave in the prison yard.

in the intent way she had of looking up into one's face when talking; while Edith looked as though she had just come from playing five sets of tennis and had not a care in the world. Despite these differences in appearance both women undoubtedly had 'that quintessential femininity that fascinates the male', as one commentator describes it.[6]

Both were remarkable women by any reckoning. For one thing, each had managed to hold her own in a highly competitive business world. Ethel rose to become head of the ladies' department at Drouet's, and later made herself indispensable as Crippen's Girl Friday. Edith Thompson was manageress-bookkeeper of a wholesale millinery firm in the City, and earned more than her husband. Of Edith her employer was to testify, 'With her business capacity she could get employment anywhere.' The truth is that both women were superior to the menfolk in their lives, which partly explains their frustrations. Percy Thompson, who was a shipping clerk in the City, had been invalided out of the army with a weak heart. He was, so far as one can make out, a dull, ineffectual, slightly pathetic little man, who vented his fits of temper on Edith. Crippen, as will be seen, came to lean more and more heavily upon Ethel LeNeve. Crippen looked to her not only for business advice, but Ethel's decisions affected their lives generally. More and more she emerges as the stronger of the two characters, the dominant partner.

From a sexual standpoint Edith Thompson appears to have been exceedingly unlucky in her choice both of husband and lover. Percy Thompson left her unsatisfied, whereas Frederick Bywaters was crude, animal-like, a brute. 'Darlingest when you are rough I go dead—try not to be, please,' Edith pleads with her lover. Sexual frustration partly accounts for Edith's retreat into the world of fiction, for she was a devourer of novels of the romantic type, novels with titles like *The Slave, Beyond the Shadows, The Way of These Women*, whose heroes are strong-limbed and clean, and whose heroines are called Deborah, Dolores or Bella Donna. Concerning the last Edith writes to her lover, 'No I don't agree with you about her, darlint—I hate her—hate . . . that sensual pleasure-loving greedy Bella Donna . . . she never knew what it was to be denied anything—she never knew "goodness" as you and I know it . . . She doesn't seem a woman to me—she seems abnormal—a monster.'

As a lover Hawley seems to have made Ethel happy, but then, aside from the phantom boyfriend who took her ballroom dancing earlier on, she had no other men with whom to compare him. She is certainly more realistic, more down-to-earth than Edith Thompson. It is hard to picture Ethel rattling on about books she has read to a bored lover at sea ('About *The Slave*, I didn't know what to make of that girl . . . She stooped low—to get back that Emerald —but darlint wouldn't all of us stoop low to regain something we have loved and lost?'). One outstanding trait the two women shared in common was their penchant for lying, even when lies were not called for. Protest as Edith would her dislike for untruths ('I hate every lie I have to tell to see you—because lies seem such small mean things to attain such an object as ours') Edith went on lying, this Madame Bovary of Ilford, from a desire to see everything writ larger than life. Ethel, on the other hand, lied from sheer perversity, probably dating back to the days when she was intent upon deceiving her father. Ethel in fact appears incapable of telling the truth; it is as though defective vision prevents her from seeing things other than obliquely, in a distorting light.

Finally, although both women managed to rise above their class, neither was able to defy that class's code of morality which is summed up by the terrible word 'respectability'. As J. B. Priestley points out, the respectability at whose altar the lower middle class worshipped did not deserve to be called puritanism. 'It did not wonder what God would think,' Priestley writes, 'but what the neighbours would think.'[7] Edith Thompson did not hesitate to break her marriage vows, but she shrank from the consequences. She could not bear to face the censure of her family and her business associates. 'I'd love to be able to say "I'm going to see my lover tonight," ' Edith writes to Bywaters. 'If I did he [the husband] would prevent me—there would be scenes and he would come to 168 [her place of business] and interfere and I couldn't bear that . . . Darlingest find me a job abroad. I'll go tomorrow and not say I was going to a soul and not have one little regret.'

In the end Ethel had more guts than her sister in extremity. For Ethel did turn her back on her family and friends, and Ethel did flee with her lover into an unknown future, with less than twenty-four hours in which to make up her mind. And Ethel did cut off her hair and put on an ill-fitting boy's suit in an attempt to make good her escape. Despite her protestations, 'I'll go tomorrow . . .

[84]

and not have one little regret', it is difficult to picture Edith stowing away aboard Bywaters' ship, which would have been roughly the equivalent of the sacrifice Ethel made for Crippen.

*　　*　　*

'I have frequently stayed with Miss LeNeve at hotels, but was never from home at nights,' Crippen was to declare later.[8] In obedience to what weird punctilio, one wonders, did Crippen return to Belle at night after making love to Ethel in the afternoon? Was it to appease the hearth gods? By spending the night under his own roof, did Crippen hope to avert their baleful eyes? Or was it simply that he was afraid that Belle might forget to feed the cats? Whether a concession to superstition or to protocol, love in the afternoon became a part of Crippen's established routine for the next three years.

Edith Thompson and her lover seemed always to be meeting after his long sea voyages in station buffets, much to the sorrow of Edith, who complained that the decor was so 'ordinary'. 'I shall always want you to come straight to our home,' she writes to Bywaters, 'and take me in both your arms and hold me for hours —and you can't do that in the street or a station, can you darlint?'

With Hawley and Ethel the trysting place was always some shabby hotel in the vicinity of the King's Cross–St Pancras rail termini. One or two afternoons a week they would steal away separately from the office and make their way by different routes to King's Cross, where they would meet by pre-arrangement. They would then go together to Argyle Square with its decaying Georgian houses converted into Bed and Breakfasts, each with its high iron palings around a dark area, its window-boxes of geraniums, its 'Vacancies' sign in the front window. Here they would register as man and wife. The routine was invariably the same: Hawley would explain to the proprietor that they had left their luggage at the station, since they were coming from Birmingham (or was it Manchester?) and were on their way to Bath (or was it Bristol?) and had a few hours to kill between trains. Ethel, who was a born conspirator, would enter into the spirit of the game by clinging to Hawley's arm like a travel-weary wife in need of a few hours' respite. Not that this rigmarole was at all necessary. The proprietors of these hostelries waxed fat off of love in the afternoon.

For Ethel these clandestine rendezvous began to pall. She grew tired of hotel rooms whose windows gave onto ventilation shafts, whose beds were lumpy, their sateen coverlets worn. On still afternoons one could hear the sounds from the nearby goods yards —the sudden shriek of a train whistle, the chuff-chuff of an engine followed by the clatter of trucks being shunted. Ethel longed, as Edith Thompson was to long, for a place of her own. Even though Hawley was no longer in love with his wife Ethel found it galling that he should have to return to Belle each night. As she told her landlady, Mrs Jackson, 'I cannot bear to see them together. When I do see them I feel my position.'[9]

Ethel began to despair that Belle would ever run off and leave her husband, as she had so often threatened to do. She began to feel that she would never have Hawley all to herself. Just such forebodings were to darken the life of Edith Thompson towards the end, as it was eclipsed by tragedy. 'Darlint,' she writes her lover, who is in Aden, 'the greatness, the bigness of the love I have, makes me fear that it is too good to last. It will never die, darlint, but I fear—how can I explain?—that it will never mature, that we, you & I, will never reap our reward . . . our love will all be in vain.'

[7]

'My Dear Sister Kate and Brother George, — So many, many thanks for the lovely photograph of your dear little, darling baby.' Thus does Belle begin a letter to her half-sister Kate, who was married to George Volkens and living in Williamsburg, South Brooklyn.[1] The letter reveals more about Belle than she had perhaps intended, for it is obvious that she was terribly lonely when she wrote it, and had yielded to a melancholic strain. As Filson Young points out, Belle, at thirty-five, 'had reached that age . . . when a woman of her race begins to realise that her youth is over, and that the time in which her attractions can still pass current in the world of men is growing short'.[2] Most of the married Polish women Belle had known in her Brooklyn neighbourhood had compensated for these losses by devoting themselves to raising their families.

'What a beauty he is,' Belle rhapsodises over the photograph of her tiny nephew. 'Really, I do think I should be quite jealous to hold him in my arms and squeeze him.'

Thirty-five was the age when women of Belle's type tended to go to fat, particularly if they were short and stocky and had a peasant's build like Belle's. The upper arms developed a certain fleshiness, there was the suggestion of a double chin. Whether it was that once having settled down with a man of their choice (and most of the Polish girls she knew in Brooklyn had married early) they simply lost interest, or that they were too beset by the problems of everyday existence to bother about their looks, Belle did not know. It could be, of course, that they no longer felt themselves desired.

'I love babies,' Belle hurries on. 'I am certain that a baby makes a great deal of difference in a family. In fact, it is not complete without a baby. So I envy you. Oh, I tell you, it makes a great deal of difference when it is your own.'

Belle herself could not have babies, owing to the ovariectomy she had undergone shortly after marrying Crippen. The operation had left a scar which had caused Belle's friend Clara Martinetti to cry out when she saw it by accident. Belle had been staying with Mrs Martinetti at the latter's bungalow on the Thames near Marlow and was dressing for breakfast one morning when her peignoir accidentlly fell open disclosing the scar to her friend, who mistook it for a wound. 'Oh, Belle, does it hurt?' Clara Martinetti had asked anxiously. Belle had said 'No,' and had explained the nature of it.

'Yes, dear mamma loved us all,' Belle's letter to her sister goes on, this time plunging into a morbid vein. 'How I wish she was here with us again. And poor Anna as well. May their souls, through the mercy of God, rest in peace.'

The association of ideas is not difficult to trace. Talk of babies inevitably calls to mind Belle's mother who, judging from photographs of her, was worn out from child-bearing by the time she reached forty. For having given birth to three daughters before Joe Mackamotzki died, including Anna, who did not live beyond childhood, the mother then bore five more children to her second husband, Fritz Mersinger.

'Yes, Katie dear, our garden is lovely, and the house is very nice, too. And I do wish that some of you lived over here to share it with us. It is so big for only us two and a woman servant and two cats. Of course we have plenty of friends, but then they are not like your own family, are they?'

'Perhaps you may visit us,' Belle writes, concluding her letter on a wistful note. 'I should be so pleased to have you all and the house full to suffocation. I like a lot of company, don't you . . .?'

The reason why Belle wanted the house 'full to suffocation' was that ever since the Ehrlich episode she could not bear to be in it alone with Hawley. On those rare occasions when they were forced to spend an evening together alone—that is, when Belle was not attending some Music Hall Ladies' Guild 'do', and Hawley was not seeing Ethel—the tension between them was so great that even the cats were jumpy. The couple continued to bicker; that is, Belle continued to give Hawley pieces of her mind. But it took two to quarrel, and Hawley spoiled it all by remaining silent to her reproaches. It was as though she were not there. It was small wonder perhaps that Belle began to drink more heavily than usual, finding consolation in cognac. Only when the Nashes or the Martinettis came to play whist, or Belle gave one of her little

[88]

supper parties, did the tension relax. They now played at being happily married more by force of habit than by conviction.

*   *   *

The Green Man was one of those Edwardian pubs, all frosted lights, cut glass and mirrors, that are divided into compartments with a fine eye to class distinctions. Not that the compartments with their eye-level partitions afforded all that much privacy. The two men standing at the saloon bar, for example, could not help but overhear snatches of conversation coming from the snug parlour adjacent, conversation that was punctuated at intervals by yelps of laughter from a heavily made-up blonde who, her face flushed, was obviously the worse for her glasses of port. There were three men sitting at her table, but the blonde appeared to be buying the drinks.

'Calls herself Belle Elmore,' one of the men in the saloon bar, a West End actor, remarked to his companion. 'Thinks she can sing and dance, too. They put her on for a few shows, and she got the bird—feathers, beak, spurs and all. Now she's an artist—resting!' Into the ultimate word the actor poured all of the scorn which the successful reserve for the flop.

'She's got a husband, too,' the actor pursued. 'Some sort of American doctor. And blimey! Look at the crowd she's buying drinks for—ain't he out of luck!'*

Crippen was out of luck indeed. Seymour Hicks, the theatrical producer, who knew the Crippens well, tells how Belle's alcoholic fugue affected what was left of Hawley's home life. 'Working hard all day in his shop, on his return home . . . he would be met by his Belle but newly risen from her bed, attired in pyjamas and with a "hangover".' 'Miserably unhappy, he would not have been human if he had not sought consolation elsewhere,' Hicks adds.[3] The neighbours too used to see Belle, her head covered with hair curlers, tottering around the backyard as she tried to shoo a tomcat away from her beloved white Persian.

Being a late riser, Belle also neglected her housework. Her friend Mrs Harrison describes the disorder that reigned in Belle's kitchen: 'I followed her into the kitchen one morning when she was busy.

* This anecdote was told by Solicitor Arthur Newton's managing clerk.

It was a warm, humid day, and the grimy windows were all tightly closed. On the dresser was a heterogeneous mass, consisting of dirty crockery, edibles, collars of the doctor's, false curls of her own, hairpins, brushes, letters, a gold jewelled purse, and other articles ... the kitchener and gas stove were brown with rust and cooking stains. The table was littered with packages, saucepans, dirty knives, plates, flat-irons, a washing basin, and a coffee pot. Thrown carelessly across a chair was a lovely white chiffon gown embroidered with silk flowers and mounted over white glacé.'[4]

*　　　*　　　*

Then too Belle had money worries which put her in a melancholy frame of mind. For things were not going well with 'The Yale Tooth Specialists'. Crippen had gone into partnership with Dr Gilbert Rylance, a young American with a New Zealand degree in dentistry, but Crippen's exact role in the firm is not clear. Rylance denied that Crippen did any of the dental work, claiming that the latter acted merely as business and advertising manager for the firm. 'In my judgment,' the dentist later told a reporter from the *Pall Mall Gazette*, 'he was a smart man and a wonderful organiser, very exact, with fine business methods; in fact, one could not have desired a straighter representative.'[5] In the interview Rylance made no mention of the £250 Crippen was asked to invest in the partnership, nor did he offer any explanation why, if Crippen was merely the business agent, his name appeared first on the door of their office thus:

Yale Tooth Specialists
American Dentists
H.H. CRIPPEN
G.M. RYLANCE

The 'Yale Tooth Specialists' shared offices on the third floor of Albion House with Munyon's, for whom Crippen continued to work on a commission basis. In addition to Ethel, the office personnel consisted of Marion Curnow, who was manageress for Munyon's, and William Long, who had been with Crippen since Drouet days, and who was now employed as a dental mechanic.

An entirely different version of Crippen's role in the dental partnership is given by Ethel's father, who as a coal canvasser, had secured the firm's business. According to Walter Neave, Crippen did the actual extractions, assisted by Ethel, while Rylance apparently did the crown work and made the dentures.* Neave writes that the sight of Crippen in his white smock 'gave nervous people a shock . . . and Ethel, by kindly and sympathetic suggestion, had to reassure the patients.' 'She would tell them that the doctor was one of the most fascinating and gentle of men,' her father continues; 'that the extraction of teeth under his skilful hands would be a painless operation; and that she herself had had over twenty false teeth put in by the doctor without suffering a single pang.' The father then quotes Ethel as soothing the patient by promising, 'I will stand by you all the time, and if he hurts you, nip my hand, and I'll soon stop him.' Neave also claims that Ethel did all the banking for the firm, and paid the bills, as well as making the appointments.[6]

What makes Neave's story sound authentic is that early in his career as a homoeopath, when times were hard, Crippen had practiced dentistry, apparently illegally, as a side-line. Also it is true Ethel had had most of her teeth—twenty-one to be exact—extracted. Moreover, she had had them extracted (by Dr Rylance, not Crippen) at one sitting, which must have been an excruciating experience. It is one more example of the strong character of this girl, whom the press later was to paint as a very delicate plant in need of protection. Ethel was convinced that the neuralgic pains in her head were due to bad teeth; therefore nothing would do but that she must have them out, all at one go.

The sight of Hawley and Ethel in their white smocks, their heads almost touching as they bent over a patient, was galling to Belle when she looked in at her husband's office on her way to the Music Hall Ladies' Guild down the hall. Doubly so, in that Belle had been opposed to 'The Yale Tooth Specialists' from the start, and had predicted a gloomy future for it. It was all the fault of 'the little typewriter', Belle felt sure. Ethel had used her influence upon Crippen to wean him away from patent medicines, which was the

---

* Filson Young corroborates Neave's version that Crippen was engaged in dental surgery. Concerning the statement which much later Crippen dictated to Inspector Dew, Young writes that it was given 'in the intervals between medical consultations and tooth-pulling; he would dictate a little of it, go out and extract a tooth, and return and dictate some more'. Young, *op. cit.*

thing he knew best, and into dentistry about which he knew next to nothing. Probably it was to spite her, Belle, that Ethel had exerted the pressure (Belle had a way of twisting issues around so that they became deeply personal). Belle's reaction was identical when she learned that Ethel was pregnant. Obviously, 'the little typewriter' had done it out of spite.

* * *

One of the most baffling of the many baffling aspects of the Crippen murder mystery is why Ethel's pregnancy has never been mentioned by any of the writers who have studied the Crippen case, and this includes Filson Young. Worse still, why was Ethel's pregnancy never alluded to at Crippen's trial where it might have shed light on the defendant's motive, if nothing else? Ignorance cannot be pleaded as an excuse either by those in charge of Crippen's defence, or by those who have written up the events afterwards. The facts were there for all to see. They are to be found in the evidence given by Ethel's landlady, Mrs Jackson; they were admitted by Ethel's defence counsel, F. E. Smith. Yet this pregnancy and its aftermath, which one might almost say were the single most important factor in the developing tragedy, have been studiously ignored.

As to Ethel's reaction there can be no doubt. She was in an exultant mood. There was no question of her not having the baby. She was fiercely proud that she was to bear Crippen's child. No doubt it satisfied a deep-felt desire for fulfilment, that being 'all in all' to one another to which Crippen alludes time and again in his letters. Then, too, a child would be a decisive weapon in Ethel's hands in her battle with Belle. Ethel of course knew of Belle's barrenness, and that this had been a reason why Crippen's marriage had been a failure. She knew also that Hawley would leave his wife once Ethel's child was born, that nothing could persuade him to remain a day longer with Belle. Who could say, perhaps Belle might vanish from the scene once the child was born—either take off for America, or set up house with some admirer.

Ethel in the months following her pregnancy was happier, more serene, more optimistic than at any other time in her life, according to those who knew her. Those who had bestowed upon her the nickname 'Not Very Well, Thank You' would not have recognised

Ethel in the radiant young woman who now appeared in charge of Crippen's dental practice at Albion House, and who bossed him around gently. By the same token, Belle had never appeared more depressed.

Then Ethel lost the child she was carrying and the whole human equation was changed.

*   *   *

There can be no doubt that it was a miscarriage and not an abortion. Mrs Emily Jackson, with whom Ethel was lodging in Hampstead at the time, was very positive on this point when two years later the landlady was called upon to testify at Ethel's trial. Mrs Jackson was closer to Ethel than the girl's own mother; in fact, Ethel called her 'Ma', and confided in her as she never would have confided to Mrs Neave. In her evidence in chief, 'Ma' Jackson said that Ethel, in one of her later fits of depression, had named Crippen as the author of her woes. 'Do you mean he was the cause of your trouble when I first knew you?' Mrs Jackson asked, to which Ethel replied, 'Yes'. In his cross-examination of the witness F. E. Smith, Ethel's counsel, was quick to pick up this point.

SMITH. Was Miss LeNeve on several occasions prevented from going to business by the state of her health? — She had to stay at home several times.

And was she several times kept away from business for two or three days? — She was at home in the first instance for three weeks.

When you spoke of her trouble you meant that soon after she came to you she had a miscarriage? — Yes.

Ethel came to 'Ma' Jackson at No. 30 Constantine Road in Hampstead, in September, 1908, and remained there until March, 1909. The landlady erred in her calculations in that March, 1909, is the date that Ethel lost her child, after which she went to stay with her aunt, Mrs Thomas Benstead, in Hove to recuperate her health and spirits. If further proof were needed that it was a miscarriage and not an abortion Crippen's letter to Ethel dated November 5, 1910, provides it. In this Crippen expresses his concern for Ethel's financial security. 'If only I could have left you well provided for,' he writes, 'I would have wished our little one had lived that you might have had what would have been part of both of us. But, like other things, it was not to be.' If Crippen had counselled abortion, he would hardly have had the tactlessness, the indelicacy to refer to Ethel's loss in this manner.

Astrologers tell us that those born under Ethel's zodiacal sign with both the Sun and Mercury in Aquarius are subject to fits of depression, periods when they long passionately for death. Whether or not this is true, Ethel's grief over the loss of her child was terrible indeed. As her landlady declared, Ethel shut herself in her room, and remained there, weeping most of the time. When 'Ma' Jackson suggested that Ethel should give Crippen up the girl replied that she would sooner kill herself. 'If I cannot have him I shall not have anybody,' she said.[7] Her despair communicated itself to Crippen, who came away from his visits to Ethel in Constantine Road feeling miserable, and helpless to assuage her grief.

As for Belle, she was not appeased. Ethel's pregnancy had rankled with her more than she had cared to acknowledge even to herself. For through Ethel she had been hit at her most vulnerable point. Was she not passionately fond of children? Had she not declared that no home was complete without babies?

Another thought struck her. Ethel's pregnancy may have terminated in miscarriage, but what was to prevent her from conceiving again? Ethel was only twenty-six, and strong and healthy, despite her protestations that she suffered from neuralgia. Would not Ethel be in a hurry to become pregnant again, if for no other reason than to spite Belle? This nightmare possibility once admitted, Belle could not get it out of her mind. There was only one thing to be done: Hawley must sack Ethel, giving her the customary month's notice. That way Belle hoped to get rid of her rival once and for all. Commenting on Belle's decision, Filson Young writes, 'though she did not want Crippen for herself, it was not in accordance with her vanity that he should enjoy the love of any other woman.'[8]

*   *   *

The emotional crisis in all three lives coincided with a worsening of Crippen's financial situation. By December, 1909, Crippen's commissions from Munyon's having dwindled to a trickle, he had given two months' notice that he was severing his connection with the firm. Meanwhile, more money was needed to keep the 'Yale Tooth Specialists' afloat. (Crippen had been siphoning income from 'Ohrsorb' and his other quack cures into the painless dental practice with the result that all of these ventures were now threatened with collapse.) In desperation Crippen now turned to Belle with the suggestion that she invest part of her savings or dispose of some of her jewels in order to bolster the dental firm. This was enough to throw Belle into a panic. As Mrs Harrison expresses it, 'She was seized with a horrible fear for her little world, and was haunted by the thought of having to give up some of her outward glitter. Her little material soul shuddered. She forgot he was the man who had given her everything in the past.'[9]

The Crippens' finances were chaotic to say the least; and given Hawley's 'fine business methods', to borrow Dr Rylance's phrase, one suspects that the fault lay with Belle. In brief, the couple had £600 on deposit with the Charing Cross Bank in the Strand. Slightly more than half of this (£330 to be exact) was in Belle's name alone, representing in part her earnings from the music hall stage, in part 'gifts' from gentlemen admirers. The balance, totalling £270, was in a joint account requiring the signatures of both depositors before withdrawals could be made.

In addition, Belle had what she thought was a secret account at the Birkbeck Bank, it was disclosed when her will was proved. She appears to have cached away some £200 in this account, although Crippen may have known about it. As for Belle's personal estate, her jewels, furs and gowns later were to fetch nearly £500 at auction. Concerning her presents from various men, Filson Young points out that 'whether these took the form of money or jewellery, or both, one can understand that she would regard them as entirely her own property and at her own disposal.'

Belle not only refused to part with a single penny of her savings, or to pawn a single one of her diamonds, but secretly she resolved to decamp, taking with her as much of their joint property as she could lay her hands on. The threat of insolvency had done wonders to stir her to action. But before Belle left Crippen for good she was determined that Ethel should go too. To this end Belle spread the rumour among the guild ladies that Ethel had had an abortion. Belle tried to make out that Ethel was a Little Miss Sly-

[95]

Boots, who, having led a fast life and been caught out, had opted for abortion because she could not decide which of several men was the putative father of her unborn child. Ethel had, to her certain knowledge, wrecked several homes, Belle told the guild ladies.

Crippen himself could take almost unlimited abuse from Belle. He was accustomed to being humiliated publicly, to having Belle use him as a doormat on which to wipe her feet; one cannot help but admire his ability to retain a semblance of dignity under these circumstances. But when it came to Ethel he drew the line. He would not stand for 'wifie' being mired. 'Hub's darling' would not become a subject of scandal if he could prevent it. Whatever else happened, Ethel must remain unharmed. There was only one way to stop the campaign of calumny directed against Ethel, he concluded, and that was to silence it at its source.

*　　　*　　　*

Thus as the year 1909 drew to a close all the ingredients of tragedy were present, or perhaps black comedy in the manner of the film *Divorce Italian Style* might be an apter description. On the one hand, the wife is preparing to scarper with the couple's life savings without a word to her spouse of sixteen years' standing. On the other, the husband is planning to commit a perfect crime, hoping not to leave a single trace. In the event, both plans were to go terribly wrong. The wife was the victim of procrastination; the time for action had long since past. As for the husband, he turned out to be a prize bungler; everything he did was technically wrong.

The black comedy began on Wednesday, December 15th, when Belle, dressed as elegantly as usual, her plump hands displaying her diamonds, called at the Charing Cross Bank off the Strand and told the manager that she would like to withdraw not only her personal savings, but the £270 held in the joint deposit account as well. A rude awakening was in store: Belle was told that because of the high interest rate paid (7%) a year's notice of withdrawal was required.* She left the bank badly shaken by the news.

---

* The bank manager would testify later in court that at the expiry of a year he was prepared to hand over the entire amount to Belle without Crippen's signature.

On December 23rd the Music Hall Ladies' Guild gave its usual Christmas party for the widows and orphans of music hall entertainers who had taken their last curtain call, and Belle was busy afterwards with the distribution of plum puddings and toys. That same night Belle was suddenly taken ill. She told Melinda May, the guild secretary, about it afterwards, how she had awakened with a strangling sensation in her throat, and had told her husband, 'Get up, Hawley, and fetch a priest—I am going to die'. When Miss May gave evidence to this effect at the inquest hearing nine months later her testimony gave rise to an amusing misunderstanding.

> JURY FOREMAN (to Miss May). When Mrs Crippen complained at Christmas-time of having been ill in the night what was it she said to her husband, 'Send for the police'?
> MELINDA MAY (hastily). Oh, no. She said, 'Send for the priest.' She was a Roman Catholic.

Belle, however, was well enough on New Year's Eve to entertain Melinda May and the John Nash's to dinner. At midnight the guests came out and stood at the top of the front steps 'to listen to the hooting of the sirens, the ringing of the church bells, the hammering of trays', Miss May records. 'Miss Elmore handed round the cocktail and we took it and expressed the usual good wishes . . .'[10]

Then Crippen made his first blunder. On Monday, January 17th, he ordered from Lewis and Burrows, chemists, five grains of hydrobromide of hyoscine. Crippen had first made the acquaintance of this drug in 1883 when, still a medical student, he had seen it administered in minute doses to calm the violently insane at London's Royal Bethlehem Hospital. Hyoscine was so toxic, however, that if more than a quarter of a grain were given it could prove fatal, he learned.

For years Crippen had dealt with Lewis and Burrows in New Oxford Street in connection with his homoeopathic preparations, purchasing from them in considerable quantities such poisons as aconite, belladonna, gelsemium and cocaine, but never hyoscine hydrobromide. The order which he now placed was therefore certain to be remembered. In fact, hyoscine was in such rare demand that Lewis and Burrows did not even keep it in stock, but had to order it for him. Two days later Crippen called round for the drug, signing the Poisons Register on this occasion.

Hyoscine is an alkaloid poison found in henbane, an annual of the nightshade family which commonly grows on waste ground. The henbane plant from which hyoscine is extracted has sticky, hairy leaves, a yellowish blossom shot through with purple-tinted veins, and it is poisonous in all its parts, the most active principle being found in the seeds. Animals without exception will not touch it.*

*   *   *

Towards the end of January there occurred an incident which may have been of profound significance so far as the unwinding of the tragedy is concerned. On Tuesday, January 25th, as near as Mr Jackson could make out, Ethel returned home from work in a state bordering upon hysteria, refused her supper, went straight to her room. 'Ma' Jackson followed her upstairs. 'At first she said nothing,' Mrs Jackson was to testify at the coroner's inquest. 'She commenced doing her hair, and finally she undressed. When she got into bed she commenced to cry and do her front hair, but she was in such a terribly agitated state of mind that she could not get the curler in, and had to keep doing it over again, clutching at it nervously. Every nerve in her body seemed to be full of suppressed agitation.'

TRAVERS HUMPHREYS (for the Crown)—Did she give any reason for her state of agitation?

MRS JACKSON—Not just then. She sat up in bed and her eyes were staring right across the room, and horrible shivers seemed to run through her whole frame. It was twenty minutes past two in the morning before I left her.

---

* In its raw stage the hyoscine is a gummy brown mass with a tobacco-like odour; but in the refined state in which Crippen sought it, the drug consisted of white, odourless crystals. Mixed with morphine hyoscine becomes 'twilight sleep', once used extensively in obstetric cases. However, in 1910 it was used chiefly as a sedative to calm the violent in insane asylums and alcoholics in the throes of delirium tremens. The dose usually prescribed was between 1/300th and 1/100th of a grain.

At Ethel's trial Mrs Jackson, under cross-examination, testified that for almost the whole of the month of January Ethel had been 'miserable and unhappy', a state which had caused her to look 'strange and haggard'. Asked what the matter was Ethel had replied that she was 'worried with the accounts in the office'. Her mental anguish then, however, was nothing to what it was on Tuesday, January 25th, when she came home hysterical. The following morning Mrs Jackson took Ethel a cup of tea, but the girl was too ill and trembling to drink it. The landlady said, 'I can't let you go to Albion House like this—I'll telephone them that you are unfit to go to business today.' Ethel said, 'You will ring up the doctor, won't you?'

After telephoning, 'Ma' Jackson returned and urged Ethel to unburden herself. 'You must have something on your mind,' the landlady declared. 'It must be something awful or you would not be in such a state. You must relieve your mind or you will go absolutely mad.' To which Ethel replied, 'I will tell you the whole story presently.' Mrs Jackson takes up the story again: 'Soon afterwards she said to me, "Would you be surprised if I told you it was the doctor?"' (Obviously Mrs Jackson was referring here to Ethel's pregnancy and subsequent miscarriage.) 'I said, "Why worry about that? It is past and gone." She said, "Oh, it's Miss Elmore—she's his wife, you know; and when I see them go away together it makes me realise my position—what she is and what I am." I said, 'Well, my dear girl, what's the good of worrying about another woman's husband?" She said that Miss Elmore had been threatening to go away with another man, and that was all the doctor and Miss LeNeve were waiting for her to do. Then he would divorce her.'

In her evidence at the Bow Street Police Court the landlady testified that at first she thought that Ethel's agitated state was due to her 'old trouble'—i.e. that she was pregnant once more. 'I thought the same thing was the matter again,' Mrs Jackson explained. She also expanded the evidence she had given at the inquest to indicate that in her heart-to-heart talk with Ethel she had blamed Crippen as the author of the girl's woes: 'I said, "Don't you think he is asking a great deal of you? At your age it seems to me to be most unfair. Tell him what you have told me." Next day she said she had told the doctor. I asked if she was sure he would marry her. She said he had told her that he would; that she would be his only wife . . . After that she seemed very much more cheerful.'[11]

When it came her turn for the rebuttal, Ethel tried to pooh-pooh the significance the landlady attached to her nervous attack, writing, 'Now, really, I find great difficulty in recalling the exact incident to which she was alluding.' 'It was no uncommon thing for me to come home from the office in a state of mental distress,' she adds. 'The life of a typist-secretary is always a hard one, and I had many responsibilities mentally harassing to a girl of my age and temperament. Many visitors would call during the day, and the doctor, trusting me implicitly, would give me full discretion to deal with them. Therefore, I often arrived home in a highly-strung condition.' 'All I know is that the much discussed incident had no tragic significance,' she concludes.[12]

The much discussed incident, when taken in conjunction with other events, cannot be dismissed so lightly. Granted that Ethel was worried about the business accounts, would this have caused her to return home on Tuesday, January 25th, shaking so badly that she could not get a curler in her hair? Granted again that her duties as typist-secretary and receptionist were arduous, what caused her to remain in bed in a catatonic state that particular night, 'her eyes staring right across the room', her frame wracked by 'horrible shivers', in the language of her landlady. Surely 'something awful', to use Mrs Jackson's expression, had happened — or was about to happen.

* * *

At four o'clock Monday, January 31st, Crippen called on the Martinettis at their flat in Shaftesbury Avenue to invite them home to dinner that night. Clara Martinetti answered the door, explaining that her husband Paul had gone to his doctor for a check-up. Clara did not know whether they could come to dinner, as usually Paul came home from the doctor feeling rather weak. But Crippen was insistent. 'Make him come,' Crippen urged. 'It will cheer him up, and afterwards we can have a game of whist.' Crippen was so anxious that he called again at six o'clock, by which time Paul had returned home. Paul did not relish going out again, for it was a bitterly cold winter's night; but he allowed himself to be persuaded, and the Martinettis arrived at No. 39 Hilldrop Crescent around eight. Just the four of them sat down to dinner, which Belle herself had prepared and which was served in the breakfast-room next to the kitchen which the Crippens used as a dining-room.

Afterwards they went up one flight of stairs to the parlour and began their game of whist. Paul, who was not feeling well, made several trips to the bathroom during the course of the evening; and his wife feared that he was coming down with a chill. At 1.30 when they decided to leave Belle urged the Martinettis to stay the night, rather than to brave the inclemency out of doors; but the couple insisted on going home. Crippen was dispatched to fetch a carriage, and it was quite a while before he found one in Camden Road. Then there was the leave-taking with the Crippens standing at the top of the steps, and Clara kissing Belle goodnight. When the latter wanted to accompany her friend down the steps to the waiting cab Mrs Martinetti stopped her, admonishing her, 'you'll catch your death'.

[8]

'I can't understand . . . his telling of his wife's death. Why? What did he gain? Why not let it stand that she had decamped and stay with that?'[1] Thus does Raymond Chandler, the creator of Philip Marlowe, puzzle over Crippen as though the latter, too, were a character of fiction. Nor does Chandler understand why Crippen, 'a man of so much coolness under fire, should have made the unconscionable error of letting it be known that Elmore had left her jewels and clothes and furs behind'. 'She was so obviously not the person to do that,' he points out.

Raymond Chandler is criticising Crippen from the standpoint of a craftsman, a writer of detective thrillers. Specifically, he is criticising Crippen for his attempt to write Belle Elmore out of the script by having her die in California six thousand miles away. The attempt was heavy-handed, amateurish, as any whodunnit writer could have told Crippen. The thing to do was to report Belle to the police as a missing person, and let the police prove that it was otherwise. That way the burden of proof would have rested with Scotland Yard. That way Crippen could have sat back and relaxed.

As it was, Crippen appears to have had no game plan. He appears never to have sat down and thought out what he was going to do next and to have planned it logically. He was like the writer of a detective serial who improvises as he goes along, unmindful of the fact that once the first instalment appears he is committed to his plot. There is no going back, no opportunity for revision, he must stick to the scenario, implausible though it may seem.

The scenario which Crippen devised, improvising as he went along, began to unfold on Wednesday, February 2nd, or two days after the dinner party for the Martinettis. On that Wednesday morning Ethel, upon her arrival for work at Albion House, was surprised to find that Crippen had been before her and had gone. Ordinarily Crippen did not show up at Albion House for his appointments until mid-morning, but went straight from his home to Craven House in Kingsway, which was a convenience address for the Aural Remedies Company. Here with the aid of Miss Ena Balham, a typist, he transacted what was known as 'Crippen business'—answering the letters of people who had written in in response to the golden promises dangled by the Aural Remedies advertisements of curing deafness and catarrh.*

On this particular morning, however, Hawley had left a note for Ethel on her typewriter enclosed with two letters and a packet. The note read:

> B.E. has gone to America. Will you kindly favour me by handing the enclosed packet and letters to Miss May as soon as she arrives at her office, with my compliments? Shall be in later, when we can arrange for a pleasant little evening.

Belle gone to America? What did it mean? Hawley had said nothing to Ethel about Belle planning a trip to America. For further enlightenment she had to wait for Hawley, who did not appear until four o'clock, according to her story. At that time the following dialogue took place, if Ethel is to be believed:

'I have your note—has Belle Elmore really gone away?'

'Yes, she has left me.'

'Did you see her go?'

'No, I found her gone when I got home last night.'

'Do you think she will come back?'

Crippen shakes his head. 'No, I don't.'

'Did she take any luggage with her?'

'I don't know what luggage she had, because I did not see her go,' Crippen replies with impeccable logic. 'I daresay she took what she wanted.' Then, as an afterthought, 'She always said that the things I gave her were not good enough, so I suppose she thinks she can get better elsewhere.'[2]

Ethel's recollection sounds plausible enough until one analyses it. What has happened is that at one stroke the fetters that kept apart these 'poor children of life', as Crippen describes Ethel and himself, have been sundered. They are free at last. Nothing now stands in the way of their happiness. This is the moment they

---

* Crippen did not show up at Craven House until the end of that first week in February, according to Miss Balham. She told a reporter from the *Islington Daily Gazette*: 'To the best of my recollection he was absent for some three days at the beginning of February, during which time his work was taken over by a Frenchman.'

have dreamt about, lived in expectation of, yet hardly dared hope for—the moment when 'grief comes to an end and happiness begins', as the fairy tale would have it. It is an occasion which calls for celebration, for wild, almost delirious joy. Instead of delirium, what does one find? Ethel and Hawley discussing in the most prosaic terms Belle's wardrobe—whether or not she took any luggage with her when she departed for good, and if so, how much. Or so Ethel would have the reader believe.

'I could not pretend to commiserate with him,' she goes on in the same vein; and when Crippen a few days later suggests they go to the theatre it is because 'he thought it would cheer us both up'. Commiserate? Ethel and Hawley in need of cheering up? The moment Ethel puts pen to paper a different, more devious side of her character begins to emerge, like writing in invisible ink does when held up to a flame. Here is a person who loves mystification for its own sake. Or is Ethel lying because she has something to hide?

*　　*　　*

The Guild committee was already in session when shortly after midday Ethel stepped along the corridor and handed the letters and documents to Melinda May in accordance with Crippen's instructions. Both letters were in Crippen's handwriting, he apparently being pressed into service as an amanuensis by Belle in her haste. The first was addressed to Miss May personally and read:

Dear Miss May,
　　Illness of a near relative has called me to America on only a few hours' notice, so I must ask you to bring my resignation as treasurer before the meeting today, so that a new treasurer can be elected at once. You will appreciate my haste when I tell you that I have not been to bed all night packing, and getting ready to go. I shall hope to see you again a few months later, but cannot spare a moment to call on you before I go. I wish you everything nice till I return to London again. Now, good-bye, with love hastily, Yours, Belle Elmore, pp H.H.C.
The second letter was addressed to the committee of the Music

Hall Ladies' Guild, and was signed 'Belle Elmore' with a crude attempt being made to copy her signature.* It read in part:

> Dear Friends,—Please forgive me a hasty letter and any inconvenience I may cause you, but I have just had news of the illness of a near relative and at only a few hours' notice I am obliged to go to America. Under the circumstances I cannot return for several months, and therefore beg you to accept this as a form letter resigning from this date my hon. treasurership . . .

The packet was found to contain Belle's passbook, a paying-in book, and the cheque book she had used as treasurer.

The committee's reaction after the letters had been read was one of stunned incredulity. 'It's so unlike dear Belle to go running off like that without a dickey-bird to anyone,' as one member expressed it. But the guild ladies were more than incredulous. 'We were at once suspicious that something was wrong . . . something indefinite which we could not understand,' Mrs Smythson later was to tell a reporter.[3]

* * *

In her autobiographical sketch Ethel, still describing the events of Wednesday, February 2nd, now comes to what even she concedes to be 'a remarkable incident': Crippen's decision to pawn Belle's jewels that very day. Here is Ethel's account of this crucial episode:

> When we had discussed the departure of Belle Elmore the doctor thrust his hand into his pocket and drew out a handful of jewels . . . 'Look here,' he said, 'you had better have these. At all events, I wish you would please me by taking one or two. These are good, and I should like to know you had some good jewellery. They will be useful when we are dining out, and you will please me if you will accept them.'

---

* Michael Bernstein, a friend of Lottie Albert, claims that Crippen started to write 'Elmore' with a double 'l', then clumsily covered up his mistake; but in the absence of the actual document the author has been unable to verify this.

I said, 'Well, if you really wish it, I will have one or two. Pick out which you like.'

Thus prompted, Crippen selected for Ethel two solitaire diamond rings, a ring set with four diamonds and a ruby, and a small diamond brooch—the so-called 'rising sun' brooch, which was to play such an important part in both their lives. There remained a pair of diamond earrings, a very large brooch set with beautiful stones in the shape of a tiara, with many rows of diamonds arranged in a crescent, a marquise diamond ring, and half a dozen other rings of varying worth. Ethel's narrative continues:

> I then asked what he would do with the remainder, as it would not do to leave them about in the house, and as we had no safe, surely it would be better either to sell them or to pawn them. Perhaps the latter course would be best, as he could redeem them whenever he was disposed to do so.
> 'That is a good idea,' he said. 'I will take your advice.'

That same afternoon Crippen went round to Messrs Attenborough, pawnbrokers, at 142 Oxford Street, and pawned the marquise diamond ring and diamond earrings for £80. He returned one week later and pawned the balance of the jewellery, including the diamond tiara brooch, for £115, making a total of £195 he received for Belle's jewels.

> It will be seen, therefore, that Dr Crippen pawned the jewels purely on my suggestion. As far as I know, at that time he was not in financial trouble, tempting him to pawn those jewels immediately . . .

But if Crippen was not in any financial difficulty why did he rush out and pawn the jewels that same afternoon? Why the great haste to dispose of them? If safe-keeping were the prime consideration, why pawn the jewels at all? Why not place them in a safety-deposit box in Crippen's bank? And if Crippen was so concerned for the jewels' safety what was he doing running around with several hundred pounds' worth of diamonds stuffed in his pocket?

An entirely different version of this episode was given by Ethel to her landlady, Mrs Emily Jackson, according to the latter's testimony at the inquest hearing.[4] Ethel told her landlady that the jewels were uncovered when Crippen, with her help, made a thorough search of the premises at No. 39 Hilldrop Crescent. Mrs Jackson's evidence was as follows:

CORONER—Did Miss LeNeve tell you during that period she had been to Hilldrop Crescent?—Yes.

Sleeping there?—No; she said she had been helping the doctor to search for a bank-book. Afterwards she told me they had found it.

Where?—I cannot be sure.

Did she tell you whether it was very valuable?—Two hundred pounds.

Did she tell you whether they had found anything else?—Yes, a diamond tiara and two or three valuable rings. She said Dr Crippen had raised £195 on them in the West End to put into his business.

If the story she told her landlady is correct then Ethel could not have waited at the office for Crippen to show up at four o'clock, but she must have met him at Hilldrop Crescent. Together they must have spent most of the afternoon ransacking the house, discovering the jewels, or part of them at least, in time for Crippen to return to Oxford Street and pawn them before Messrs Attenborough, the pawnbrokers, closed their doors.

The rationale Ethel advances to justify her acceptance of Belle's jewels is an intriguing one. 'It has always seemed to me,' she writes, 'that any woman with a spark of pride, any wife abandoning her husband for someone else, would scorn to pack up the things she had been bought by the one whom she no longer loved.' Crippen must have let on that the jewels were all his presents to Belle, and not those of gentlemen admirers, for Ethel writes: 'After all, as regards the jewels, they had been bought by Dr Crippen as an investment. It was impossible for Belle Elmore to have paid for them.' And how did Ethel know that some of the diamonds at least were not bought with Belle's own money? 'I have seen her contracts, and I know that even when engaged on tour her salary amounted at the most to £3 a week, out of which she had to pay her agent's fee and other expenses.' So while rooting around in drawers in search of the missing bank-book Ethel presumably had found time to go through some of Belle's private papers. The impression left is one of meddlesome prying.

One basic assumption underlies all of Ethel's actions on that Wednesday, February 2nd: Belle Elmore had vanished from Ethel's life and Crippen's for ever. But how could Ethel be so certain about this? How could she be sure that Belle would not return, if for no other reason than to reclaim her diamonds? And her furs—apparently Belle had walked away from No. 39 in the dead of winter leaving behind several expensive fur coats, not to mention her fur neckpieces and stoles, in fact, taking nothing with her except the clothes she stood in.

Confident that she had nothing further to fear from the usurper, Ethel that same night slept under the roof of No. 39 for the first time—Crippen was positive about the date later. She was in no hurry to move in permanently, however, spending two or three nights a week at No. 39 until shortly before Easter when she left Mrs Jackson for good to take up her abode with Crippen.

* * *

Meanwhile, Crippen, who was being asked more and more questions about Belle's sudden departure, was beginning to get rattled. He had said nothing about her impending departure when, on Tuesday, February 1st, the morning after the dinner party for the Martinettis, he had called upon them to enquire after Paul's health. Clara Martinetti said that her husband was no worse, and, in turn, inquired after Belle. 'Oh, she is all right,' Crippen had assured her, whereupon Clara charged him, 'Give Belle my love.'

Clara Martinetti was cross when Crippen saw her a week later. 'Well, you're a nice one,' she scolded. 'Belle gone to America, and you don't tell us a thing about it.' 'Why didn't you send us a wire?' she persisted. 'I would have seen Belle off at the station and brought her some flowers.' Crippen said there had been no time, that they had received a cable late Tuesday night saying that one of them must go to America. 'As she wanted to go I let her.' The rest of the night they had spent packing. 'Packing and crying, I suppose?' Mrs Martinetti remarked sardonically. 'Oh, we have got past that,' Crippen replied.

Paul Martinetti elicited the further information that Belle had gone to America 'on legal business which might lead to a title'. Filson Young thinks that this refers to a title-deed, but most probably it refers to the story the Crippens had put about that Belle was descended from Polish nobility, and one day might come into her own as the Baroness Mackamotzki.

Clara Martinetti, in turn, complained that Belle had not sent her a postcard from the boat. 'I suppose she will write from New York,' she added. 'Oh, she does not stop in New York,' Crippen quickly replied. 'She goes straight on to California.' The next moment Crippen most likely could have bitten off his tongue, for Mrs Martinetti knew that all of Belle's relatives lived in and around New York. So why would Belle be going to California to see about a title? It was Crippen's family who lived in California.

Crippen made one more mistake before taking his leave of the Martinettis on this occasion. Clara Martinetti asked him if he were going to the charity ball being given by the Variety Artistes' Benevolent Fund at the Criterion restaurant on Sunday, February 20th. 'Paul can get you two tickets from the club,' she added. Crippen could not very well wriggle out of taking two tickets, for Belle, as he knew, had planned to sell programmes at the Ball. Having been manoeuvered into the position of buying the tickets he should have flushed them promptly down the nearest toilet. But, thanks to a puritan upbringing which taught that waste was sinful, Crippen could never bear to throw anything away. His attendance at the charity ball with Ethel LeNeve on his arm was to prove the biggest blunder of all. Overnight it was to transform the previously amiable members of the Music Hall Ladies' Guild into self-appointed Furies. It was to set their tongues wagging with suspicion, suspicion which ultimately would lead to Crippen fighting for his life in the dock at the Old Bailey.

* *

'Neither of us was very anxious to go,' Ethel writes, with her customary flair for understatement. 'I said that I was not very keen, as I had not danced for some years, and I had not a suitable dress.' In the end Ethel, with her own money, bought herself a pink gown at Swan and Edgar's ('People have said that I went to the ball in one of Belle Elmore's frocks,' she writes indignantly. 'Nothing of the kind.')

At Clara Martinetti's table Crippen sat uneasily between his hostess and Ethel, with the Nashes—Lil Hawthorne and her manager husband—opposite, and Paul Martinetti on Ethel's right.

Mrs Smythson, who was also present at the ball, observes, 'Miss LeNeve was not formally introduced to anybody, but Crippen secured partners for "My friend".'[5] As for Mrs Martinetti, she was to testify that she did not speak to Ethel all evening—Belle's hatchet job on her rival's reputation had been a thorough one. The irony was that Ethel, who still made excuses to her landlady when she slept at No. 39, told Mrs Jackson that she would be staying the night with Mrs Martinetti, 'who was going to do her hair for her (for the ball) and trim it with silk ribbon.'[6]

The cause of the glacial atmosphere which descended upon the party when Ethel joined it was not far to seek: it was the 'rising sun' brooch she wore on her bosom. Who was it who first spotted this tell-tale piece of jewellery? Marie Lloyd's biographer claims that it was Miss Lloyd herself, and that she immediately called it to the attention of other members of the Music Hall Ladies' Guild; however, this is incorrect, as Marie Lloyd did not attend the Criterion ball.* The chances are that the brooch was spotted by several of the guild ladies almost simultaneously.

The brooch itself, consisting of a central diamond cluster from which extended zigzag arms of brilliants like the rays of the sun, was unmistakable. The effect upon the ladies on seeing the brooch sparkling on Ethel's bosom was likewise unmistakable. 'They were amazed and indignant,' Mrs Smythson observes. 'Belle never in a thousand years would have allowed another woman to wear her jewels,' as one of the guild ladies expressed it. What before had been a vague feeling that something was wrong, 'something indefinite which we could not understand', in Mrs Smythson's words, now took root as deep, well-founded suspicion. To make matters worse when *The Performer* appeared with a write-up of the ball Ethel and her escort were listed among the guests as 'Mr and Mrs Crippen'. Before he left the ball Mrs Smythson made a point of stopping Crippen and asking him for Belle's address, to which he replied that she was in the California mountains. 'Has she no settled address?' Mrs Smythson persisted, and Crippen said, 'No, but when she is settled I will let you know.'[7]

'After this,' Ethel writes, 'I noticed that the members of the Music Hall Ladies' Guild were showing marked curiosity in my

* Naomi Jacob, in *Our Marie*, makes this error, which is repeated by Daniel Farson in his biography of Marie Lloyd.

movements.' 'Often when I went along the street with Dr Crippen
I remarked people staring at me in a curious way. "Good gracious!"
I said, "do they think I haven't paid for these clothes I am wearing?" ' What insensitivity, one wonders, blinded Ethel to the fact
that the guild ladies' hostility was due to her having stolen Belle's
husband, not her clothes?

*   *   *

Crippen was now anxious to move out of No. 39 as soon as
possible, telling Paul Martinetti that he intended to sell the furniture. On March 16th Crippen gave the owner of the house three
months' notice of his intention to vacate the tenancy 'because he
had been left property in America'.

There is some confusion as to whether Ethel shared Crippen's
desire to move. 'From the first I took a dislike to the house,' she
writes in her autobiography. 'It was so big,' she explains, 'and,
without a servant, I found it almost impossible to keep it as tidy
as I should like.' Her father, however, tells a different story. 'Ethel
was very fond of the garden,' he writes, 'and always objected to the
idea of leaving. She had got it [the garden] full of lovely flowers.
. . . All the same, the doctor was always urging her to leave the
place.'[8]

Like it or not, Ethel delayed moving into No. 39 until Crippen
had got rid of some of the furniture and all of Belle's theatrical
costumes. 'In spite of the extravagant way in which Mrs Crippen
dressed . . . the house was, I thought, furnished in a higgledy-
piggledy way,' Ethel writes. Early in March, therefore, a van
pulled up in front of No. 39 and removed two loads of furniture,
including a dining-room suite and a large deal chest containing
silverware, to Albion House, where they were stored. The van then
dropped off five large cardboard boxes containing ladies' clothes
at a theatrical costumier's in Shaftesbury Avenue. This done,
Ethel installed herself as chatelaine at No. 39 on Saturday, March
12th, telling Lydia Rose, a girlhood chum, that the house had been
left to Crippen 'by a relative of the doctor's, who . . . had gone
to America'.[9] To her dressmaker whom she called on earlier Ethel
was more specific. 'His [Crippen's] aunt has gone to America and
left the house in Hilldrop Crescent for him to dispose of, and also
left me all these things.'[10] 'These things' referred to lengths of

silks and satins which Belle had never bothered to have made up into frocks, and which Ethel now fished out of the wicker baskets at No. 39. 'I remember I thought it funny that the American aunt should go away and leave all those things behind,' the dressmaker is quoted as saying. 'I mentioned it to her, and she said, "I expect she did not want to pass the Customs with all those goods."' Ethel was quick-witted if not wholly convincing.

*   *   *

Meanwhile, Crippen, having told Belle's friends that she was in the California mountains where she could not be reached by letter, was faced with the task of writing her out of the script once and for all. 'Killing off' a character — particularly if she is the heroine — is no easy task, as the writers of magazine serials will bear witness. The groundwork has to be laid carefully, the 'killing' foreshadowed, so that the reader is prepared in advance, and the actual 'death' comes as not too great a shock to his sensibilities. The scenario worked out by Crippen with its attendant time-table was as follows:

March 15, 1910: Crippen calls on the Martinettis to say that he has had disquietening news concerning Belle. 'I cannot make it out,' he declares. 'I have had a letter from my relations to say that Belle is very ill, and has something the matter with one of her lungs. At the same time I got a letter from Belle to say that I must not worry, she is not as bad as they say.'

March 21, 1910: Clara Martinetti receives the following letter, dated Sunday, March 20th, from Crippen: 'Dear Clara and Paul, — Please forgive me not running in during the week, but I have really been so upset by very bad news from Belle . . . and now I have just had a cable saying she is so dangerously ill with double pleuro-pneumonia that I am considering if I had not better go over at once.' Paul Martinetti then calls on Crippen and advises him, 'Doctor, if I were you I would take the first steamer and go home to America,' to which advice Crippen shrugs his shoulders, makes no reply.

March 23, 1910: Clara Martinetti informs the Music Hall Ladies' Guild at their weekly meeting of Belle's illness, whereupon the ladies send along the hall to Crippen's office for Belle's address.

Bumping into Clara Martinetti and Annie Stratton in the lobby of Albion House after the guild meeting, Crippen tells them that it is no use their trying to get in touch with Belle, as hourly he is expecting a cablegram to say that she is gone. 'If anything happens to Belle I will go to France for a week for a change of air,' he announces.

March 24, 1910: Clara Martinetti receives the following telegram from Crippen sent from Victoria Station, London: 'Belle died yesterday at six o'clock. Please phone to Annie [Mrs Stratton]. Shall be away a week.'

March 26, 1910: The following obituary notice appears in *Era*, the theatrical weekly: 'ELMORE—March 23, in California, U.S.A., Miss Belle Elmore (Mrs H. H. Crippen).'

When Crippen wired Mrs Martinetti from Victoria Station, Ethel and he were about to join Easter holiday-makers on the boat train to Dieppe. For the two of them it was to be in the nature of a honeymoon; for had not Ethel, who was wearing a new travelling costume of *vieux rose* as part of her trousseau, told her dressmaker that Dr Crippen and she were to be married on Easter Saturday, March 26th? (Ethel gave a different version to her mother and her friend Lydia Rose, telling them that she married Crippen 'a week or two before Easter' at the St Pancras Registry Office.) In Dieppe they registered at a small hotel in the rue de la Marinière as 'Mr and Mrs Crippen'.

Ethel was to claim later that she knew nothing about Belle's supposed death in California until Tuesday, March 29th, the day Crippen and she returned from Dieppe. 'In course of time the doctor told me that Mrs Crippen had caught a chill, and had died of pneumonia in America,' Ethel writes. 'Trusting him as I did, of course I believed it. He was the man to whom I had looked up for ten years, and he had been the soul of honour to me. I put implicit faith in all he said and did.'[11]

[9]

The Furies of antiquity, those 'daughters of earth and shadow', as Sophocles calls them, are usually depicted in blood-smeared garments, and with snakes twined among their dishevelled tresses. Their descendants, however—those demiurges of the Music Hall Ladies' Guild who met for tea on Wednesdays—were nothing if not impeccably groomed. In place of snakes these avenging goddesses wore cartwheel hats on which everything in Proserpine's garden in the way of flowers and fruit, not to mention feathers and birdwings, was tastefully displayed. For chlamys they covered their shoulders with stoles of mink and sable; and in lieu of the scourges with which the Furies traditionally are pictured little jewelled purses dangled from their wrists.

Despite the impression of outward calm and well-being which these Furies exuded, they now proceeded to harry Crippen as effectively as though their appearance had been designed to strike terror to his heart. No sooner had Crippen returned from the Dieppe 'honeymoon' and changed into mourning clothes (Ethel sewed the black armband to his sleeve) than Mesdames Smythson and Martinetti were on his doorstep demanding information concerning Belle's death. To their questions as to where and how Belle had been taken ill, Crippen replied, 'It was on the boat. Belle never could take full care of herself, and finally, when she got to her destination, she became worse, until I got the sad news that she was dead'.

Clara Martinetti spoke up: 'Then you yourself will have to go to America to transact the business?' 'Oh, no,' Crippen said, 'she managed that before she died.' Telling him that the guild wanted to arrange for a wreath of everlasting flowers to be placed on Belle's grave, Mrs Smythson asked the doctor for the address where Belle had died, but Crippen said that the wreath would be unnecessary as Belle was to be cremated and her ashes to be sent to London 'where you ladies can have a little ceremony.' Mrs Smythson was insistent ('I was not going to leave him without knowing something definite'), so Crippen gave her the address of his son, Otto Crippen, living at 1427 North Hoover Street, Los Angeles. 'Was your son with Belle when she died?' Mrs Martinetti quickly asked, to which Crippen replied, 'Yes.'

The news that Belle's remains were to be cremated caused some consternation among the Furies, for they knew that Belle's relatives, the Mackamotzki-Mersinger tribus, were all Catholics, and as such not likely to have given their consent to the cremation.

A few days after this interview Clara Martinetti took a taxi to No. 39, this time accompanied by Annie Stratton and Mrs Stratton's nephew. The ladies did not get out of the taxicab, Crippen being summoned by the nephew, and coming down to talk with them. 'We asked him what boat Belle left by, and he mentioned some name which I do not remember,' Mrs Martinetti testified later at the Old Bailey. 'It was something like "La Tourenne" or "La Touvée".' In point of fact Crippen named the French liner *La Touraine*, which sailed regularly from Le Havre to New York. A check with the offices of the Compagnie Générale Transatlantique disclosed the fact that *La Touraine* had been on the high seas from New York on February 2nd, and did not arrive at Le Havre until February 4th, when it went into dry dock immediately 'to repair sundry damage', according to *Lloyds Weekly Shipping Index*. It did not sail for New York again until March 12th.

At this point Michael Bernstein, a friend of Lottie Albert, who described himself as 'an amateur detective', entered the picture briefly. At Miss Albert's request, Bernstein checked with various shipping lines, but could find no trace of Belle on the passenger list of any liner sailing for America early in February. Interestingly enough, Bernstein claims that he tailed Crippen for a while. 'Often I have kept watch on Dr Crippen in the hope of learning something which would give me a real clue to the mystery,' he writes, adding, 'It was necessary that I should act warily.'[1]

While Mesdames Martinetti and Stratton were checking on the steamship lines, two other guild ladies—Mrs Smythson and Louie Davis—were interviewing the neighbours on either side of No. 39 Hilldrop Crescent. The neighbours, though wanting to be helpful, could not remember when they had last seen Belle, nor could they recall seeing any luggage being taken away.

Meanwhile, two letters had gone forward from Albion House to

Crippen's son Otto in Los Angeles. The first was from Melinda May on behalf of the Music Hall Ladies' Guild, and asked for details of Belle's death. The second was from Crippen himself, to his 20-year-old son, and was so brief that Otto later could quote it from memory: 'Dear Son, I am very sorry to write you that my beautiful wife died recently in San Francisco. She went there to attend an estate and while en route contracted pneumonia. She died in San Francisco suffering from pleuro-pneumonia.'[2]

Both letters as it happened were sent to the wrong address. Otto Crippen, who was employed as a linesman by the Pacific Telephone and Telegraph Company, had married the previous year, and had moved with his bride from North Hoover Street to Holmby Avenue in Hollywood. By a further irony the couple had just lost their first-born; and by the time Miss May's letter was finally forwarded to him from the County Clerk's Office Otto was too upset to reply immediately.

The delay of nearly two months before Otto's reply was received in London was to throw the Furies into some confusion; however, on Thursday, March 31st, exactly one week after Crippen had wired Mrs Martinetti from Victoria Station that Belle was dead, Louise Smythson went to Scotland Yard on behalf of the Music Hall Ladies' Guild. Mrs Smythson asked to see a detective inspector, and was ushered into an office where presently Chief Inspector Walter Dew waited upon her.

'I told him of my suspicions, which were becoming stronger in the direction of foul play,' Mrs Smythson relates. First she detailed the circumstances surrounding Mrs Crippen's mysterious disappearance, then she described the Criterion Ball, where Ethel had been seen wearing the missing woman's jewels. She also spoke of the many conflicting stories Crippen had told concerning his wife's death. 'Am I overstepping the law by conveying these suspicions to you?' she asked the inspector, to which he replied, 'No.'[3]

But Dew was anything but encouraging. Pointing to a steel filing cabinet behind him, the inspector claimed that it was chock-full of reports of missing persons, some, he didn't mind saying, originating with busybodies who might occupy their time better. He then gave her a brief lecture. Wives ran away from husbands for no other reason than that they could not get a divorce. Did Mrs Smythson realise how difficult it was, how well nigh impossible for a woman to get a divorce?* Husbands were seen dancing with their secretaries, who, in some cases, were decked out in the absent wife's jewels. The police could do nothing about it. They were not custodians of morals.

As for the conflicting stories concerning Mrs Crippen's death in California, had Mrs Smythson stopped to consider the state of the husband's mind when he received the sad news? Perhaps he was suffering from shock. Perhaps he was too numbed by grief to remember the exact details of time and place. Or again, maybe Crippen was reticent. 'Maybe he doesn't believe in telling his business to the world,' Inspector Dew suggested. The upshot was that the police were not prepared to move in the matter unless Mrs Smythson preferred a definite charge. 'And I was under the impression that Scotland Yard kept their eyes on all suspicious persons,' Mrs Smythson comments bitterly.[4]

*   *   *

Mrs Smythson need not have despaired, however, for Crippen's actions had aroused the suspicions of Isabel Ginnett, the president of the Music Hall Ladies' Guild, who, as it will be recalled, was then based temporarily in Roselle, New Jersey, while her husband toured the States with his equestrian act. Although three thousand miles away Mme Ginnett was thoroughly conversant with the events surrounding Belle's mysterious disappearance, thanks to an intelligence network which would have done credit to the Mafia. Having learned of Belle's death from Melinda May, Mme Ginnett, wrote first to the Los Angeles police; then, getting no answer, she prevailed upon a New Jersey justice of the peace to write to them on his official notepaper. Back came the answer from Los Angeles: no such person as Belle Elmore or Mrs Cora Crippen had died within the county precincts. To Lil Hawthorne and her husband John Nash, who happened to be passing through New York early in May, Mme Ginnett imparted this information, along with her own private misgivings concerning Belle's fate.

* In 1910 all a man had to do to obtain a decree nisi was to present convincing proof of his wife's adultery, but a woman had to prove some additional offence, such as cruelty, incest, bigamy, rape, sodomy or bestiality, to get a divorce.

Meanwhile, unaware of the enquiries the guild ladies had under-
taken, Crippen had begun to breathe more easily. He found time
to write on black-bordered notepaper to Dr John Burroughs,
whose wife Maud was active as a guild member ('My dear Doctor,
I feel sure you will forgive me for my apparent neglect, but really
I have been nearly out of my mind with poor Belle's death . . .');
and to Belle's half-sister Louise ('The shock to me has been so
dreadful that I am hardly able to control myself. My poor Cora
is gone . . .'). Then on May 18th Crippen ran into Mrs Smythson
in a shop in Tottenham Court Road. 'Miss LeNeve was with him,'
Mrs Smythson testified later. 'I went over and asked him if he
had heard anything more about his wife's funeral, and he said,
"Yes, it is all over, and I have her ashes at home".'

On the Whitsun Bank holiday week-end of May 20th–21st Crippen and Ethel slipped across the Channel to Boulogne. They
brought back from Boulogne 16-year-old Valentine Lecoq both to
act as *au pair* girl and to tutor Ethel in French. 'I have a fair knowledge of the language,' Ethel writes in her autobiography, 'but I
am afraid my pronunciation of it is not all that it should be.'

On May 24th Melinda May received from Otto Crippen in Los
Angeles the long-delayed reply to her query concerning Belle's
death as follows:

Los Angeles, Calif., May 9, 1910
Dear Madame, — Received your letter forwarded to me from
the County Clerk, April 23, 1910. Owing to many misfortunes,
sickness, and death of our son, I overlooked your letter until
this date.

The death of my stepmother was as great a surprise to me as
to any one. She died in San Francisco, and the first I heard of
it was through my father, who wrote to me immediately afterwards. He asked me to forward all letters to him, and he
would make necessary explanations. He said he had, through
a mistake, given out my name and address as my stepmother's
death-place.

I would be very glad, if you found out any particulars of her
death, if you would let me know of them, as all I know is the
fact that she died in San Francisco. H. Otto Crippen.

*   *   *

A revolver mounted on a polished oak base was the sole ornament above the fireplace in Superintendent Frank Froest's office at New Scotland Yard, it being in the nature of a trophy of war. If pressed, Froest, the executive head of the Criminal Investigation Department, would tell visitors the story behind the weapon. It had once been the property of a train robber whom Froest, after a chase half way across America, finally had cornered in London at Gatti's Restaurant in the Strand, and had disarmed singlehanded. His friends John and Lil Nash knew the story, but on Thursday, June 30th, as they sat facing Superintendent Froest across an expanse of mahogany desk, the trophy was there on the wall to remind them, if reminder were needed, of the detective's fearlessness and of his strength (Froest could tear a pack of playing cards across with his hands). It was less than a week since the Nashes' had returned to London from a triumphant vaudeville tour in America. But now, troubled by the growing mystery concerning Belle's death, they had come to the detective superintendent whom they knew socially, with their questions and their doubts. Froest, his blue eyes alert, his moustache waxed to bayonet sharpness, in turn had listened attentively to what the Nashes had to say. He had then summoned Chief Inspector Dew to his office to meet the couple.

'They have called,' the superintendent explained, 'to see me in connexion with the disappearance of a friend of theirs, a Mrs Cora Crippen, better known on the stage as Belle Elmore. She is the wife of Dr Crippen living out Holloway way.' (Whether or not Dew connected this visit with the one he had received earlier from Mrs Smythson acting on behalf of the Music Hall Ladies' Guild he does not say in his autobiography.)

'Mr and Mrs Nash are not satisfied with the story the husband has told,' Froest pursued. 'Perhaps you had better listen to the full story.'

John Nash, who spoke with a Texas drawl, told about an interview he had had with Crippen on Tuesday, June 18th, right after the Nashes had returned from New York. The Nashes, who had been among Belle's closest friends, and who had been deeply shocked by the news of her death, had paid a call to express their sympathy to Crippen, 'who seemed very cut up, very nervous and distressed, and who sobbed'. The Nashes, in turn, were upset to catch Crippen out in a number of lies. Having given out at first that Belle had died at the home of his son in Los Angeles, Crippen now switched his story. 'Belle died in some little town near San Francisco,' he told Nash, not knowing that the latter had once lived in the San Francisco Bay region. 'It was a town with a Spanish name, but it slips my memory,' Crippen added. When Nash suggested Alameda, the doctor appeared to reflect for a moment, then said, 'Yes, I think that was the town.'

'Doctor, do you mean to tell me you don't know where your wife died?' Nash had asked incredulously.

'I think it was that town,' Crippen replied evenly.

'You say that you have received her ashes from the crematorium?' Nash prompted.

'Yes, I have them in my safe.'

'But from what crematorium?'

Crippen was not to be drawn. 'There are about four crematoria near San Francisco, and I cannot tell you which one,' he had maintained.

'But surely you received a death certificate?'

'I have got it here somewhere.' For the first time Crippen had shown signs of nervousness.*

That night Nash talked the matter over with his wife, who agreed that they should go to Scotland Yard. 'You did exactly right,' Froest assured the couple. After the Nashes' statement had been typed up the superintendent noted on the docket, 'Have the doctor seen and shaken up by a Chief Inspector.'[5]

*　　　*　　　*

The trouble was that Inspector Dew had done too thorough a job of shaking up 'the little man', as he refers to Crippen in his memoirs, the result being that Crippen took fright and fled. But then perhaps it needed only the slightest jar to send Crippen in the jittery state he was in scurrying for cover.

Inspector Dew, accompanied by Detective-Sergeant Mitchell, had called first at Crippen's home, and then not finding him there, at his office in Albion House on Friday, July 8th. After introducing himself, Dew explained, 'We have called to have a word with you

* The above account is based upon John Nash's evidence at the inquest hearing of July 18, 1910.

about the death of your wife.' If the inspector had expected Crippen to blanch he was disappointed. 'He was as calm as I was,' Dew comments. 'Looking back, it is quite plain to me that Crippen had anticipated . . . the visit of a police officer. A clever man, he had thought out in the fullest detail the story he was going to tell.'

'I suppose I had better tell you the truth,' Crippen began. Dew said he thought that that would be the best course. 'The stories I have told about my wife's death are untrue,' Crippen pursued. 'As far as I know she is still alive.' Afterwards, the three men went into Crippen's private office, and a statement from him was taken down in writing which he later signed.

In that statement Crippen, giving a good imitation of a man anxious to make a clean breast of things, admitted that he had lied. He had lied in his teeth, and lied in his bowels, first in telling the guild ladies that Belle had been called away suddenly to America on business, then that she had died of pneumonia in California. All the business about cremation and having the ashes sent to London — that was a pack of lies, too. So far as he knew Belle was not only alive, but enjoying the best of health. To the best of his knowledge, she had gone to Chicago to join her lover, an ex-prize fighter named Bruce Miller. Crippen had lied about Belle's disappearance because he could not bear to be sneered at as a cuckolded husband, or so he claimed.

Most regrettably he had lied to Miss Ethel LeNeve, who even at that moment was living with him as his wife at No. 39 Hilldrop Crescent.

'His very frankness was misleading,' Inspector Dew records. 'By admitting things which in normal circumstances men like to hide from others, he hoped to convince me that he was telling the whole truth and had nothing to hide.'

The two men had hit it off so famously that, in the midst of drawing up the statement for Crippen to sign, they had knocked off work to have lunch together, for all the world like two members of the same Oddfellows lodge holding a reunion. 'We went to a small Italian restaurant only a few yards from Albion House,' Dew declares, adding, 'Crippen made a hearty meal. He ordered beefsteak and ate it with the relish of a man who hadn't a care in the world.'[6]

After getting Crippen to sign the statement he had given, and after taking a short statement from Ethel LeNeve, the inspector accompanied the couple home to No. 39, where he and Sergeant Mitchell made a cursory search of the premises. Dew then collaborated with Crippen in drawing up the following advertisement to be inserted in an unspecified American newspaper, presumably in the Chicago area where it would come to Belle's notice:

MACKAMOTZKI. Will Belle Elmore communicate with H.H.C. or authorities at once. Serious trouble through your absence. Twenty-five dollars reward to anyone communicating her whereabouts to Box No. ——.

Before taking leave the inspector felt it necessary to address a few stern remarks to Crippen for the latter's benefit. 'Of course I shall have to find Mrs Crippen to clear this matter up,' the detective warned Crippen, to which the latter had replied, 'Yes, I will do everything I can.'

If Crippen had sat tight, and had been content to bide his time, quite likely the investigation involving him would have been dropped. The head of Scotland Yard's CID has admitted this. Sir Melville Macnaghten, writing in 1914, declares that 'if his [Crippen's] nerves had remained unshaken, and he had had the courage to take a long lease on the house which held his guilty secret, he might still be alive . . .'[7] Inspector Dew has agreed that this is so. 'If Crippen had stood his ground and continued to live quietly at Hilldrop Crescent,' Dew writes, 'my difficulties would have been infinitely greater. Maybe the mystery would never have been solved.'[8] But Crippen did not stand his ground. On Saturday, July 9th, the day following Dew's interview with him, he cut and ran, taking with him an albatross in the form of Miss LeNeve.

V

CAPTAIN
KENDALL

'You can't beat a British crime,
The hunt and the trial,
And the hanging all in style
Is better than a pantomime.'

*—from 'Belle or the Ballad of
Doctor Crippen'*

'It is arguable, even if amoral, that
Doctor Crippen provided more popular entertainment by murdering his
wife than Harry Tate in his music-hall
sketch "Motoring".'

—MACDONALD HASTINGS[1]

'. . . somehow I don't think he would
have minded the fact that his name
was to become a rather macabre music-
hall joke . . . as, for instance, one well-
known comic, discussing in his patter
his discomforts as a lodger, ended up
by saying, "Cor blimey! You ought
to see the landlady—what a face—
Crippen was innocent!" '

—CLARKSON ROSE[2]

[10]

Wednesday, July 20th, dawned with one of those coastal fogs that are soon burned off by the sun. The 5,431-ton cargo vessel *Montrose*, bound for Canada, had cleared the port of Antwerp and was steaming down the River Scheldt on its way to the sea when Captain Henry Kendall, glancing through the porthole of his cabin, saw something that arrested his attention. Standing behind a lifeboat were two men who held hands as though each could not bear to let the other go. 'The younger one squeezed the other's hand immoderately,' Captain Kendall recalls. 'It seemed to me unnatural for two males, so I suspected them at once,' he adds, though of what he suspected them he does not say.*

The *Montrose* was what was known as a 'steerage' vessel; that is, the bulk of its passengers—some 280 in all—were travelling 'steerage' in what had once been refrigerated holds, but had been fitted out since with bunks to accommodate human cargo. These holds had carried troops to Capetown during the Boer War; more recently they had been transporting immigrants to the New World in search of gold-paved streets. There were no first-class passengers, and only twenty passengers in the second class, which meant that the odd couple whom the captain had seen lurking behind the life-boat stood out prominently from the start.

Captain Kendall was kept busy most of the morning, so it was not until shortly before noon when the *Montrose* had reached the open sea that he was able to introduce himself to the pair and to invite them to take lunch at his table. The elder of the two men, who spoke with an American accent, introduced himself as John Philo Robinson, merchant, taking his 16-year-old son to California for the boy's health.† Dutifully, the son coughed and otherwise gave signs of having a severe cold. There were several things about

---

* Captain Kendall's account of events appeared first in the *Montreal Star*, then was picked up in London by the *Daily Mail*.

† The derivation of this alias is not hard to find. Crippen's uncle was 'Harvey Robinson', and he had a cousin named 'Philo Robinson'.

the boy which did not ring true to the captain. The boy's voice, for one—it began in a low register, became progressively higher as he talked. The boy's figure, for another—it was all curves where there should have been angles, and appeared about to burst the seams of clothes that were too small for him.

As for the father, he was wearing a grey frock coat and trousers, with a white wide-awake hat which seemed inappropriate attire for a sea voyage even for a vessel as modest as the *Montrose*. J. P. Robinson was clean-shaven and wore no spectacles, though tell-tale red marks on either side of the bridge of his nose made the captain think that he had but lately discarded them. He was also inclined to be garrulous, commenting on the weather, the scenery, the ship's accommodation, the passengers, in marked contrast to the son, who remained as though struck dumb. Captain Kendall had heard all about the murder of Belle Elmore. The newspapers, notably the Continental Edition of the *Daily Mail*, had been full of it while he was ashore at Antwerp. Although the captain does not admit this, the chances are that he twigged the Robinsons' true identity the moment he laid eyes upon them.

While the Robinsons were at lunch at his table that first day Captain Kendall made some excuse for absenting himself and slipped down to their cabin to examine their luggage. There was pitifully little of it, the couple having only one small suitcase between them. The boy did not even have an overcoat. Captain Kendall noted that the senior Robinson's hat was stamped 'Jackson, blvd du Nord, Bruxelles', while the boy's hat bore no label, but was packed with tissue paper round the rim to make it smaller. Also, the boy apparently was using the sleeve of a woman's under-garment as a face-cloth.

*   *   *

Captain Henry Kendall liked to think of himself as an amateur criminologist. Perhaps he had read too many Dead-Eye Dick novels as a lad when he first shipped to sea from Liverpool. Or again, his imagination may have been fired by stories of real-life criminals. Whatever the cause, Kendall had developed his powers of detection to an unusual degree. Aboard the *Empress of India*, where he had been Chief Officer before joining the *Montrose*, those powers had been given scope, for the *Empress* had been infested with card-sharpers, and Kendall had been instrumental in exposing these 'bounders', as he called them, at the rate of at least one a voyage.

The opportunity which now presented itself to play detective made collaring card-sharpers seem small beer indeed, but the captain was hesitant. Was the evidence of his eyes and ears enough 'to justify me in sending a message involving myself, my ship, and my company in this sensational affair?' as he expressed it later.[3] Would the Canadian Pacific Line thank him for his pains? Supposing he were wrong, supposing Scotland Yard demanded further proofs — what then? There was no time to dither, for the radio transmitter of the *Montrose* had a range of only 150 miles, and every minute was bearing the ship further away from land receivers where a message from her might be picked up. 'If I was to act at all, it had to be soon,' the captain writes.

First, however, he decided to conduct a simple experiment. He fished among the copies of the *Daily Mail*, Continental Edition, which he had saved to read aboard ship until he found the one for Thursday, July 14th, which contained a portrait of Crippen, together with an account of the 'North London Cellar Murder'. With a piece of chalk he found in a desk drawer the captain carefully 'whited out' the rims of the spectacles Crippen was wearing in the press photograph. Then he did the same with Crippen's straggly moustache until the upper lip in the photograph appeared clean-shaven. The resultant 'Photo-Fit' picture bore an uncanny resemblance to 'J. P. Robinson, merchant'.

Delighted with his artistic endeavours, the captain next turned his attention to a portrait of Ethel LeNeve.* It showed Ethel wearing a toque with an aigrette sprouting from a jewelled ornament that would have made any Grand Vizier proud. The face tucked beneath was anything but that of an oriental potentate, however. It was Ethel at her most dreamy-eyed, giving the photographer her 'soulful expression', as her friends called it.

This time Captain Kendall took a pair of calipers from his desk drawer, and, after measuring Ethel's face carefully with the dividers,

* The *Daily Mirror* had 'scooped' not only rival newspapers but Scotland Yard in obtaining the LeNeve photograph. By merest chance a *Mirror* photographer named Parker learned that Ethel's cousin lived in the flat above his at Clapham, so while the cousin was out he simply went into her bedroom and lifted the photograph off the wall.

transferred the measurements to a piece of cardboard. He then cut a hole in the cardboard and placed it on the photograph in such a way that the template completely masked the toque Ethel was wearing, as well as her piled hair. The resultant face which stared from the printed page was that of 'Master Robinson'.

'I said nothing to the officers till the following morning, when I took my Chief Officer into my confidence,' the captain records. 'I warned him that it must be kept absolutely quiet, as it was too good a thing to lose . . .' The *Montrose* had steamed 130 miles west of the Lizard when Captain Kendall handed the radio operator the message directed to the ship's owners in Liverpool that was to electrify the world: HAVE STRONG SUSPICIONS THAT CRIPPEN LONDON CELLAR MURDERER AND ACCOMPLICE ARE AMONG SALOON PASSENGERS. MOUSTACHE TAKEN OFF, GROWING BEARD. ACCOMPLICE DRESSED AS BOY. VOICE MANNER AND BUILD UNDOUBTEDLY A GIRL. BOTH TRAVELLING AS MR AND MASTER ROBINSON. (Signed) KENDALL.

* * *

'Of one thing both Irving and I were convinced, if Crippen had cared to throw over his companion . . . he might have made good his escape,' writes Edward (later Sir Edward) Marshall Hall, the eminent barrister, who was to take such a keen interest in Crippen.[4] (The Irving referred to was H. B. Irving, son of the actor Sir Henry Irving, and himself a student of criminology.) Sir Melville Macnaghten agrees. 'If he had gone away alone he might have baffled the police,' Sir Melville observes, 'but as soon as he determined to take his lady friend with him, the rope was already dangling round his neck, and it very perceptibly tightened when he dressed her up as a boy.'[5]

For one who made such incredible errors Crippen's luck had held amazingly well, up to the moment Ethel and he boarded the *Montrose* at least. In travelling from London to the Continent via Harwich and the Hook of Holland the fugitives had easily got lost in the holiday crowds pouring abroad at the height of the summer season. In Rotterdam they had stopped long enough for Ethel to visit a Dutch barber and to get her hair trimmed, for Crippen's efforts with scissors to give Ethel a boyish bob had been rough and ready. In her memoir Ethel tries to turn the ordeal with the

Dutch barber's clippers into a lark. 'Good gracious!' she writes, 'how startled I was when I first felt the little instrument running up and down my head, and my hair scattering upon the floor. "Heavens alive," I thought, "I shall soon have no hair left at this rate!" . . . When I came out with a poll as closely cropped as Jack Sheppard we both burst out laughing.'[6]

Their luck held, too, when they arrived in Brussels. They were fortunate enough to choose a hotel whose *concierge* was a reader of novels of the feuilleton variety, and who immediately wove a romance round them. The Hôtel des Ardennes was a leprous-looking, greystone building in the rue de Brabant, frequented mostly by country folk who came to Brussels only on market days, and by commercial travellers with an early morning train to catch at the nearby Gare du Nord.

The 'Robinsons, *père et fils*', who registered Sunday afternoon, July 10th, answered neither of these descriptions, M Delisse, the patron, quickly decided. The son in particular puzzled the inn-keeper. After showing the pair to their room, on the third floor, a room whose big double bed scarcely left them space to turn around, M Delisse hastened downstairs to describe the boy to his wife. 'He has large hips, small feet, and wears girl's shoes,' as M. Delisse explained, mimicking Ethel's mincing walk. A Ganymede, was M Delisse's verdict; one of those unfortunates who suffer from a hormone deficiency, or a glandular disorder.

Robinson *père* had explained that his son was deaf, but a moment later, when the patron had turned away to the key rack, the father forgot himself, whispered something into the boy's ear.

Mme Delisse divined the true sex of this changeling the moment she laid eyes on Robinson *fils*, and immediately dubbed the newly-transformed girl 'Titine'. 'We saw that her hands were beautiful and white, with well-kept nails—a woman's hands quite obviously,' the patronne was quoted as saying.[7] By the same token Robinson *père* became 'Old Quebec', in madame's parlance, because he could talk of nothing but Quebec, and of the necessity of getting his son there as quickly as possible. 'My son is ill, it's his chest, you know,' the soi-disant father would explain. 'Besides, the sea voyage will do him a world of good,' he would add, patting the 'lad's' cheek.

Madame decided that 'Old Quebec' was, in reality, a professor at a girl's convent who had fallen madly in love with 'Titine', his pupil, and that the two were eloping with the girl's parents in pursuit. Did not the schoolgirl heroines of the novels Mme Delisse read invariably run away with the fatherly types who were their professors? As she watched the couple take their breakfast coffee the patronne developed a protective feeling towards them. At the same time their escapade thrilled her to the core of her romantic being.

The elopers took their breakfast in the hotel bar on the ground floor, whose banquettes were covered with oil cloth. In a wall rack were long-stemmed, numbered clay pipes for the regulars; behind the comptoir there was a show of bottles containing green and yellow liqueurs; and copies of *L'Etoile Belge*, *Le Patriote*, and *L'Indépendance Belge* were scattered over the tables. Mme Delisse noted how anxiously 'Old Quebec' scanned the morning papers—no doubt to discover whether the girl's parents had gone to the police.*

After breakfast the Robinsons were gone from the hotel for the rest of the day. Brussels in July was host to an International Exhibition that had attracted visitors from all parts of the world. So with no fear of attracting attention the couple mingled with sightseers admiring the gothic splendours of the Hôtel de Ville in the Grand Place. They made a pilgrimage to the Mannikin Pis, and Crippen explained how, during rag week, the students dressed the little urchin as a Garde Civique and paraded him through the streets. But mostly they enjoyed picnicking on the lawns of the Bois de Cambre 'listening to the band and the singing of the birds', if Ethel is to be believed. 'It all seemed very beautiful, very peaceful, and they were happy days,' she writes in her autobiography.[8] Does Ethel, one wonders, really expect her readers to swallow this?

Shortly after their arrival in Brussels Crippen had stopped by a shipping office and had booked passage aboard a Red Star liner sailing from Antwerp for Montreal on July 31st. He had insisted upon having a cabin for the exclusive use of himself and his son, explaining that the son was ill. Then on Friday, July 15th, after reading an item in *L'Indépendence Belge*, Crippen had suddenly changed his mind. Calling at the shipping office again, he explained that his son's condition had worsened, which meant that they must return to Canada as soon as possible, and would the agent please

---

* The story of 'Titine' and 'Old Quebec' is based upon interviews M and Mme Delisse gave to the London *Daily Mail* and to the *Montreal Star*.

change the reservation to the *Montrose* sailing on Wednesday, July 20th. The item Crippen had read in *L'Indépendence Belge* had been headed '*ACTRICE ASSASSINÉE*'.

*   *   *

Sir Melville Macnaghten had just finished dressing for dinner on Friday, July 22nd, when he received an urgent telephone call from Scotland Yard. Inspector Dew was on the line apologising for disturbing the Assistant Commissioner, but he had just received, through the Liverpool police, a marconigram from a ship at sea which he thought Macnaghten should see at once. At the latter's invitation, Dew took a cab and drove to the Macnaghten residence, where he showed the CID chief the wireless message Captain Kendall had sent. As he read Macnaghten's eyebrows knit with perplexity. Suppose the captain of the *Montrose* were wrong? Suppose it was a case of mistaken identity? If Scotland Yard acted upon the captain's information and it turned out to be erroneous 'then the case would have been hopelessly messed up, and I didn't care to dwell on the eventualities of the future,' Macnaghten confesses in his memoirs. In his indecision Sir Melville turned to Dew for his opinion, the latter records.

'I feel confident it's them,' I replied.

'So do I,' agreed Sir Melville, and then. 'What do you suggest?'

'I want to go after them in a fast steamer,' I said eagerly. 'The White Star liner *Laurentic* sails from Liverpool to-morrow. I believe it is possible for her to overtake the *Montrose* and reach Canada first.'

Sir Melville Macnaughton [sic] smiled ... Then he moved to his desk, sat down and started to write. A few minutes later he handed me a document which authorised me to pursue just the course I had suggested ...

'Here's your authority, Dew,' he then said, 'and I wish you all the luck in the world.'[9]

The *Laurentic*'s running time to Quebec was seven days, whereas it took the *Montrose* eleven; so even though the latter had a three-day head start, there was every possibility of it being overtaken by the faster liner. It was as 'Mr Dewhurst' that the detective inspector sailed aboard the *Laurentic* the following morning. So intent was he upon keeping his voyage secret that not even his wife was made privy to the nature of 'Operation Handcuffs', the police code name for the mission, the inspector telling her only that he had to go abroad 'on a matter of great urgency'.

Not all the Yard chiefs were agreed as to the wisdom of the course now being pursued. One 'highly-placed official' quoted by the *Daily Mail*, in casting doubt whether the transvestite aboard the *Montrose* was Ethel LeNeve, advanced the po-faced argument, 'It is by no means an uncommon practice for young women in long-distance liners to pass as boys in order not to lose, by confinement in the female quarters, the company of a father or brother.'[10] 'Operation Handcuffs', however, had the blessing of Sir Edward Richard Henry, the Police Commissioner, and the Yard chiefs breathed more easily after photographs of the missing couple sent to Brussels were positively identified by a travel agent as the 'father and son' who had booked passage on the *Montrose*.

*   *   *

The sea chase which followed captured the imagination of the world. As a cliff-hanger it rivalled the account of Sherlock Holmes grappling with Professor Moriarty above the falls at Reichenbach. Would the *Laurentic* overtake the *Montrose*? Would the couple aboard the latter whom Captain Kendall 'strongly suspected' of being Dr Crippen and Ethel LeNeve in fact prove to be them? Newspaper readers in most parts of the world scanned their favourite dailies each morning for the answers to these posers. The press for its part assured readers that Inspector Dew was gaining on Dr Crippen at the rate of $3\frac{1}{2}$ miles per hour, and to prove its point, published diagrams, maps, projections showing the relative positions at sea of the ships bearing the two men.

What gave the drama its extra dimension was wireless telegraphy. Marconi's recent invention was all set to prove itself as a powerful adjunct of the law, having already given convincing demonstration of its usefulness in sea rescue.* As J. B. Priestley observes, 'The

---

* On January 23, 1909 more than 1,600 passengers were rescued as a result of wireless SOS messages after the White Star luxury liner *Republic* and the Italian steamer *Florida* collided in fog off the Ambrose Lightship. Fortunately, the *Republic* was equipped with a Marconi set.

people, who have a sure instinct in these matters, knew they had seats in a gallery five hundred miles long for a new, exciting, entirely original drama: *Trapped by Wireless!* There was Crippen and his mistress, arriving with a smile at the captain's table . . . While they were looking at the menu, several million readers were seeing their names in the largest type.'[11]

As for Captain Kendall, he proved to be not only an amateur Sherlock Holmes, but a first-class reporter. The dispatches which he wirelessed to the *Montreal Star* via Belle Isle, and which in turn were relayed by cable to the *Daily Mail* in London, made vivid reading over the breakfast table. Thanks to Kendall, the public learned that Dr Crippen continued to shave his upper lip, but that his beard was coming along nicely ('I'd often see him stroking it and seeming pleased,' Kendall wirelessed, 'looking more like a farmer every day.') The mark on Dr Crippen's nose, caused through wearing spectacles, 'has not worn off since coming on board,' the captain observed. As for Ethel, her table manners— the way she handled her knife and fork, and took fruit off a dish with two fingers—gave away her 'Master Robinson' disguise at every turn, according to Kendall. 'Crippen keeps cracking nuts for her and giving her half his salad, and is always paying most marked attention,' the captain added.

Not only were the world and his wife witness to the drama, but, like the Olympian gods, they knew its outcome. Mercifully, this foreknowledge of doom was kept hidden from Crippen and his paramour. 'They have been under strict observation all the voyage, as, if they smelt a rat, he might do something rash,' Captain Kendall wirelessed the *Montreal Star*, adding, 'I have noticed a revolver in his hip pocket.' Again, 'When my suspicions were aroused as to Crippen's identity I quietly collected all the English papers on board the ship which mentioned anything of the murder . . .' Crippen, who, contrary to Captain Kendall's surmise, was unarmed, could no more have escaped from the *Montrose* at sea than he could have escaped from the moira which the fates had spun for him, and which even at that moment Atropos was getting ready to snip with her shears. It was this inevitability which gave the drama its Greek dimension.

On July 29th Captain Kendall wirelessed: ETHEL'S TROUSERS ARE VERY TIGHT ABOUT THE HIPS AND SPLIT A BIT DOWN THE BACK AND SECURED WITH LARGE SAFETY-PINS. Suddenly the tension snapped. Where before there had been silence, broken only by the crackle in the wireless operator's cabin as the bluish sparks leapt from end to end of an induction coil, now there was laughter, slow at first, but increasing in volume. Somehow one could not take seriously a heroine of tragedy whose modesty hung by a safety-pin. Music hall comedians were quick to mirror the new mood with ditties such as:

> 'Oh Miss LeNeve, oh Miss LeNeve,
>   Is it true that you are sittin'
>   On the lap of Dr Crippen
> In your boy's clothes,
> On the Montrose
>   Miss LeNeve?'

*　　　*　　　*

Meanwhile, aboard ship, Captain Kendall, continued to play detective, even though by now he was satisfied as to the odd couple's identity. For example, having read in the police description of Crippen that he had false teeth, the captain told 'Robinson' a funny story, so that when the latter opened his mouth to guffaw, he [Captain Kendall] could look for dentures. Having read that Crippen had lived at one time or another in San Francisco, Detroit and Toronto, the captain drew him out in conversation about these cities to find that the doctor knew them well. In particular, Crippen spoke sadly about the San Francisco earthquake and fire of 1906, which had destroyed the city as he knew it as a boy.

Continuing his cat and mouse games, Captain Kendall records that 'on two or three occasions when walking on the deck I called after him by his assumed name, "Mr Robinson", and he took no notice. I repeated it, and it was only owing to the presence of mind of LeNeve that he turned round. He apologised for not hearing me, saying that the cold weather had made him deaf.'

But mostly Dr Crippen was content to doze on deck wrapped up in a steamer rug. Occasionally he would gaze aloft at the wireless aerial and listen to the Marconi operator send his crackling electric spark messages, according to Captain Kendall. 'What a marvellous invention it is!' the doctor would exclaim. 'How privileged we are to be alive in an age of such scientific miracles.'

Crippen might have changed his tune had he known the burden of the messages that were being transmitted and received. For two days Captain Kendall had been kept in suspense, not knowing whether his marconigram to the ship's owners in Liverpool had been relayed to Scotland Yard. The first intimation that Scotland Yard had got his message and was acting on it came when at 3 am, Monday, July 25th, the wireless operator awakened the captain to say that he had picked up a message from a London newspaper to the *Laurentic* asking, 'What is Inspector Dew doing aboard? Is he playing games with passengers? Are passengers excited over chase?'

The *Laurentic* was not alone in being pestered by reporters. As soon as it became known that Crippen was thought to be aboard the *Montrose* the ship was inundated with queries from the world's press.* 'Is it true Crippen and LeNeve are on board disguised as clergyman and son?' wirelessed the London *Daily Mirror*, referring to a report in the rival *Daily Express* that Crippen in a dog collar and disguised as the 'Reverend Mr Robinson' had been arrested aboard ship, and was being held in his cabin. The London *Daily Mail* came straight to the point with: 'Kindly wireless on business terms good description of how Crippen and LeNeve arrested.' As for the *New York World*, this enterprising journal by-passed Kendall to appeal to the main protagonist directly. 'Will gladly print all you will say,' the *World* offered hopefully.

Then at midnight Wednesday, July 27th, the *Laurentic* overtook and passed the *Montrose* in mid-Atlantic, and the latter's skipper received the message for which he had been waiting. 'Will board you Father Point,' Inspector Dew wirelessed. 'Please keep any information till I arrive there strictly confidential.' 'What the devil do you think I have been doing?' was Captain Kendall's testy reply.

*   *   *

Meanwhile, Dr Crippen was riding an emotional switchback. At

* More than 50 messages from American, British and Canadian newspapers were in the bundle of marconigrams received by Captain Kendall, and sold at auction by Bonham's of Knightsbridge on July 30, 1974 for £1,600. Shortly before his death in 1965 Kendall had given the wireless messages to his friend Sir Norman Vernon.

one moment his spirits would be high, buoyed no doubt by the thought of the life that lay ahead for Ethel and himself when they landed in Canada. The next moment he would be down in the trough, and Ethel had her work cut out to arouse in him even a semblance of cheerfulness. Crippen was in one of his manic moods at the ship's concert, when he and Ethel joined in the sing-song. 'He spoke to me next morning,' Captain Kendall writes, 'saying how one song, "We all walked into the shop", had been drumming in his head all night, and how his "boy" had enjoyed it and had laughed heartily when they retired to their room.'

But as the voyage neared its end Dr Crippen grew more and more restless. 'During the day he would often look at the track chart, which shows the ship's position,' according to Captain Kendall, 'and count the number of days remaining to the end of the passage.' Once, after listening to the Marconi operator send a dispatch, Crippen, vaguely alarmed, asked him who the message was for. The quick-witted operator replied that he had wirelessed the skipper of the *Royal George* whether any ice had been spotted near Belle Isle.

Ethel, on the other hand, not only remained composed, but actually enjoyed herself, if her story is to be credited. 'It never entered my head,' she writes, 'that they [the ship's officers] had discovered my disguise . . . I remember there was one nice English boy with whom I got rather chummy. We used to talk football together! Afterwards Dr Crippen laughingly said, "How nicely you are getting on!" '[12]

Ethel was a heroine to one passenger at least. Mrs Nepher, a Belgian lady, was on deck and playing with her small son when the boy slipped and would have fallen through the railing into the sea had not Ethel caught him. In doing so Ethel had let out a shrill scream, which had dispelled all doubt concerning her sex so far as the child's mother was concerned. 'I felt sorry for her,' Mrs Nepher later declared. 'She used to play with my little boy, although she never spoke to him or me. She was very kind and sweet.'[13]

Mostly the fugitives kept to themselves, shunning the other passengers. When a Canadian named Husmer tried to get up a whist game with Dr Stewart, the ship's surgeon, and the 'Robinsons', Ethel begged off, pleading neuralgia. On another evening the pair did not appear at the ship's concert in the saloon, and the next morning Crippen apologised to the captain, saying 'that he wanted to come, but the young fellow did not feel well and would not let him come, as he did not like to be left alone.'[14]

*   *   *

Was it Captain Kendall who placed in Crippen's hands a copy of *The Four Just Men*, one wonders? Or did the doctor find this detective thriller all by himself in the ship's library? However it happened, Crippen, tucked up in a steamer rug on deck, was soon absorbed in this novel, Edgar Wallace's first. *The Four Just Men* is about four anarchists who plot to assassinate the British Foreign Secretary in order to right a social injustice. After the anarchists plant a bomb in the Member's smoking-room of the House of Commons, the government puts a price on their heads of £1,000, exactly four times the reward the police offered for the capture of Crippen. The thriller, one of Wallace's best, is full of realistic descriptions, such as the following, which tells how Londoners reacted to the anarchists' reign of terror:

> Blood-red placards, hoarse news-boys, overwhelming head-lines, and column after column of leaded type told the world . . . People stopped talking about wars and famines and draughts and street accidents and parliaments and ordinary every-day murders and the German Emperor, in order to concentrate their minds upon the topic of the hour . . .

Did this description set up an echo within Crippen? Certainly it was not unlike the public hysteria which had greeted the discovery of the remains in the cellar at No. 39. Did the doctor identify the fictional Detective Superintendent Falmouth with the real-life Inspector Dew? What did Crippen make of the fate which awaited the anarchists if and when they were captured? 'Here are men arrogating to themselves the Divine right of superior judgment,' the British Prime Minister is made to comment. 'If we catch them they will end their lives unpicturesquely . . . in a little shed in Pentonville Gaol . . .'

The novel's climax occurs when the hour fixed by the assassins for the Foreign Secretary's murder approaches, and Westminster is cordoned off by police:

All that afternoon a hundred thousand people waited patiently, seeing nothing, save, towering above the heads of a host of constabulary, the spires and towers of the Mother of Parliaments, or the blank faces of the buildings. In Trafalgar Square, along the Mall as far as the police would allow them, at the lower end of Victoria Street, eight deep along the Albert Embankment, growing in volume every hour, London waited, waited in patience, orderly, content to stare steadfastly at nothing, deriving no satisfaction for their weariness, but the sense of being as near as it was humanly possible to be, to the scene of a tragedy. A stranger arriving in London, bewildered by this gathering, asked for the cause. A man standing on the outskirts of the Embankment throng pointed across the river with the stem of his pipe.

'We're waiting for a man to be murdered,' he said simply, as one who describes a familiar function.[15]

*　　*　　*

Ethel was struck by the change that came over Hawley as the ship neared the end of its voyage. In her biographical sketch she writes:

Two days before we reached Father Point, just off Quebec, he came down to the cabin very serious. Before we left London I had handed him all my money, now changed into notes, and amounting to £15.

'My dear,' he said, 'I think you had better take charge of these.'

'Why?' I exclaimed, 'I have nowhere to put them except in these pockets. You can keep them, can't you, until you get to Quebec?'

'Well,' he said, hesitatingly, 'I may have to leave you.'

'Leave me!' I said. I was astounded. It seemed to me incredible that I should have come all this way and then should be left alone.

'Listen, my dear,' he said. 'When you get to Quebec you had better go on to Toronto. It is a nice place and I know it fairly well. You have not forgotten your typewriting? and you have got your millinery at your fingers' ends?'

It then occurred to me that what he meant was that he should go ahead and prospect the country in order that we might settle down in peace in some out-of-the-way spot.

But her lover was contemplating a longer journey than Ethel realised. Was Crippen contemplating suicide? Although later he was to deny it vigorously, a clear indication that he planned to take his life on the eve of the *Montrose*'s docking at Quebec is to be seen in a suicide note found on him at the time of his arrest.* The note was written on the back of one of the calling cards Crippen had had printed in Brussels with the legend 'E. Robinson & Co., Detroit, Mich., presented by Mr John Robinson'. Written in Crippen's pencilled handwriting, the message read: 'I can't stand the horror I go through every night any longer, and as I see nothing bright ahead and money has come to an end, I have made up my mind to jump overboard to-night. I know I have spoiled your life, but I hope some day you can learn to forgive me. With last words of love, your H.'†

Having written the note, why did Crippen not go through with his plan? What caused him to draw back? Or had he timed it wrong? Did his arrest occur before he could put his plan into operation?

*   *   *

'Since Mr H. M. Stanley discovered the missing missionary

---

* At his trial Crippen's story was that a friendly quartermaster had tipped him off that police were waiting to arrest Ethel and himself at Quebec, whereupon Crippen concocted the suicide hoax. The quartermaster, Crippen declared, had promised to stow him away and smuggle his ashore at Montreal. Meanwhile, the police would be handed the suicide note indicating that the doctor had jumped overboard at sea. In the witness-box Crippen, however, could not give the quartermaster's name. 'My belief is that Crippen really did intend to take his life,' Inspector Dew writes in his autobiography.

† On a second card found on him at the time of his arrest Crippen had written, 'Shall we wait until to-night about 10 or 11? If not, what time?' This has led some observers to conclude that Crippen and Ethel had made a suicide pact. Ethel, however, pooh-poohed the idea, writing in *Lloyd's Weekly News* of November 13, 1910: 'I had no great trouble, and I looked forward with keen delight to an adventurous life in Canada.'

with the remark, "Dr Livingstone, I presume", no meeting has ever been equal to that of Chief Inspector Walter Dew with the murderous doctor on the deck of the *SS Montrose*,' writes Sir Melville Macnaghten. Certainly the 'Good morning, Dr Crippen', with which Dew greeted his quarry was as banal as Stanley's opening gambit. The inspector then watched the startled emotions that chased across the doctor's face. 'For a second longer doubt and uncertainty were registered on his face,' Dew records. 'Then a sudden twitching of his Adam's apple told me that recognition had come to him.'

Wearing the brass-buttoned pea-jacket and the visored cap of the pilot service and accompanied by Canadian police similarly disguised, Dew had boarded the *Montrose* early Sunday morning, July 31st while the ship lay off Father Point. Dew made straight for the bridge, shook hands hurriedly with Captain Kendall, who directed the detective's attention to a little man in a grey frock coat just then emerging from behind a funnel on the deck below. The figure looked familiar, but at that distance Dew could not be certain. 'Captain Kendall was watching me closely, but he said no word,' Dew recalls. 'Together we moved in the direction of the man now walking slowly up and down ... Presently only a few feet separated us. A pair of bulgy eyes were raised to mine. I would have recognised them anywhere.'[16]

The actual arrest was a Canadian show, inasmuch as the *Montrose* was now in Canadian waters. As he was being hustled towards the stairs leading to the deck below, Crippen asked the arresting officer, Chief Constable McCarthy of the Quebec police, 'Have you a warrant? What is the charge?' When McCarthy produced the warrant, Crippen grabbed it before the police official could prevent him, and scanned it rapidly. 'Murder and mutilation, oh, God!' he muttered, throwing the warrant onto the deck. He then held out his hands to be manacled, and passively allowed himself to be led away to a vacant cabin below. Five minutes later a woman's shriek informed the ship's officer personnel that Ethel LeNeve, too, had been placed under arrest. She had been reading curled up on her bunk when Inspector Dew and the Canadian police had burst through the door. No sooner had she recognised Dew than she gave a cry and fainted. The novel which fell from her lap to the floor was *Audrey's Recompense*, by Mrs Georgie Sheldon, the author of *Wedded by Fate* and *Ruby's Reward*.

Three blasts from the *Montrose*'s siren was the signal for the pilot boat *Eureka*, loaded to the gunwales with journalists, to approach. The reporters came swarming over the deck of the *Montrose* like a boarding party of pirates. Soon they were to be seen button-holing bewildered passengers, very few of whom spoke English. The principals of course were nowhere to be seen. The *Daily Mail* pictures the representatives of the world's press 'scurrying hither and thither for facts, writing them down on pads of paper which were crushed into wads and thrown on the deck of the *Eureka*, many feet below, or crushed in bottles with little flags in the cork, to be cast overboard . . . and picked up by a chartered despatch-boat.'[17] Meanwhile, the *Montrose* proceeded up the St Lawrence to Quebec, where the two prisoners were hurried ashore through the crowds that thronged the quay.

VI

HAWLEY

'I think he was one of the nicest men I ever met.'

—MRS EMILY JACKSON[1]

'. . . there was something almost likeable about the mild little fellow who squinted through thick-lensed spectacles, and whose sandy moustache was out of all proportion to his build.'

—CHIEF INSPECTOR WALTER DEW[2]

'Of all the criminals we ever defended there was never one who so compelled my sympathy as Crippen.'

—ARTHUR NEWTON'S
MANAGING CLERK[3]

'I too always felt some inexplicable sympathy for him.'

—SIR EDWARD MARSHALL HALL, KC[4]

'You can't help liking this guy somehow. He was one murderer who died like a gentleman . . .'

—RAYMOND CHANDLER[5]

[11]

'Crippen crucified between two thieves . . .' Thus did a Garrick Club wit describe the scene which presented itself when, during a court recess, Hawley Harvey Crippen conferred briefly with his advisers. It was Tuesday, October 18, 1910, the opening day of Crippen's trial in the oak-panelled Court No. 1 of the Old Bailey with Lord Alverstone, the Lord Chief Justice, presiding.

As he leaned over the railing of the prisoner's dock to confer with his solicitor in the well of the court below Crippen easily dominated the tableau. Always the dandy, he wore a well-cut black coat with silk facings, a dove-coloured waistcoat showing a great deal of white shirt-front, and a neat black bow tie. His hair was carefully brushed to cover the bald spot on top. 'His pink cheeks had a fresh, healthy look,' notes a *Daily Mail* reporter. For one who was about to stand trial for his life Crippen bore the approaching ordeal lightly, betraying 'not the slightest trace of care or emotion of any kind', according to this same *Daily Mail* reporter. He wrung no hands, mopped no perspiring brow, nor otherwise gave sign of anxiety as Day One of his trial unfolded.

Standing slightly apart from Crippen and his solicitor as they conferred was the lesser of the two thieves, Horatio Bottomley, who had obtained a press ticket to the trial by virtue of the fact that he was the proprietor and editor of *John Bull*, a muck-raking weekly magazine. Swindler, demagogue and some-time Liberal Member of Parliament for South Hackney, Bottomley, who himself looked like the John Bull of the newspaper cartoons, had a vested interest in Crippen, for he had put up £50 for the latter's defence (he was to put up another £150 later on for the appeal). A *quid pro quo* was involved, to be sure: Bottomley's magazine was to have exclusive rights to anything that could be wrung from Crippen in the way of 'copy'. But that would come later, after the trial: for the moment Bottomley was content to beam upon the little man in the dock with a proprietorial air.

More in the guise of a jesting Pilate than that of the unrepentant thief did Arthur John Edward Newton, solicitor, appear on the opening day. Newton, however, did not hold with Pilate's hand-washing routine, preferring instead to wear kid gloves of a dove-grey colour (he ordered them by the gross from a glove-maker in Jermyn Street) when he appeared in police court proceedings. Once twitted about this sartorial foible Newton had protested, 'But in our profession it is so difficult to keep one's hands clean.' Arthur Newton found it more difficult than most.

A tall, heavy-set man of fifty with a pugnacious thrust of jaw, Newton is shown wearing the tell-tale gloves with a morning coat of matching grey in a *Vanity Fair* cartoon by Leslie Ward ('Spy'). Newton's speciality was 'defending young men about town from the consequences of youth and folly', in the words of one critic.[6] In 1895 Newton had figured prominently in the two trials of Oscar Wilde, when he was retained to represent Wilde's co-defendant, Alfred Taylor. Five years earlier Newton had been retained to represent the younger son of the Duke of Beaufort, Lord Arthur Somerset, accused of patronising a male brothel in London's Cleveland Street. As an aftermath of the so-called Cleveland Street Scandal, Newton was gaoled for six weeks for having 'conspired to defeat the ends of justice' (he had attempted to spirit out of England three telegraph boys who were prepared to testify that Lord Arthur had committed acts of gross indecency with them). Luckily for him, the Law Society did not strike his name from its rolls.

Newton's mismanagement of Crippen's defence was on a par with his involvement in the Cleveland Street Scandal. In fact, it was so disgraceful that it was to result in the kid-gloved solicitor being suspended from practice for twelve months in an action brought against him by the Law Society in the King's Bench Division of the High Court of Justice. In concurring with the suspension order, Mr Justice Darling held that, if anything, it erred on the side of leniency. 'Crippen was not defended as he should have been,' Mr Justice Darling observed, adding that Crippen's case 'was conducted very largely for the purpose of making "copy" for the newspapers.' 'Even the greatest criminal is entitled to have his case conducted from first to last with the sole view to his interest,' the High Court Justice concluded.[7]

Newton 'captured' Crippen as a 'professional speculation' in order to help pay off his racing debts, which ran into hundreds of pounds, according to W. E. Henchy, Newton's managing clerk. 'I have known him to borrow from money-lenders at exorbitant interest merely to pay bookmakers,' Henchy declares.[8] This, however, was not the story Newton gave out to the press.

'I was on the eve of starting a short holiday,' Newton told a *Daily Mail* reporter, 'when an old business friend of Dr Crippen came to my office yesterday (August 2nd) and asked me if I would undertake his defence, saying he would do all he could to supply the necessary expenses for him.'[9] The business friend in question was that prince of quacks Eddie Marr, alias 'Professor' Keith-Harvey, alias 'Professor' Elmer Shirley, alias W. S. Hamilton, obesity specialist, who, when last seen was busy scraping Crippen's name off the office door in Craven House where the Aural Remedies Company did business.

It is doubtful, however, whether Marr came to Newton's office in Great Marlborough Street, whose fittings were in green leather, and whose cigar cabinets were stocked with the choicest Havanas. More likely the solicitor sought out Marr in a shake-down operation designed to persuade Crippen's shady friend to cough up money for the latter's defence. The upshot was that Marr agreed to advance £100, and on the strength of this Newton sent the following cablegram to Crippen, then under arrest and held in a Quebec prison: 'Your friends desire me to defend you and will pay all necessary expenses. Will undertake your defence, but you must promise to keep absolute silence and answer no questions and do not resist extradition. Reply confirming. Arthur Newton.'

Crippen, unaware of all of the backstage manoeuvres, was only too eager to avail himself of Newton's services, and cabled accordingly, agreeing to all the latter's stipulations. Commenting on his employer's offer, Newton's managing clerk writes, 'It would have been worth taking on a case of this kind for its publicity value alone. Newton saw his way to get the publicity and the money, too.'[10]

*　　　*　　　*

Looking back it is evident that Crippen's only chance of escaping the gallows—and admittedly it was a slender one—lay in securing the services of the barrister who not only was recognised as the leading advocate in criminal cases of this kind, but who (inestimable advantage) actually believed in Crippen's innocence. He was Edward (later Sir Edward) Marshall Hall, KC. Three years earlier Newton had briefed Marshall Hall in the so-called Camden Town Murder in which a young artist was accused of murdering a prostitute by cutting her throat. Marshall Hall, against almost impossible odds, had secured the acquittal of this young man. The murder had excited much public interest.* It is not surprising therefore that Newton's first call in the process known as 'hawking the brief' should have been at Marshall Hall's chambers in the Temple Gardens.†

Unfortunately for all concerned, Marshall Hall was on holiday abroad. Almost certainly he would have intervened personally to secure the brief, instead of leaving the matter to the discretion of his managing clerk. For Marshall Hall, as has been said, strongly believed in Crippen's innocence. Moreover, the advocate, whom one of his friends described as 'a walking chemist's shop', considered himself an expert on poisons in general, and on hyoscine in particular; and he had devised a defence which he felt sure would result in the charges against Crippen being reduced from murder to manslaughter, a defence which is discussed at length in the next chapter.

In Marshall Hall's absence, negotiations with Newton were conducted by the advocate's managing clerk, A. E. Bowker, and quickly foundered on the question of money. 'We discussed terms,' Bowker writes, 'but when he [Newton] said that he was not prepared to pay any of the fees until the case was over, I became suspicious and insisted on a cheque with the brief. We haggled for a time, for I wanted the case badly,' Bowker adds. 'The defence

---

* It also inspired Walter Sickert to do an extraordinary series of paintings from his imagination picturing the murdered woman in her squalid surroundings.

† In the episode that follows it is as well to bear in mind the division of labour that exists between the two branches of the British legal profession, barristers and solicitors. A barrister has the exclusive right to practice in the superior courts of England and Northern Ireland (in Scotland he is called an advocate). However a client cannot consult a barrister directly, but must do so through a solicitor, who instructs the barrister in a 'brief'. Barristers who are appointed King's Counsel have the letters 'KC' after their names and are said 'to take silk'—they wear gowns made of silk on ceremonial occasions to distinguish themselves from ordinary members of the Bar.

of Crippen offered just the sort of challenge that would spur Marshall Hall to one of his great efforts of advocacy; but I continued to demand a cheque and would not budge.'[11]

In the long run it made little difference, for Crippen, determined upon martyrdom, would never have allowed Marshall Hall to put forward the defence which might have saved him from the gallows, and which incidentally the advocate believed to be the truth. By the time Marshall Hall returned from holidaying on the continent the committal proceedings at the Bow Street Police Court were already over, and, on Crippen's specific instructions, a line of defence had been adopted which the eminent barrister considered to be suicidal. As Marshall Hall expresses the dilemma: 'Can counsel . . . take the responsibility of defending a man, of whose innocence he is convinced, if that man ties him down to a line of defence which that counsel knows to be a plea of "guilty"? . . . I could not have defended Crippen on those lines.'[12]

Refusing to pay the barrister's fees in advance, Newton, a hot-tempered man, 'banged out of the chambers, shouting,' according to Bowker. 'He walked up the Middle Temple Lane . . . furious at his failure to obtain the services of Marshall Hall. Three doors up the lane from Temple Gardens he saw the name of Alfred Tobin, and stopped. Newton knew quite well that Tobin . . . was not within miles of being a leading criminal "silk". Newton's temper, however, had got the better of his judgment, and ten minutes after leaving me he had arranged for Tobin to lead for the defence of Crippen.'[13]

Thus, as a result of Newton's personal pique, did Crippen get saddled with one of the dullest, the most plodding advocates in the business. Alfred (later Sir Alfred) Tobin may have built up a fair practice as a junior on the Northern Circuit, but, as Bowker points out, he could not touch the hem of Marshall Hall's robe when it came to criminal advocacy. He was strictly a bargain basement choice.

* * *

Any defending barrister, however, would have had his work cut out to ensure a fair trial, so great was the hostility that had been built up against Crippen by an unfriendly press. From the beginning the press had been at no pains to conceal its belief that Dr

Crippen was guilty. Thus as far back as July 17th *Reynolds's News-paper*, the London weekly, had described Crippen as a 'degener-ate'. 'One must search for a weakling,' *Reynolds's Newspaper* advised, adding, '*Mens sans in corpore sano* is scarcely a description one would apply to the husband of a woman whose corpse lay mouldering for months under the floor almost over which the widower entertained and made high revel.'

In the exciting sea chase which followed Captain Kendall's wireless message the big dailies vied with one another, their re-porters going off into the realm of pure fantasy to scoop a rival. Thus while the *Montrose* was in mid-Atlantic the *Daily Express's* omniscient correspondent was able to report that Dr Crippen had been arrested disguised as a clergyman and wearing false eyebrows ('Crippen was immediately searched and deprived of a revolver, a number of cartridges, and a pen-knife, while Miss LeNeve burst into tears.')

With Dr Crippen safely behind iron bars, press mendacity rose to new heights. The *Montreal Star* in a story datelined Quebec, Tuesday, August 3rd, reported, 'Crippen has made a full con-fession of the murder of his wife. This is an absolute fact.' The same paper was back the following day with a direct quote from Inspector Dew, 'Crippen will be a dead man in two months.'

Inspector Dew, after the dust of the Crippen case had settled, was to reap a rich harvest from nine separate libel actions which he brought against newspapers for misquoting him to the detriment of his professional reputation.[*] 'There is no longer any doubt that Crippen had made a confession to Inspector Dew,' writes the *Daily Chronicle*'s reporter in Quebec, adding, 'I not only have the very best authority for saying this, but I also have the admission of Inspector Dew.' The *Daily Chronicle* then goes on to quote Dew as saying, 'Yes, Crippen has now told me the complete story of the crime and how her body was disposed of. He also related to me exactly how the murder occurred.' The *Chronicle*'s 'Special Correspondent' then declares 'from a source which I know to be authoritative' that the confession was made Monday, August 1st,

---

[*] Among the newspapers sued for libel by Dew were the *Montreal Star*, the *Daily Chronicle*, the *Evening Standard*, the *Pall Mall Gazette*, and the *Westminster Gazette*, the latter four being London dailies. Most of the actions were settled out of court for undisclosed sums, but Dew was awarded £400 damages plus costs from the *Daily Chronicle*.

in the presence of Dew and three other police officers after the statutory caution had been given. Crippen is then quoted as saying, 'It is true. I did kill my wife . . . I will say nothing until I return to England, and then I shall prove that I am not a murderer. I make this confession in order to free Miss LeNeve from suspicion.'

The story of the alleged confession was picked up by Reuters and widely reprinted throughout the United Kingdom. 'The papers,' Crippen writes to Ethel from Pentonville prison, 'have treated us so shamefully they all owe us a great reparation, which we shall never get. It is impossible to deny that everyone was prejudiced by the newspaper lies.'

*   *   *

As if popular prejudice were not enough, defence counsel had Crippen himself to contend with in its efforts to make a good showing. For Crippen appeared to be bent upon self-destruction.

Most legal experts are agreed that Crippen's only hope of escaping the hangman's noose lay in entering a plea of guilty, making play of such mitigating circumstances as there were, then throwing himself upon the mercy of the court. Marshall Hall's biographer quotes him as saying 'there was only one possible defence for Crippen, and that was to admit everything except the intent to murder.'[14] In so doing Crippen stood a chance of having the charge reduced from murder to manslaughter. As another distinguished jurist, Sir Travers Humphreys, points out, 'In another country he [Crippen] would I feel sure have been given the benefit of "extenuating circumstances" .'[15]

A guilty plea would have involved telling the truth and shaming the devil—that is, dragging into the open the whole sordid story of Crippen's married life with Belle, of her shrewishness, her addiction to alcohol, her infidelities. The risk, of course, was that the strategem might boomerang, and far from incurring their censure of Belle's behaviour, might have awakened the jurors' sympathy for the dead woman whose name was being blackened. Ethel would have to be called as a witness, and the story of Crippen's affair with Ethel—including her pregnancy and miscarriage— would have to be developed through her testimony in open court, and as a consequence, she would be exposed to the deadly cross-fire of the prosecution. She would be lucky if there were even a fig-leaf to clothe her nakedness when she stepped down from the witness box.

Crippen of course would not for a single moment hear of calling Ethel in his defence. 'Tell Ethel not to worry,' were Crippen's instructions to Newton's managing clerk, when the latter came to see him in prison. 'Tell her I will take all the blame. Give her my heart's love.'[16]

The decision to protect Ethel at all costs was not a hasty one. 'I would have been ready any time and at all times to lay down my life and soul to make you happy,' Crippen was to write to Ethel from his death cell. When had this determination formed in his mind? Was it in the early days of their 'courtship', as he called it, when the two lovers sat in a corner at Frascati's listening to the palm court orchestra? Was it that rainy Sunday in the summer of 1903 of which Crippen recalled, 'How happy we were together, with all sunshine in our hearts'?

Whenever it was, Crippen, once he had opted for martyrdom, was not to be cheated of it if he could possibly help it. He would plead not guilty, go into the witness box and lie. He would maintain under oath that Belle Elmore had left the domestic hearth to fulfill her oft-repeated threat of running away with another man. He would just as solemnly affirm that he knew nothing about the remains found in the cellar at No. 39 until told of their discovery by his solicitor. 'Do you really ask the jury to understand,' the Lord Chief Justice would ask somewhat incredulously, 'that . . . without your knowledge or your wife's, at some time during the five years, those remains could have been put there?' Without blinking an eye, Crippen would reply, 'It does not seem probable, but there is a possibility.' The big lies would be bolstered by smaller lies, until in the end Crippen would be tangled up in a skein of lies from which it would be impossible to extricate himself.

Henchy, Newton's managing clerk, recalls Crippen's utter indifference to his fate during the numerous pre-trial consultations he had with the accused. 'He couldn't seem to concentrate on his own case,' Henchy writes. 'He began to ask us about Ethel directly we arrived and he would still be talking about her when we left. Moreover what he did tell us was of little real use to the defence.'[17]

*   *   *

Unfortunately the Crippen trial was robbed of that dignity which usually accompanies justice. From the beginning it was treated more as a spectacle than as a judicial hearing where a man's life was at stake. This was evident in the boisterous, holiday mood of the crowd that queued for gallery seats on the opening day, 'some begging, pleading, wheedling, arguing, lying to gain admission', in the words of the *Daily Mail*, 'others knowing the hopelessness of such endeavours, trying for no more than to catch sight of some of the people prominent in the case . . .'[18] Inside, the confusion was no less marked. The demand for seats in the body of Court No. 1 had been so great that, in true music hall fashion, a two-house-a-day system had been inaugurated; thus in the corridor outside the courtroom there was much shouting of 'Red tickets this way', and 'Blue tickets over there', and one half-expected an usher to announce, 'Ladies and gentlemen, will you kindly take your seats—the curtain rises in two minutes.'

Whether or not it was out of respect for Belle Elmore's memory, the theatrical profession had turned out in force, headed by actor-managers Sir Herbert Beerbohm Tree and Sir John Hare. (At the earlier Bow Street committal proceedings W. S. Gilbert had been assiduous in his attendance. 'Gilbert,' as his biographer Hesketh Pearson points out, 'always attuned to popular emotion, could not keep the subject out of his conversation and remained on tenterhooks until Crippen was convicted.')*

No doubt members of the Music Hall Ladies' Guild too felt 'attuned to popular emotion' as they chatted, exchanged smiles, even waved to one another across the crowded courtroom. Some of the guild ladies—notably Melinda May and Mesdames Martinetti and Smythson—were not in the courtroom, but awaited below in the witness room their turn to give evidence against Crippen. Now that Crippen had been brought to justice, they no

---

* The Crippen case was to inspire Gilbert to write *The Hooligan*, a one-acter about a condemned man awaiting execution in a prison cell. Nat Solly, the man in question, is a far cry from Crippen, however, as is made clear by his Cockney background ('My faver was a high toby cracksman, my muvver was a prig, and did two stretches, my bruvvers and sisters was all prigs . . .').

[153]

longer thirsted for vengeance. They even found kind things to say of the doctor personally, though their cumulative evidence against him was damning. Thus Clara Martinetti declared, 'He always appeared kind-hearted and exceedingly courteous towards his wife.' Their only concern now was to see justice done.

Not to see justice done, but to savour the full drama of it—this was the reason given by one pretty ingenue for being present in court. 'This,' she confided to the man sitting next to her, 'is our real dramatic school.'* By 'this' the actress with a sweep of her hand indicated not only the prisoner in the dock, the row of be-wigged counsel who sat facing one another with their law books piled beside them, but the Lord Chief Justice, Lord Alverstone, whose full-bottomed wig and scarlet and ermine robe she might have supposed had been rented from a costumier in Shaftesbury Avenue.†

The high point in theatricality was reached when actress Phyllis Dare, who not long previously had been toasted as 'The Belle of Mayfair', was invited to share the Bench with his lordship, and accordingly took a seat to the left of the Lord Chief Justice and directly beneath the Sword of Justice whose gold-inlaid scabbard shimmered on the wall high above her head. This was too much for *The Times*. 'A criminal court is not a showroom,' *The Times* sternly reminded its readers; 'nor is such a trial of the nature of a matinee; the Old Bailey is not a place to which fashionable ladies may fitly go in search of the latest sensation, where actors may hope to pick up suggestions as to a striking gesture or a novel expression, or where descriptive writers may look for good copy.'[20]

While actors and extras alike strutted and postured on the im-provised stage of the courtroom, Hawley Crippen, in the prisoner's dock and screened from the public by a glass partition, contrived to remain aloof. 'To all outward appearance he might have been a client slightly perturbed at the prospect of a summons for riding

* The incident is reported in a letter to *The Times*, October 28, 1910.
† In point of fact the actress would not have been far wrong. Lord Alverstone *was* a performer of sorts. His rich baritone had graced the choir of St Mary Abbot's, Kensington for forty years, and he was a shining light of the Old Madrigal Society. 'I cannot speak too highly of the pleasure which I derived from the study of part music,' his lordship writes in his memoirs, adding, 'There is no more refining and interesting pursuit.'[19]

a bicycle without a light,' in the words of Newton's managing clerk.[21]

*　　*　　*

The trial quickly resolved itself into a forensic duel, with one set of medico-legal experts pitted against another. At issue was a piece of skin, eight inches long, horseshoe-shaped, and fringed by short, dark hairs. The Crown experts who examined the skin found that it had all the characteristics of a scar, namely no hair follicles or sebaceous glands, but only fibrous tissue. The fringe consisted of pubic hairs, indicating that the skin had come from a woman's abdomen, they would claim. The scar, the Crown would maintain, corresponded to that left on Belle's body after one of her ovaries had been removed. The defence, through the medical witnesses it would call, would contend just as vehemently that the so-called scar was no scar at all, but merely a mark made by a folding of the skin.

The horseshoe of skin was lifted from its formalin with pincers by pathologist Dr Augustus J. Pepper, a short, black-haired man with a heavy moustache, and gold pince-nez. It was then placed in a soup-plate, and passed along the jury-box, causing a *Daily Mail* reporter to have stomach twinges. None was more interested than Crippen who, as the dish was carried by an usher to the defence counsel's table, rose to his feet and leaned over the rail to look at its contents with the intelligent curiosity of a student of anatomy. Indeed, the Lord Chief Justice might almost have been rebuking a prankish member of such an anatomy class when he suddenly snapped at Mr Tobin, 'You have taken an inky pen.' In order to point to some detail of the skin fragment, Tobin in fact had snatched up the nib with which he had lately been making notes.

The Crippen case marked the public debut of Bernard (later Sir Bernard) Spilsbury, then 33, who was to become the most famous pathologist of his day. 'To the man in the street he [Spilsbury] stood for pathology as Hobbs stood for cricket or Dempsey for boxing or Capablanca for chess,' writes Edgar Lustgarten, adding, 'His pronouncements were invested with the force of dogma, and it was blasphemy to hint that he might conceivably be wrong.'[22]

But in October, 1910, when he went into the witness-box the

plump, pink-cheeked Spilsbury was unknown except to a restricted circle at St Mary's Hospital, Paddington, where he had done his work in pathology. In order to nail down the Crown's case for the piece of skin being scar tissue, Spilsbury invited the jurors to adjourn to an adjacent courtroom and there to peer through microscopes at slides he had prepared from the supposed scar. It was a theatrical *tour de force* which struck Coroner S. Ingleby Oddie as being 'as futile as it was unusual'.[23] But it captured the imagination of reporters covering the trial. In the next quarter of a century Spilsbury would give evidence at nearly every important murder trial held in the south of England, including the celebrated 'Brides in the Bath' case, in addition to conducting 25,000 post-mortems.

*   *   *

How Arthur Newton tricked two eminent pathologists into giving evidence for the defence forms one of the sorrier episodes of the trial. Newton was acquainted with Dr Gilbert Turnbull, director of the Pathological Institute of the London Hospital. Newton was also aware of a certain animosity which the London Hospital pathologist felt towards his more illustrious colleagues at St Mary's, Paddington. He was to use this knowledge with a skill born of low cunning. At a bridge party at which both Dr Turnbull and he were guests Newton suggested to the former that he might like to examine the disputed piece of skin 'as a matter of interest'. 'Having done this, rather perfunctorily, Turnbull was so foolish as to sign a report to the effect that the skin came from the thigh, not the abdomen, and that the supposed scar was a fold,' as Spilsbury's biographers point out.[24] Turnbull also got the concurrence of his friend and colleague, Dr Reginald Wall. The understanding had been that neither man would be called as a witness, but the unsuspecting scientists little reckoned with the craftiness of the man with whom they were dealing.

Dr Turnbull in particular, was both stunned and angry when he was subpoenaed as a defence witness, for after a further examination of the skin and a study of the Pepper and Spilsbury depositions he had begun to entertain doubts about his first opinion. 'Horrified to learn that he had been tricked into giving evidence at the trial, he [Turnbull] telephoned Spilsbury for advice. Spilsbury recommended him to withdraw the report. Finally, however, Turnbull determined to stand by it.'[25] Foolhardily Doctors Turnbull and Wall submitted to the Crown's devastating cross-examination, to emerge with their professional reputations badly dented. 'To me at least it was a painful sight to see two men of undoubted probity and of considerable eminence in their profession one after the other having to admit that they had signed a statement . . . which they both had to admit was quite incorrect,' writes Travers Humphreys, one of the Crown counsel at the trial.[26]

For one other person it was a painful business. Crippen was to write to Ethel later, 'Today at the appeal I realised more and more that the medical evidence for my defence was so mismanaged that it told against me rather than for me. This I saw at the Old Bailey in the judge's summing up and again today in the summing up of the Appeal. I am powerless now, and can do nothing more, but bow to the inevitable,' he added.[27]

*　　　*　　　*

Finally there remained only Crippen himself facing the Crown prosecution in the person of Scottish-born Richard (later Sir Richard) Muir. So formidable was Muir's reputation that Crippen is said to have muttered, upon learning that Muir was to lead for the Crown, 'I wish it had been anybody else . . . I fear the worst.'[28] The son of a Clydeside shipbroker, Muir had come to London originally with the intention of going on the stage, but had been talked out of it by an older brother, who persuaded him that the law was more suitable to his talents. Traces of the would-be matinee idol were discernible in the profile, with its long, straight nose and prematurely silvered hair, which Muir now turned to the jurymen as he rested his arm on the jury box.

Faced with a defendant such as Crippen, who appeared determined to commit *felo-de-se* in the witness-box, Muir's present task was not such a difficult one, as is evident from Crippen's answers to the first six questions put to him in cross-examination.

MUIR (to Crippen) — In the early morning of the 1st February you were left alone in your house with your wife? — Yes.

She was alive? — Yes.

And well? — She was.

Do you know of any person in the world who has seen her alive since? — I do not.

Do you know of any person in the world who can prove any fact showing that she ever left that house alive? — Absolutely not; I have told Mr Dew exactly all the facts.

And so it went on hour after hour, this relentless rebuttal, with Crippen being led over the minefield of his own lies, which were exploded, one by one, under his unwary feet. For Muir was a master of over-kill, as his notes on the Crippen case make evident.* 'Muir's playing cards,' they were called, these notes written in four or five different coloured pencils on small, numbered cards. Muir pored over his 'playing cards' night after night until the case against Crippen was foolproof, and until 'everybody connected with the prosecution of Crippen heartily cursed his [Muir's] name,' according to his biographer.[29]

Occasionally the Lord Chief Justice intervened to clarify a point. For example, Crippen testified that on Friday, July 8th, immediately after he had been questioned by Inspector Dew he contemplated fleeing London with Ethel LeNeve. His line of thinking he explained as follows: 'If there is all this suspicion, and I am likely to have to stay in gaol for months and months and months, perhaps until this woman is found, I had better be out of it.' (Note how he refers to his wife as 'this woman'.)

LORD CHIEF JUSTICE — Mr Crippen, do you really mean that you thought you would have to lie in gaol for months and months? Do you say that? — Quite so, yes.

MUIR — Upon what charge? — Suspicion.

Suspicion of what? — Suspicion of — Inspector Dew said, 'This woman has disappeared, she must be found.'

Suspicion of what? — Suspicion of being concerned in her disappearance.

What crime did you understand you might be kept in gaol upon suspicion of? — I do not understand the law enough to say.

---

* The notes are reproduced in their entirety in Sidney T. Felstead's biography of Muir.

From what I have read it seems to me I have heard of people being arrested on suspicion of being concerned in the disappearance of other people.

The disappearance of other people? — Well, I am doing the best I can to explain it to you. I cannot put it for you in a legal phrase.

LORD CHIEF JUSTICE — Nobody wants you to put it in a legal phrase. The simple question is, What was the charge that you thought might be brought against you after you had seen Inspector Dew? — I could not define the charge, except that if I could not find the woman I was very likely to be held until she was found. That was my idea.

MUIR — Because of what? — I cannot say why. I can only say that no other idea than that entered my head. If I could not produce the woman —

Yes, what would be the inference? — Mr Dew told me that I should be in serious trouble. Well, I could not make out what the inference would be.

And that was why you contemplated on the afternoon of 8th July flying from the country? — Quite so; that, and the idea that I had said that Miss LeNeve was living with me, and she had told her people she was married to me, and it would put her in a terrible position. The only thing I could think of was to take her away out of the country where she would not have this scandal thrown upon her.

The cross-examination lasted for three hours, at the end of which Crippen, not visibly shaken, stepped down from the witness-box. To complete the illusion of the trial as a theatrical spectacle, the comments on Crippen's demeanour as a witness read like the notices of a stage performance. 'Marvellous was the calm which he maintained throughout the trial . . . the demeanour of innocence so counterfeited as to deceive any one who forgot the evidence . . .' (*The Times*). 'He had given a marvellous exhibition of nerve power under the strain of a terrible ordeal' (the *Daily Mail*). 'He stood up to it . . . with wonderful composure and calmness' (S. Ingleby Oddie). 'The most amazing feature of the trial was the absolute coolness and imperturbability of Crippen in the long and terrible cross-examination' (Filson Young).

*　　*　　*

The jury retired shortly after the lunch recess on Saturday, October 22nd, returning to the courtroom twenty-seven minutes later. A hush fell over the spectators as the jurors filed into the jury box. Then the Clerk of the Arraigns asked, 'Gentlemen, have you agreed upon your verdict?' To which the jury foreman replied, 'We have.' At this point the mask of tragedy, insecurely held throughout the trial, slipped once again when it was discovered that the jury was about to discharge its office in the absence of the accused. 'One moment,' the Lord Chief Justice cried, holding up a hand to halt the proceedings. 'The prisoner is not in the courtroom.' At this signal Crippen suddenly appeared into view from up the stairs of the cell beneath the dock. It was as though he had been sprung through a trap-door. Crippen walked briskly towards the rail where he stood, wedged between two warders, facing the judge.

'Do you find the prisoner guilty or not guilty of wilful murder?' the clerk intoned.

'We find the prisoner guilty of wilful murder.'

A *Daily Mail* reporter, whose eyes, like those of the other spectators, were fixed upon Crippen, describes the latter's reaction. 'The little man's intertwined fingers tightened in the effort to preserve his self-command,' the reporter observed. 'A pallor spread over his forehead and cheeks. The bald patch at the back of his little, flat head became a dull white . . . The face showed no trace of emotion.' The question whether the prisoner had anything to say before sentence was passed had to be repeated before Crippen replied in a firm voice, 'I still protest my innocence.'

The judge's marshal then placed the black cap on his lordship's wig; the usher with a loud 'Oyez, oyez, oyez' commanded silence; and the Lord Chief Justice, declining to dwell upon the 'ghastly and wicked nature of the crime', ordered Hawley Harvey Crippen to be 'taken from hence to a lawful prison, and from thence to a place of execution, and that you be there hanged by the neck until you are dead'. Then it was all over. The court rose, his lordship left the Bench, and the condemned man disappeared as suddenly as he had appeared.

[12]

The reference in the opening chapter to the 'Crippen Murder Mystery', may have occasioned some surprise, for it will be argued that Crippen was convicted 'upon evidence which could leave no doubt in the mind of any reasonable man', in the words of Lord Alverstone, the Lord Chief Justice. Was there ever a more open-and-shut case? Quite so, and yet certain doubts creep in, certain questions which remain to be answered.

There is the question of motive, for example. Hawley Crippen was condemned to death without the Crown having made any but the most feeble attempt to supply a motive for the murder of his wife. The Crown of course was under no necessity to tell why Crippen committed murder, it being enough to identify the cellar remains as those of Belle Elmore, and to weave a circumstantial case around Crippen which would lay those remains at his door. This the prosecution did through the forensic evidence which it called. In the voluminous notes which he made for use in court Richard Muir dismisses the question of motive in two sentences, writing, 'Belle Elmore stood between him [Crippen] and the closer relations he wished to establish with Ethel LeNeve. Belle Elmore's money (and other property convertible into money) would enable him to keep Ethel LeNeve'.[1]

In his final address to the jury Muir was scarcely more expansive, relying upon bluster to bridge this gap in the prosecution's case. 'No motive?' Muir cried with mock astonishment. He then proceeded to supply two possibles. 'Love,' he said, 'if they dignified it by that name; lust, if they gave it its true appellation . . . Money to gratify that lust—immediately on 2nd February the wife's jewels were pawned.' 'And it is suggested that there is no motive,' he finished scornfully.

But Crippen and Ethel had been lovers by their own admission for at least three years prior to the murder. If Crippen had wanted to indulge his 'guilty passion' (the words are those of the prosecution) for Ethel without let or hindrance from his wife why had he waited so long to eliminate said interference? 'When a man is in love with a woman who is not his wife,' writes Filson Young, 'the time at which he is most likely to desert the wife for the mistress is at the beginning of the new relationship . . . And if this is true of mere desertion, how much more it is of murder . . .'[2] The truth is that Belle knew all about the affair from the beginning but was in no position to object to it, being occupied with her own extra-marital love life.

As for the motive of financial gain, which Muir appears to have offered as make-weight, this is too ridiculous for extended consideration. Muir could not have been serious in asking the jury to believe that Crippen, who at one time had been earning £2,500 a year, and who at the time of the murder had a healthy balance in a savings account, would poison Belle for the paltry £195 which he got from pawning her jewellery. Belle's penchant for collecting china dogs and pinning pink velvet bows on paintings would have been more convincing as a motive for murdering her than pawning her jewels.*

Chief Inspector Dew, who had ample opportunity for studying Crippen, comes closer to the mark when he writes, 'I believe he harboured an intense hatred for his wife'. That hatred had lain dormant for years. It was activated not when Belle attacked Crippen—he could bear any amount of ridicule himself, even as a cuckolded spouse. No, the critical temperature was reached when Belle directed her attacks upon Ethel, causing the latter acute mental distress, threatening Ethel's future happiness and well-being. It was then that Crippen decided to act.

*　　　*　　　*

What did Belle have for dinner on that Monday night, January 31st, when she entertained the Martinettis? Did she cook the dinner herself? What did they talk about at table, and afterwards when they went up to the parlour to begin the whist game? What was Crippen's attitude towards his wife during the evening? Did the Crippens give the appearance of being a loving couple? What

---

* Arthur Binstead, editor of the *Sporting Times*, or the 'Pink'un', as it was better known, was of the opinion that had Belle's penchant for tie-ing velvet bows on paintings been better known a verdict of 'Justifiable Homicide' would have been returned against her husband.

did the party have to drink? How much did they drink? This is the minutiae that a novelist requires in order to build up a picture of events, and it was just this minutiae that was not forthcoming at Crippen's trial (for reasons not explained Paul Martinetti was not even called as a witness at the Old Bailey although he had testified at the inquest).

Above all, what happened after the door closed on the Martinettis at approximately 1.30 am, Tuesday, February 1st, and the Crippens found themselves alone? The Crown made no attempt to reconstruct events leading up to the murder, and for good reason —the only witness to these events other than Crippen was dead. That Crippen was not in a good mood when he shut the door is likely; he had been out in the cold night and had had great difficulty in finding a carriage for the Martinettis in the Camden Road.

Belle, too, was in a vile mood, if Crippen is to be believed, and for the most trivial of reasons. During the evening Paul Martinetti had wanted to use the lavatory. 'As I thought he knew the house perfectly well, having been there many times during eighteen months,' Crippen testified, ' I thought it was quite all right that he should go up himself. When he came down he seemed to have caught a chill . . . Immediately after they had left my wife got into a very great rage with me, and blamed me for not having gone upstairs.' This most flimsy of pretexts had then developed into the bitterest of quarrels, with Belle threatening to leave him, according to Crippen's statement to Inspector Dew. 'She abused me, and said, "This is the finish of it. I won't stand it any longer. I shall leave you to-morrow, and you will never hear of me again." ' 'She had said this so often that I did not take much notice of it,' Crippen added. When he returned home from work between five and six on Tuesday, February 1st, he had found that Belle had gone, gone to join her lover in Chicago, he supposed. If nothing else, Crippen's version of events shows how totally devoid of imagination he was.

Suppose for a moment that Crippen, after standing in the doorway with his arm round his wife's waist, shut the door after the Martinettis drove off, and, turning to his wife, said quite civilly, 'Belle, how about a night-cap? Let me fix you a brandy and soda?' This more closely approximates the reconstruction of events as Sir Edward Marshall Hall saw them. Sir Edward used to dine out on the ingenious theory he had developed to account for the sudden death of Mrs Crippen. It was a theory which he would have used in court had he been briefed to defend Crippen, and would have used successfully, he claimed. He was convinced that he could have got the charge reduced to manslaughter.

The anti-aphrodisiac theory, to give Marshall Hall's defence a handy label, is based upon the following assumptions: That Crippen continued to cohabit with Belle though with growing distaste up to the time of her death. That Belle was a nymphomaniac, and that her amative demands upon Crippen were such as to undermine his health. That Crippen 'devoted as he was to his mistress, found himself the victim of a double demand to which the poor little man's frail physique and advancing years rendered him unequal', in the words of Filson Young. That Crippen, caught in this double bind, had taken to administering hyoscine bromide as a sexual depressant to Belle unbeknown to her and most likely in her drinks, increasing the dosage as time went on. That Crippen's knowledge of this drug, which Marshall Hall's biographer describes as 'new and rare', was imperfect to say the least, with the result that on the night of January 31st–February 1st he had given his wife an overdose. 'When, instead of falling quietly asleep, Mrs Crippen, to the horror and surprise of her husband, incontinently died,' writes Filson Young, 'he was so frightened . . . that he cut up, burned, and otherwise disposed of the remains.' What it meant was that Crippen killed his wife by accident. 'If when she died he had run out and told a policeman of his dreadful mistake, he would have been an object of sympathy rather than of legal vengeance,' Young concludes.[3]

Edward Marjoribanks, who spent an 'enthralling' afternoon listening to Marshall Hall expound this theory, adds an important gloss to it. According to Marjoribanks, Marshall Hall believed that Ethel may have been hiding in the house when Crippen administered the fatal dose, or that Crippen had fixed a rendezvous with her for later that night, either at the house or elsewhere, and was impatient to keep it. (The prospect of this rendezvous accounted for Crippen's cheerfulness at the dinner-party, according to the advocate.) Marshall Hall was further of the opinion that Crippen and his mistress met often and made love under the same roof with Belle while the latter was drugged and unconscious ('She would be there, and she would not be there,' is the way Marshall Hall expressed it.)[4]

Marshall Hall had acquired his knowledge of hyoscine from his father, who was a doctor; and he himself had administered the drug once to an importunate client who had insisted upon seeing him at his home instead of going through the usual channels of consulting a solicitor.* As the man refused to take no for an answer, Marshall Hall resorted to the desperate expedient of slipping him a dose of hyoscine in his coffee cup, thinking that the effect would wear off in about an hour. At the end of two hours the man was still sleeping. 'A very worried Marshall Hall went to bed, leaving the man asleep and wondering whether he would have shortly to defend himself on a murder charge.' However, the man rallied the following morning, and Marshall Hall packed him off to a solicitor none the worse for the experience.

Certain fundamental objections to the anti-aphrodisiac theory immediately spring to mind. To postulate that Crippen continued to cohabit with Belle up to the time of her death is manifestly absurd. The desire for separate bedrooms and for separate beds was, as has already been shown, the principal reason why the Crippens moved to No. 39 Hilldrop Crescent in September, 1905. Besides, it is nonsense to represent Crippen as the victim of the inordinate demands of wife and mistress. 'These are two fires between which a man in his situation cannot really be forced to remain,' as Filson Young points out. 'Although Courts of law continue to make orders for the restitution of conjugal rights, no method of enforcing them has so far been discovered . . .'5 Marshall Hall's gambit also ignores the fact that since December 6, 1906 at least, when Crippen and Ethel plighted their troth in a secret 'wedding' of their own devising, Crippen no longer recognised Belle as his wife. She was the usurper, while Ethel was his real spouse, and sacredly so, thanks to the secret 'marriage'.

All the same it is a pity that Marshall Hall was never given the opportunity of developing his theory in court. Who knows, he might have swayed the jury, and succeeded in getting the charge reduced if not an outright acquittal. Lord Birkenhead, one of his warmest admirers, writes of Marshall Hall, 'The élan with which he swept down upon a doubtful jury, brushing aside their preju-

---

* Marshall Hall told the anecdote to a group of barristers on their way back to London from the Kent Assizes, and it is repeated in Robert Jackson's biography of Sir Bentley Purchase, the coroner.

dices, and persuading them against their will . . . into accepting his own sanguine view of his client's innocence, won many a day which a more timorous, if not less skilful, advocate must have given up for lost'.[6]

As to why Crippen did not avail himself of this line of defence, which was of course open to his counsel Alfred Tobin to develop as well, Marshall Hall himself has some interesting comments. Crippen turned it down because 'he considered that it would have made Miss LeNeve his accomplice,' Marshall Hall told his biographer. 'If she was in the house with him at the time that Mrs Crippen lay dying or dead from a drug administered to her by Crippen, it would have been very difficult for her to escape from the charge of complicity with him . . . if the defence were to go wrong and he were convicted of murder, what might not happen to her at her trial?' 'Crippen,' the advocate concluded, 'loved Miss LeNeve so tenderly and wholeheartedly that he wished her to escape *all* the legal consequences of his association with her . . . to ensure her complete scathelessness he was willing to die for her.'[7]

*   *   *

A more plausible reconstruction of the murder is put forward by S. Ingleby Oddie, for many years coroner for Central London. Oddie held that Crippen planned the murder to look as though Belle had died a natural death. Weight attaches to Oddie's views owing to the fact that he was both a qualified doctor and a barrister, and thus brought to the study of the murder the insights of those two disciplines. More important still, Oddie as Treasury counsel assisted the Crown in the prosecution of Crippen at the Old Bailey, and the examination of such key witnesses as Dr W. H. Willcox, the Home Office analyst who tested the cellar remains for hyoscine, was entrusted to him. As the chief prosecutor's assistant Oddie was in possession of facts which did not come out in court. As such his witness is precious to an understanding of the case.

'I believe he [Crippen] intended to poison her with hyoscine,' Oddie writes, 'and to say that she had often had attacks of heart failure before, owing to her weak heart, and particularly after heavy meals, and that she had had such an attack on the night of the 31st January, which had unfortunately proved fatal.'[8] Fatty degeneration of the heart would almost certainly have been found in a person of Belle's age, weight and habits, Oddie argues. His theory of course is certainly consonant with Crippen's careful preparation of the ground for murder, his insistence that the Martinettis came to dinner, even though Paul Martinetti had been to the doctor that very afternoon, and obviously was in no position to enjoy a game of whist. (At this point the novelist once more interrupts to ask, What did Belle give the Martinettis for dinner? Did Belle herself eat heartily? Did Crippen urge her to have another helping of plum duff, treacle pudding or whatever the sweet was?)

One bit of supporting evidence appears to have escaped Oddie's notice (curiously the Crown made no use of it either at the Old Bailey trial). At the inquest Melinda May testified that around Christmas time Belle had been so ill that she thought she was dying, or so Belle had confided to her. Belle told the guild secretary that she awoke one night with a sort of strangling sensation in her throat. She had immediately aroused Crippen, telling him, 'Get up and fetch a priest, I am going to die.'[9] Inasmuch as the incident occurred around Christmas time the probability is that the Crippens had been to a party that night, and that Belle had eaten and drunk too well — that is, always supposing that Crippen did not put something in her food or drink to make her ill. When she became ill more than likely Crippen gave her a bismuth preparation to ease her heartburn or indigestion (Belle did not tell Melinda May whether her husband had given her any medicine on this occasion). But the incident, again assuming that it had not been deliberately instigated by him, would certainly have registered on Crippen's mind.

If Crippen were planning to poison Belle and to make it appear that she had died of a heart attack, what would be more natural than that he should speak of this incident to Belle's friends, in particular to Dr John Burroughs, who was the honorary physician to the Music Hall Ladies' Guild? In talking of the incident Crippen might be expected to dilate upon it to make it appear that Belle had been dangerously ill.

Returning to the night of January 31st, after Belle had swallowed the hyoscine disguised in a brandy toddy or some such nightcap and her respiration had ceased, it was Crippen's intention to send for a doctor in the early hours of morning, according to Oddie. Dr Burroughs, already apprised of Belle's previous attack, would in all likelihood ask no questions, but certify her death as having been due to natural causes. In so certifying, Burroughs would be relying upon the word of a medical colleague, for he looked upon Crippen as such.

With the groundwork so carefully laid, what went wrong? Where did Crippen blunder? One can only conclude that Crippen's fatal error lay in an imperfect understanding of the nature of hydro-bromide of hyoscine.

Pace Marshall Hall, hyoscine was not all that 'new and rare' in 1910. 'I have seen it used extensively in asylums to calm violent or troublesome maniacs,' Toxicologist A. W. Blyth had written as early as 1884.[10] When Crippen, as a student of homoeopathy, had come to England the previous year he had had the opportunity to observe the use of hyoscine as a tranquillizer on patients at the Royal Bethlehem Hospital for the Insane. Here its calming effect was almost immediate. Within fifteen minutes of the patient being dosed with hyoscine 'the face flushes, and pupils dilate', according to Dr Blyth; '. . . all muscular motion is enfeebled, and the patient remains quiet for many hours, the effects of a single dose not un-commonly lasting two days'.[11] As a homoeopath making use of such poisons as aconite, belladonna, rhus toxica, and gelsemium in minute dosages, Crippen had experimented with hyoscine in the preparation of a nerve tonic, he testified in the witness-box, using the drug in the proportion of 5/480ths of a grain to a drop of water.

But in medicine as in other branches of learning a little know-ledge may prove to be dangerous. For hyoscine is a highly un-stable poison. When administered in large dosages the opposite of sedation takes place, according to chemists Louis Goodman and Alfred Gilman, the authors of *The Pharmacological Basis of Therapeutics*, a standard work: 'The mouth becomes dry and burns . . . The patient is restless, excited and confused and exhibits weakness, giddiness and muscular inco-ordination. Gait and speech are disturbed. Nausea and vomiting are sometimes noted . . . Memory is disturbed, orientation faulty, hallucinations (especially visual) common . . . The syndrome described persists for many hours and may completely disappear only after several days have passed.[12] As little as one quarter of a grain can prove fatal, death resulting from the gradual paralysis of the respiratory centre after a period of coma. Thus death by an overdose of hyoscine is a long drawn-out process accompanied by dramatic changes.

Dr W. H. Willcox, senior scientific analyst to the Home Office, testified at the Old Bailey that he had found two-fifths of a grain of hydrobromide of hyoscine in the organs submitted to him, which would correspond to more than half a grain in the whole body—enough to produce the wild delirium just described. S. Ingleby Oddie is of the opinion that after the Martinettis left Crippen administered the hyoscine in a nightcap which he prepared for Belle. 'Then shortly afterwards Mrs Crippen became hysterical under the influence of the hyoscine, and started running amuck, shouting and shrieking the house down ... I believe Crippen shot his wife in the head with the revolver ... to stifle her cries which were also likely to arouse the whole neighbourhood.'[13]

Inspector Dew, it will be recalled, had found a six-chambered revolver and a box containing forty-five ball cartridges when he searched the bedrooms at No. 39 Hilldrop Crescent. The revolver might have been explained as a burglary precaution, given the amount of jewellery which Belle kept lying about. Whatever the reason, the Crown attached so little importance to the weapon that it was not even introduced as an exhibit for the prosecution, nor was any ballistic evidence forthcoming as to when it last had been fired.

In conclusion, Oddie gives two reasons for holding with his reconstruction of Belle's murder. 'In the first place,' he writes, 'shrieks were heard in the house on that fatal night, and in the second a loud noise like a pistol-shot or a door banging was heard by one of the neighbours.' Oddie is referring to Mrs Louisa May Glackner, who kept an oil and paint store in Brecknock Road, and whose garden overlooked the Crippen's backyard. Mrs Glackner was never called as a witness, either at the inquest, the Bow Street Police Court hearing, or at the Old Bailey; nevertheless she talked freely to reporters about the screams in the night which she had heard at about the time of the murder. 'I was awakened in the night,' Mrs Glackner told an *Evening News* reporter, 'by a woman's piercing scream from the houses opposite to my bedroom window ... The terrible shriek was repeated and I got out of bed and threw up my window to see what was the matter.' 'The screams,' she added, 'certainly came from the direction of Crippen's house, and they seemed to come from some person in the greatest extremity. My son also heard them, and mentioned the fact to me the next morning.'[14] (This was confirmed by Mrs Glackner's son.) In telling her story to the *Daily Mail* the storekeeper added the information that she also heard the imploring words, 'Oh don't! Oh, don't!' coming from No. 39.[15] In her press interviews the shopkeeper made no mention of having heard a pistol-shot on the night in question, but she did volunteer the information to a *New York American* reporter that Crippen used to practice with his revolver by firing at targets in the back garden; that is, up to the time of the scream — after that she never saw him fire the weapon again.

It may be argued that Mrs Glackner was an unreliable witness, possibly a gossipy old woman who was confused about dates, and that this was the reason the Crown did not call her. In which case, why did S. Ingleby Oddie, who was associated with the Crown in prosecuting Crippen, attach so much importance to her statements? In the absence of such vital parts of the body as the head, it was impossible to establish with absolute certainty the exact cause of Belle's death, though hyoscine poisoning was strongly indicated. In his charge to the jury the Lord Chief Justice acknowledged that Belle might have died of a gunshot wound. 'It is possible, of course, that the woman may have been stabbed, or shot, or something else,' his lordship declared, adding, 'but the remarkable thing is that there is no wound on the part of the body that is there . . .'

*   *   *

Assuming that Crippen had shot Belle in the head to stifle her screams, he was now faced with the herculean task of getting rid of her body so as to leave no trace of the crime. It was a task he had certainly never bargained for in planning Belle's death to look as though it were from natural causes.

The finding of the remains in the cellar has led the unthinking to assume that murder took place in the kitchen adjacent to the cellar, the kitchen being transformed into an operating theatre for the grand guignolesque dissection which followed. If the killing had occurred in another part of the house — in the upstairs rooms, for example — how could Crippen, who was neither robust nor in the pink of youth, have dragged Belle's body, or those portions of it which were found buried, down the stairs to the coal cellar? it is argued.

This reasoning overlooks one important piece of evidence: the Hinde curler with the strand of hair attached which was found buried with the remains. Does not this suggest that Belle was murdered in her bedroom, where a short time before she had been seated at her dressing-table doing up her hair? The total absence of bloodstains—and one may be sure that forensic experts had gone over every inch of the house with a magnifying glass looking for the same—suggests that the actual dismemberment took place in the bathroom adjoining Belle's bedroom, and more specifically in the enamel bath, where the blood could have drained away. (The adult human body contains about five quarts of blood, which constitutes about 1/13th of the body's total weight; hence, Belle's body would have been considerably lightened by the loss of blood.)

That Crippen was possessed of a certain amount of surgical skill may readily be conceded, though he himself was at pains to deny it when examined by his own counsel.

TOBIN—Have you ever gone through a course of surgery?—Not a practical, but a theoretical course.
Have you ever performed a post-mortem examination?—Never.

Alfred Hitchcock once remarked that 'in all cases involving mutilation . . . the biggest problem for the police is to locate the head'[16]—understandably so, since the head is the surest means of identifying the murder victim.* Hitchcock had in mind the case of Patrick Herbert Mahon, a married man who in April, 1924, murdered his pregnant mistress Emily Kaye in a cottage on that

---

* To get rid of the head of Stanley Setty, a car dealer whom he stabbed to death after a quarrel in October, 1949, ex-R.A.F. pilot Donald Hume hired a plane and dumped the head together with the dismembered legs in the English Channel, from which they were never recovered. Hume forgot that his victim had a criminal record. When the victim's torso with the arms intact was washed ashore in the Essex marshes some weeks later it was readily identified by the fingerprints as that of Setty.

lonely stretch of seafront near Eastbourne known as the Crumbles. Mahon then dismembered Emily's body, and burnt it piece by piece in an effort to obliterate all traces of the crime. In Brixton prison while awaiting trial he told a fellow inmate how he had burnt the head on a stove in the middle of a thunder-storm. 'The intense heat caused the eyes to open, and appalled, Mahon had rushed from the house.'[17] He later returned, however, to finish the job.

In Belle Elmore's case likewise, the head and limbs were never recovered. Did Crippen, like Mahon, burn them in the kitchen grate, afterwards pulverising the bones before dumping them with the clinkers into the dustbin? Officialdom appears to have rejected this hypothesis. Concerning the disposal of Belle's head, Sir Melville Macnaghten writes:

'About a week after the murder, Dr Crippen went over to Dieppe by the night boat. Did he drop a dirty clothes bag (or something of the sort) over the side of the vessel?'[18]

The answer is: not likely. A check of Crippen's movements shows that it was not a week, but more nearly two months after the murder that he travelled to Dieppe with Ethel.

A much more plausible suggestion is that Crippen wrapped up the head, weighted it with stones, and dropped it from one of the bridges over the Regent's Canal, which was half a mile from Hilldrop Crescent. An even more convenient repository was the reservoir which in 1910 stood where Camelot House now stands in the Holloway area bounded by Camden Park Road, Cliff Villas and Cliff Road. This was only a few minutes' walk from Hilldrop Crescent. Is it not possible that Crippen disposed of the limbs as well as the head in the reservoir, making several trips at night with his grisly parcels? I have been unable to find any record of the police dragging this reservoir in an effort to recover the missing parts, although this would seem to have been an elementary part of the police investigation. The question is, Why did not Crippen make a thorough job of disposing of the remains? Why did he bury Belle's torso, wrapped in the pyjama jacket, beneath the cellar floor, and in a shallow grave at that? Did he sicken, tire of his labours? If one knew the answers to this riddle one might have a better understanding of Crippen's complex personality, and there would be no Crippen Murder Mystery.

On a recent visit to Scotland Yard's famous Black Museum I

had opportunity to examine the exhibits which the Crown used to send Crippen to the gallows. Crippen occupies a place of honour to the right of the door as one enters, and not far from where Frederick Seddon, the callous insurance agent who murdered his female lodger for her gold, is memorialised (some of the fly-papers he rendered of their arsenic in order to poison the lodger are on display). There in a glass case they all are: the pyjama top with its label 'Jones Brothers, Shirtmakers, Holloway' in which Belle's remains were wrapped; the spade which Crippen allegedly used to dig the cellar grave for those remains; a photograph of the cellar itself showing the open grave with the remains, a compact, glutinous mass, *in situ*, surrounded by buckets used to remove the earth, and a basin with a candle stuck in the centre of it.

The exhibit which arrests the attention is the metal Hinde hair curler containing a tuft of Belle's peroxide blonde hair which was likewise found with the remains. Today the hair is so badly discoloured that it is no longer possible to distinguish where the natural dark brown colour left off and the peroxide began ('The hair is the last thing to decompose', the rather lugubrious museum keeper remarks.)

This artefact made the tragedy startlingly vivid to myriads of housewives, I was told by one of them, a woman now in her eighties, who recalls Crippen's trial and conviction. Thus, while husbands pored over the accounts of Crippen's dalliance with Miss LeNeve, while the breakfast coffee grew cold, dreamed perhaps of themselves with Miss Brown of the typing pool, their womenfolk puzzled over that Hinde curler. For did not these same wives roll on beds of pain nightly with these same metal bobbins screwed tightly to their heads? Why, if Belle and her husband had quarrelled bitterly on her last night on earth, had she bothered to do her hair up in curlers, and at 1.30 in the morning? Most women made themselves attractive with some man in mind. Did Belle have still another lover, whose name did not come out in court?

The curler itself, such a commonplace article on their own dressing-tables, suddenly in the imagination of these housewives took on a sinister significance. Had it been wrenched from the poor woman's head while she was still alive? Had the hair been torn out by the roots? Had Belle literally been scalped? And the head itself, which the women could picture jingling with dozens of tiny, metal clasps — where was that head now?*

Such, I am assured, were the feminine preoccupations in London semi-detached and suburban bijou bungalow alike during the latter part of October, 1910, when Crippen fought for his life in the witness box. Brought face to face with a hatred so ferocious that it could encompass scalping and beheading, the wives shuddered, looked questioningly at their spouses, now engrossed in the sports news or stock market reports, as they enquired, 'More coffee, dear?'

---

* There was some excitement in September, 1962 when workmen digging an excavation unearthed the skull of a woman aged between 35 and 45 in Busby Place, Camden Road, about 300 yards from Hilldrop Crescent. However, after examining the skull, Pathologist Dr Francis Camps pronounced that it was a specimen of the type that is used in the teaching of anatomy.

[13]

When Ethel LeNeve's trial on charges of being an accessory after the fact of murder opened Tuesday, October 25th, in the same courtroom where four days earlier Crippen had been condemned to death, her counsel, Frederick Edwin Smith, K.C., was faced with a dilemma. Should he put Ethel into the witness box to testify on her own behalf? To do so was to risk having her credibility destroyed under the relentless cross-examination of Richard Muir, who again would be leading for the Crown. On the other hand, if Ethel remained silent might not her silence be commented upon adversely by the judge? Worse still, might not the jury interpret it as a sign that she had something to hide?

In opting for the bolder course, Smith was frank with the jury. 'I am not prepared,' he declared, 'after what that woman has gone through, in the state of health in which she is, to submit her, on facts like these and on evidence such as that which has been presented, to the deadly cross-examination of my learned friend . . . Knowing that she is a young and inexperienced woman, without any knowledge of the world, that she is dazed and shattered, I have taken the responsibility upon myself, and I am content to support it.'*

Ethel, profiting by Crippen's mistakes, gave Newton a wide berth; instead she engaged Hopwood and Sons as her solicitors, and asked them to instruct F. E. Smith to defend her. In 1910 Smith was not yet known as 'the cleverest man in the kingdom', which was Lord Beaverbrook's description of him, but he was well on the way to earning this accolade. Called to the Bar in 1899, the handsome, witty, flamboyant Smith in eight years had become the youngest King's Counsel in Britain. He went on to become the youngest Lord Chancellor in modern times, Solicitor General, Attorney General, Secretary of State for India, all before the age

---

* After Ethel's trial the Lord Chief Justice was said to have remarked to Smith, 'I think you ought to have put her into the box', to which Smith made the enigmatic reply, 'No, I knew what she would say. You did not'.

of fifty-three. 'Not even Wellington had such a career as this,' as one of Smith's biographers observes.

In 1910, however, Smith was quite happy to accept the brief to defend Ethel LeNeve, with the opportunities it offered for displaying his forensic skill, and this despite the fact that Ethel proved to be 'a maddening client', according to Smith's son. For no sooner did Ethel learn of the fate that awaited her lover than she became hysterical, crying, 'I know nothing! I know nothing!' 'That is true,' Smith reassured her, patting her arm. 'Now we will get you freed. But you must let me help you, Miss LeNeve. Your life is at stake.'¹

Whether or not it was Smith's calming influence, Ethel had completely regained her composure by the time she stood before Lord Alverstone, the Lord Chief Justice, to answer charges of being Crippen's accessory in that she 'did feloniously receive, comfort, and maintain him'. Among the courtroom spectators was Winston Churchill, then Home Secretary, who followed the proceedings with avid interest.

From the outset it was obvious that the Crown's case against Ethel was shaky, to put it mildly, so much so that rather than to prove Ethel guilty, Richard Muir tried to shoulder the burden off onto Smith to prove his client innocent. But 'F.E.', to use the cognomen by which Smith was popularly known, was having none of it. So confident was 'F.E.' that there was no case to answer that he called no evidence on Ethel's behalf, but relied solely upon his persuasive powers with the jury to carry the day. It was to be one of his finest hours.

To begin with Smith had made a careful study of the jury, concluded that most of the jurors were middle-class family men, some with daughters of nubile age. Not just family men, but *hommes moyen sensuels*—there was not a lofty brow among them—with a taste for the meretricious in art and literature, novels like George du Maurier's *Trilby*, for example, which had also enjoyed an enormous success as a stage play. It was as Trilby, that pathetic little songstress who falls under the hypnotic spell of the evil genius Svengali, that Smith presented Ethel to the jury.

In Smith's mind, as he revealed it to the jury, Ethel was still a schoolgirl of seventeen. It mattered not that Ethel was older by exactly one decade. Ethel had in fact got stuck in the time continuum so that she was still 'this defenceless child' and 'this young and inexperienced person without any knowledge of the world'. At seventeen, 'an age when I need hardly remind you young girls in happier circumstances are going to a finishing governess', Ethel had been forced to earn her living as a typist. 'You know what are the temptations to which . . . a young and attractive girl is exposed going to the city as a typist.' The jurors stirred uneasily as though they did indeed know what those temptations were. In Ethel's case 'she had the extreme misfortune to come across the path of one of the most dangerous and remarkable men who have lived in this century . . . a compelling and masterful personality . . . fearing neither God nor man.' And yet Hawley Harvey Crippen could be 'insinuating, attractive', for all his godlessness. Crippen had in fact taken advantage of his position to force his attentions upon Ethel ('He was the doctor, and she was the typist.')

On and on Smith led the jury through the scenario of Ethel as the wronged working girl, turning many of the arguments which the Crown had offered as proofs of guilt against the prosecution. The 'rising sun' brooch, for example. If Ethel had known about the murder, would she have gone to the Criterion ball, at which many of Belle's friends were certain to be present, wearing the dead woman's jewellery? And Ethel's moving into No. 39 Hilldrop Crescent—'does anyone believe that the girl went . . . to live in this house knowing that its last tenant had been murdered by the man she was going to live with?' Smith asked. 'I say in all history there have been very few women capable of such wickedness.'

In his peroration Smith reminded the jury that when Ethel left the dock, acquitted by their verdict, as he was confident would be the case, she would be a most unhappy woman. 'She will be known all over London, and all over England, as one who has been the mistress of this murderer.' 'I do not ask you for mercy,' he concluded. 'I only ask you for justice, and I am content you will judge her in her hour of agony with that consideration that you would wish shown to a daughter of your own if she were placed in the same position.'

It took the jury only twenty minutes to reach a verdict of not guilty, after which Ethel hurried down the stairs at the back of the dock and into a taxicab waiting at a side door. ('Oh! how relieved I was to be out in the streets of London once more,' she writes.) There remains only this one little anecdote told by Smith's son to add to the record. 'The gratitude of accused persons to counsel who have extricated them from a terrible position of course varies widely,' the son writes. 'It is worth recording that after this case F. E. Smith received no communication whatever from Ethel LeNeve.'[2]

*   *   *

Ethel's acquittal was a great consolation to Crippen as he awaited the outcome of his own appeal against conviction. He could have had no illusions as to whether that appeal would succeed. 'The impression formed in my mind was that he was a fatalist; that he knew he was doomed,' writes S. Ingleby Oddie.[3] Nevertheless, he strove to comfort Ethel, counselling her not to despair. 'There is yet the appeal,' he writes on October 28th, 'and friends are coming forward to help. One here in England tells my solicitor he does not consider I had a fair trial, and offers to pay all expenses, and, just think, Munyon has awakened to his old friendship for me and cabled he will spend £12,000 for me if necessary.' Professor Munyon of Philadelphia had indeed bestirred himself, and was full of plans, abortive as it turned out, to apply through the U.S. State Department to the British Home Secretary for a stay of execution pending an investigation of reports that Belle Elmore had been seen recently in Chicago.*

Meanwhile, the governor of Pentonville prison had taken quite a liking to Crippen. Major H. E. Mytton-Davies, of the 22nd, the Cheshire Regiment (ret), was not the type one thinks of as a prison governor. A sensitive, cultured man, Major Mytton-Davies, upon his retirement from the army, had applied for the post of City Marshal, but had been turned down because he was not a cavalry officer (the City Marshal is required to sit a horse in a soldierly manner upon ceremonial occasions). Thereafter he had applied to the prison service as second choice. 'My father found Crippen to be a very mild, inoffensive little man who never gave anyone any trouble,' the major's son, Cynric Mytton-Davies, who lives in Castle Caereinion, Wales, tells me. Cynric was only a small boy at the time of the Crippen trial, but his father never forgot Crippen,

---

* On November 12th Reuter's in a dispatch cabled from Canada reported that a woman answering Belle's description had been seen in Alix, Saskatchewan. She was said to have fainted upon hearing that Crippen was scheduled to be hanged.

and talked about him to the family often afterwards. It is startling to learn that the major believed Crippen innocent. 'Father thought that Crippen was an unlikely type to commit a murder,' the son declares. 'He believed that Crippen was covering up for the real culprit, and was going to his death on that person's behalf.' 'Only the strongest personal loyalty could inspire such a sacrifice,' Cynric Mytton-Davies adds.

Not only the prison governor, but the warders who watched Crippen day and night as a precaution against his attempting suicide found him no trouble. According to Filson Young, who was allowed to examine the duty book in which the warders recorded Crippen's conduct from hour to hour, it was evident that they 'looked upon him not only with respect, but with something like affection'. 'He never . . . showed any concern or asked for any benefit for himself; all his concern and all his requests were for the woman he loved.'[4] Crippen spent the interim before the appeal court decision writing to Ethel, or reading, but even as he read his thoughts wandered to his absent love. 'All day I sit here by a table with my eyes on a book,' he writes to her, 'and I suppose the guards believe me to be reading, but over and over again the words are only a blank before my eyes and the book with pictures of ourselves together.'

Of the eleven letters to Ethel that have been preserved, in only two does Crippen make any reference to his innocence, and then the reference is perfunctory.* 'Should I be spared,' he writes earlier on, 'we must look forward to time to prove my conviction as unjust.' But later, on the eve of his execution, Crippen feels 'We can safely leave to the Hand of a just God the production later on, if necessary, of further evidence.' The letters mostly contain protestations of undying love for Ethel interspersed with business injunctions ('Do not forget to insist on having the trunk of silver', 'About the diamonds, I want you to have them') looking towards securing Ethel's future financially. As a result of Crippen's efforts, Ethel at the time of his death had enough to tide her over for the next two years. He even went so far as to write out the formula for a new pain-killer called 'Sans Peine' from which he was hoping that Ethel might benefit ('You may be able to make a valuable deal with someone to put it on the market for you, either buying it outright, or paying you a percentage on the sales . . .').

* The letters are reprinted in the Appendix.

As one commentator observes, 'No condemned cell can have witnessed a stranger spectacle than that of a quack doctor inventing a quack remedy to provide funds for the woman from whom Death was soon to separate him for ever.'[5]

Crippen was so concerned to secure Ethel's future financially because he wanted her to remain independent, and not to be rushed into marriage through fear of want, or 'be led into any false step through obligation to anyone', as he more delicately put it. 'I want my wifie's life to be a happy and comfortable one. That is the greatest desire of my heart,' he writes. In a subsequent letter, dated November 5th, Crippen clarifies his position. 'I am not so selfish, darling, as to wish you not to marry again,' he declares, 'but inasmuch as you have been the one woman who has had all my heart, so do I believe you will ever keep me in your heart.' That Crippen had had to struggle against the temptation to exact from Ethel a promise that she would remain faithful to him even in death is evident from one of his last letters to her. 'My love for you,' he explains, 'has become so great, so absorbing that I was afraid I should ask of you, in my longings to be all in all to you, what would be unreasonable.' 'But no, dearest,' he concludes, 'I shall only think now that as I would have been ready any time and at all times to lay down my life and soul to make you happy, so you too are mine for ever.'

Elsewhere he does put forward the pathetic suggestion that Ethel should take his name ('wifie dear, it would please me so much if you would take my first name or my second Christian name, which you prefer—probably you prefer Hawley—and add "Mrs" to it . . .'). He next writes, 'My heart rejoices in the promise that you will always bear the name you have taken, no matter what comes.' If she did make such a promise she never kept it. In the coming years Ethel, in an effort to live down her notoriety, was to use several aliases. 'Mrs Hawley' was not among them.

*   *   *

Crippen's last days were saddened by clamours from the outside world which managed to penetrate the thickness of Pentonville's walls, and into the death cell. The first of these was the failure of the Charing Cross Bank in which Crippen's life savings were tied up. Ironically, the bank failed to open its doors on

Tuesday, October 18th, the day Crippen's trial opened at the Old Bailey. Due to fraudulent land speculations in Canada, the bank had gone broke owing over £2,500,000 to depositors. These latter were mostly of 'the poorer classes', according to *The Times*, which pointed out that the bank's high interest rates 'were sure to attract numbers of ignorant and thoughtless people'. Subsequently, a number of these 'ignorant and thoughtless' depositors, unable to face the workhouse, chose death as the easier way out. A retired Yorkshire engineer took his life by swallowing ammonia, while in Dublin a coachman hanged himself from a beam in the coach-house ceiling.

At first Crippen had been optimistic, assuring Ethel that the bank 'must pay some dividend, and if only 1/4, that would mean a good sum.' But after receiving a letter from Arthur Newton to the effect that his chances of recovering anything from the bank were remote, Crippen writes of 'the bitterness of this terrible disappointment'. 'My greatest grief has been the disappointment in not being able to put *all* in your hands *at once* . . . and make you independent of *all.*'

Another source of grief was Lady Isabel Somerset who, on the eve of Crippen's appeal being heard, threatened an ill-conceived publicity campaign on his behalf. Wealthy Lady Somerset (her husband from whom she was separated was the second son of the Duke of Beaufort) was a born busybody, whose twin causes were temperance and fallen women.* It was as one of the latter that her ladyship looked upon Ethel, in offering Ethel a home at the hostel for 'soiled doves' which Lady Somerset had founded near Reigate, and which she regarded as her crowning work. Ethel, for her part, cordially disliked her ladyship. Undoubtedly it is to Lady Somerset that Ethel refers when she writes that among the 'unscrupulous people [who] were eager to obtain access to him in prison' was 'a lady whom Dr Crippen and myself were led to believe was a philanthropist . . . when we discovered her real identity we refused to have anything to do with her'.[6]

---

* After being involved in a homosexual scandal her husband, Lord Henry Somerset, was forced to live abroad. When he returned to England for Edward VII's Coronation Lady Somerset had him watched by detectives. Lord Henry is not to be confused, however, with his brother Lord Arthur Somerset, who was involved in the so-called Cleveland Street Scandal as the patron of a male brothel.

Crippen was so alarmed by Lady Somerset's publicity campaign, which involved confidences given in an unguarded moment, that he sought and obtained permission from the prison governor to write to her ladyship in an effort to head her off. 'I must protest against you giving anything from my letters publicity whatever!' Crippen writes; '. . . and also not to give away any facts whatever to newspaper people until after the appeal is over.' 'I understand your kind wish is to help me,' he adds, 'but please do not publish anything yet and do nothing to break confidences I have given to you in writing.'*

Crippen's concern stemmed from the fact that exclusive rights to any public utterances he might care to make had already been auctioned off by his solicitor Arthur Newton, ostensibly to raise funds for the appeal. What is not clear is whether Crippen knew the identity of the highest bidder. In an earlier letter Crippen writes of 'friends coming forward to help', including 'one here in England [who] tells my solicitor he does not consider I had a fair trial, and offers to pay all expenses . . .' Three days later Crippen writes to Ethel, 'my solicitor distinctly told me a friend had come forward and guaranteed payment of the expenses of the appeal with the understanding I would, in return, do certain things that were not to be unreasonable . . .'. Did Newton keep Crippen in the dark that the 'friend' was none other than Horatio Bottomley, publisher of *John Bull*? Such would seem to have been the case, for had Crippen known his benefactor's identity, he certainly would have not kept the secret from Ethel.

While in Brixton prison awaiting trial, Crippen had begun writing his memoirs, which he had handed over to Newton. Later he claimed that he had signed a contract with the ·Hearst newspaper, the *New York American*, for publication of these memoirs, and that he was to receive £500 (about $2,500) upon delivery of the manuscript. What happened to this life story is a mystery upon which the Home Office has been unable to shed any light.†

* This letter was once in the possession of Eric Barton, Richmond bookseller, together with a petition calling for Crippen's reprieve and bearing the signatures of Lady Somerset, her daughter, and a student named Maurice Crocker.

† In response to the author's query, H. G. Pearson, the Home Office departmental record officer, writes: 'It appears that Crippen provided his legal advisers with an account of his life for publication and while in

Newton had been making other deals right and left in order to maximise his client's financial potential. According to Newton's managing clerk, a New York syndicate earlier had paid the solicitor £1,000 on the understanding that if Crippen were acquitted he, Crippen, would carry out a two-months' lecture tour in the States.

Ethel, too, had been making her deals. Notably, she had sold her life story to *Lloyd's Weekly News*, the first instalment appearing on November 6th, and the story later being published in book form. Concerning this first instalment Crippen writes to congratulate her, declaring, 'You have, my wifie dear, most ably set forth important facts that must tell with great weight in the minds of the unprejudiced.'

*   *   *

On Saturday, November 5th, the Court of Criminal Appeals found against Crippen, who for the first time gave way to despair. The new date for his execution was set for Wednesday, November 23rd. 'The Appeal has decided against us,' he writes to Ethel. 'Hope has completely gone, and your hub's heart is broken. No more can he hold his wifie in his arms, and the life he planned to devote to making your life comfortable is rapidly drawing to its end.' It was one of the few times during the month-long ordeal following his conviction that Crippen had broken down. 'Death has no terror for me,' he continues, '. . . but, oh! wifie, my love, my own, the bitterness of the thought that I must leave you alone, without me in the world, to those who can never, I am sure, love you, cherish you, and protect you as I would have done hereafter as in the past . . . I did not intend to write so mournfully, but my heart overflows . . .' The balance of the letter is taken up with business matters, Crippen's instructions being more frenzied now that his time is drawing to a close. He is making a new will in Ethel's favour; he wants her to have all of his personal property, including his watch, chain, plain band ring. If it were possible he would like to be cremated and to leave his ashes to 'wifie dear', he tells her.

---

prison he was given permission to sign an agreement selling the publication rights to an American newspaper in order to raise funds for his defence. It is regretted, however, that the name of the newspaper is not recorded, nor is it clear that an agreement was actually signed.'

What was 'wifie dear's' reaction to the shattering news that Crippen's appeal against conviction had been turned down? By a strange coincidence Sir Seymour Hicks, the actor-manager, was in the Bow Street police station seeing a detective friend on the day that Crippen's appeal was heard. 'Ethel LeNeve was in here a moment ago,' the detective confided to Hicks. 'She came in to know if she could borrow the pair of trousers she wore when she was arrested on board ship disguised as a boy.' Ethel claimed she had been offered a sum of money by a newspaper to be photographed in them, the detective explained. 'While I was discussing the matter with her the news came through that Crippen's appeal had failed and that he was to hang. The only comment she made was "Oh!" '⁷ The photograph of a rather sullen-faced Ethel LeNeve in her boyish disguise, a fedora hat pushed to the back of her head, one hand in her trousers' pocket, the other on her hip, duly appeared in *Lloyd's Weekly News* on November 20th, three days before Crippen was due to be hanged. The same issue carried Crippen's 'farewell letter to the world' in which he protested Ethel's innocence in moving terms.

Another episode in which Ethel figures during these last hectic days in Crippen's life throws a different light on her character, indicates that she was not so indifferent to her lover's fate as Hicks would have one believe. Two days before Crippen was due to be executed Ethel made an unexpected call at the prison governor's house, which was located just outside the gates of Pentonville. Major Mytton-Davies was not at home, but his wife was, according to the son. 'Ethel LeNeve had the gall to ask mother to use her influence with father to obtain Crippen's reprieve,' Cynric Mytton-Davies declared. 'Apparently father was to use his persuasive powers with the Home Secretary to this end,' the son explains, adding, 'Of course mother should never have admitted LeNeve in the first place, but mother, who was somewhat naive, did not know the protocol in these matters.'

In the middle of the interview Major Mytton-Davies returned home. 'Father was furious at finding LeNeve and ordered her out of the house. Just then a newsboy ran down the street shouting, "Crippen confesses all". LeNeve turned white and obviously was very frightened. "Is this true?" she asked. Father drew himself up to his full height and icily replied, "You, if anyone, should know".'

*   *   *

The impending execution did not fail to generate macabre incidents. Two days after Crippen's appeal had failed an elderly soldier walked into a Cambridge courtroom and asked to be hanged in place of Crippen, holding that the life of a medical man was more valuable than his own. According to *The Times*, the magistrates could not resist making a sick joke, observing that although Crippen probably would not object to the exchange the application must be made in London, not Cambridge. That same day a wax effigy of Crippen went on show in Madame Tussaud's Chamber of Horrors, the little doctor taking his place beside William Palmer, the mass poisoner; Charley Peace, burglar and murderer; and Burke and Hare, the Edinburgh 'resurrectionists', who strangled their victims, then sold their cadavers for £10 a time to the Edinburgh Medical Academy.*

On November 17th petitions urging that Crippen be reprieved and bearing 15,000 signatures were transported to the Home Office in a taxicab by Arthur Newton, who, in his covering letter to the Home Secretary, observed that 'literally hundreds of other signatures are coming in by every post . . .'

Then on Friday, November 18th, came news from Los Angeles that Crippen's father, aged 83, had died. The *Coldwater Courier*, under a Los Angeles dateline, carried a pathetic story indicating that Myron Crippen's death had been due to privation. 'Since the doctor's arrest . . . his father has been penniless and dependent upon charity,' Crippen's regular allowance to his father having ceased, according to the *Courier*. The story goes on to say: 'He [the father] has haunted the news-stands for weeks, awaiting every edition containing news of his son. With a few pennies he was able to purchase the papers, leaving none for food, and he broke down from worry last week. He was delirious last night. He cried for his son, mumbling, "It will not be long before I go, but my son is innocent. He was a good boy".' As far back as August 1st the father had told a reporter, 'This is killing me. My mind will break with it all.'[8]

The blows now fell with the rapidity of a trip-hammer. At ten

* Crippen's effigy was modelled by the founder's great-great-grandson Jack Tussaud, who attended Crippen's trial and took pictures of him with a camera concealed in a bowler hat, according to the museum staff.

o'clock Saturday night, November 19th, Major Mytton-Davies, the prison governor, brought Crippen the news that the petition for a reprieve had been turned down by Winston Churchill, the Home Secretary. 'I never at any time dared hope,' Crippen writes Ethel; 'yet deep down in my heart was just a glimmer of trust that God might give us yet a chance to put me right before the world and let me have the passionate longing of my soul.' He then praises the governor of Pentonville for his thoughtfulness: 'He was so kind and considerate . . . in breaking the shock as gently as he could . . . and left me at last with, "God bless you; good night".' 'When he had gone I first kissed your face in the photo, my faithful devoted companion in all this sorrow . . . in spite of all my greatest efforts, it was impossible to keep down a great sob and my heart's agonised cry.'

*   *   *

Fortunately for him, Crippen, on the eve of his execution, was spared the full impact of two of the worst blows aimed in his direction, and the knowledge that both of them emanated from his own solicitor. Horatio Bottomley was involved in the first of these episodes. The ebullient Bottomley, who had contributed towards Crippen's defence without visible return, now began demanding his pound of flesh. In an 'Open Letter' published in *John Bull* on November 19th, Bottomley invited Crippen to 'relieve your burning brain, confiding to me the name of your accomplice'. 'Did someone else administer the fatal drug? And, in your fright, and horror, did you then lose your mental balance?'

Bottomley then wanted to know 'by what superhuman strength' the 'half-blind, elderly, weak' Crippen had managed to drag Belle's heavy body downstairs, and to 'dig the floor, remove the clay, cover up, rebrick and make good . . . Did you alone get rid of the head, the legs, the arms, powder the bones and skull? And all in twenty-four hours!'

Clearly, Bottomley expected Crippen to reply. On November 21st Newton visited Crippen at Pentonville and asked him if he had seen the 'Open Letter' but Crippen knew nothing about it, the prison governor in his wisdom having kept *John Bull* from him. When Newton imparted this information to Bottomley the latter's response was, 'Well, I'll soon remedy the situation.' Thereupon

Bottomley called in his secretary, a Mr Wray, and dictated the reply that Crippen should have made to the 'Open Letter'. 'Dear Sir,' the forged letter, which was published in *John Bull* for November 26th, begins, 'I am extremely grateful to you for the interest you have taken in me, and I am much touched by some of the passages in your letter ... I wish, however, to say most emphatically that under no circumstances shall I say anything which would bring trouble to others.'

Ethel, through her solicitors, denied that the letter had been written or signed by Crippen: 'No such letter was sent out of prison.' Moreover, the forgery was to land Arthur Newton in hot water, result in him being suspended from practice for twelve months for professional misconduct. Later in an action against Newton initiated by the Law Society, the King's Bench Division of the High Court would find that the solicitor had 'aided and abetted' Bottomley 'to disseminate false information' concerning Crippen.

While 'aiding and abetting' Bottomley, Newton had been planning his most audacious coup: no less than a forged Crippen 'confession'. Newton sold the 'confession' for £500 to the *Evening Times*, a fly-by-night London daily, which published it as genuine on the day Crippen was hanged. It was a discreditable episode in which Edgar Wallace figured, and the full story is told by Margaret Lane in her biography of the thriller writer.[9] Ever canny, Newton used a go-between in approaching the newspaper with his offer. 'A few days before November 23rd,' Miss Lane writes, 'a man called at the *Evening Times* office and asked to see the editor. He was reticent and evasive in manner, but finally, under urgent promises of secrecy, confided ... that Crippen had made a confession to his solicitor, Mr Arthur Newton, and that the said Mr Newton was willing to consider selling the confession to the *Evening Times* for £1,000.' Interviewed by the advertising manager, Arthur Findon, Newton quickly scaled down his price to £500, stipulating that it should be paid to him in gold sovereigns. Newton explained that the confession was not a written document signed by Crippen, 'but had been made verbally by his client during his imprisonment, and was embodied in the notes taken by himself.'

On the strength of this agreement the *Evening Times* blanketed London with posters announcing the confession. But when Findon went to keep a last interview with Newton at the Langham Hotel he found that the latter had got cold feet, and, fearing that the Law Society had got wind of his intentions, now wanted to back out of the deal. At this point Findon got tough: either Newton delivered the goods or the *Evening Times* would publish the whole story of the solicitor's approach, together with the fact that he had already accepted £500 for the confession. Cornered in the small hours of the morning, Newton agreed to dictate the confession to a friend, who in turn would deliver it at Arthur Findon's flat within a few hours.

When the mysterious friend whom Miss Lane does not identify arrived at about 3 am with the written narrative, he refused to let it out of his hands, but insisted upon dictating it, destroying the original manuscript page by page as soon as he had read from it. 'Findon and another member of the *Evening Times* staff took it down from his dictation, and in some anguish watched him throw the original copy on the fire,' Miss Lane records. 'The partially burned remains of it they rescued as soon as he had gone, to serve as some sort of evidence of the authenticity of the confession.'

It is at this point that Edgar Wallace, who was racing editor of the *Evening Times*, enters the story. For when the so-called 'confession' arrived at the newspaper's office at 5 am, Wallace, who had been alerted to stand by, was told by the editor to improve it with 'half a column of good human intro'.

With copy boys snatching each page as soon as he finished typing it to rush the copy to the printers, Wallace gave the 'confession' the imprimatur of authenticity. 'The statement printed below,' he wrote, 'is Crippen's own statement . . . It is unnecessary to say that no journal — even the least responsible of journals — would print this confession of Crippen's without unimpeachable authority. That authority we possess.' (Wallace no doubt had in mind the charred bits of paper which Findon had managed to fish from the fireplace.) The master of detective thrillers then went on to describe the 'confession' as 'one of the most remarkable and thrilling narratives which all the annals of crime can furnish'.

What followed hardly lived up to the expectations thus aroused. To begin with, it was told in the third person, the explanation for this being that 'Dr Crippen, before he died, confessed his guilt to a friend who, unable to hold his awful secret any longer, has given the full facts to the *Evening Times*.' Secondly, the concoction contained almost nothing that could be described as either 'remarkable' or 'thrilling', to borrow Wallace's adjectives. Crippen had poisoned his wife by administering two doses of hyoscine in indigestion tablets manufactured by Munyon's. He had then cut up her body with a surgeon's post-mortem knife which he had purchased in Holborn a few days before, and which he afterwards had hidden in the garden of an empty house in Hilldrop Crescent. Newton's imagination turns out to have been as impoverished as that of his client Crippen.

It is pleasant in the circumstances to be able to report that the 'confession' brought about the ruination of the *Evening Times*. For no sooner had the edition containing the forgery hit the streets than the prison governor was denying in the most emphatic terms that Crippen had made any such statement. Challenged to produce its proofs, the *Evening Times* remained strangely mute. The paper, whose circulation was never more than 100,000, had sold a million copies of the edition in which the 'confession' appeared, but the next day its circulation had slumped to 60,000, and within a few months the paper was dead. As for Arthur Newton, he was forced to crawl most ignominiously. 'So far as I personally am concerned,' Newton cautiously told reporters, 'I can say nothing about the confession. I personally knew of no confession, but beyond that I cannot discuss the matter.' Unrepentant, Edgar Wallace was to write in his autobiography twenty-two years later, 'That Crippen did admit his guilt and describe the circumstances of the crime to our informant there is no doubt whatever.' Wallace finishes lamely by saying, 'We were in a position that we could not explain the source of our information.'[10]

'How shameful to be hounded in our last moments, so sacred to us, by newspaper men, and that they should continue to publish lies,' Crippen complains in one of his last letters to Ethel, who apparently had told him about the *Evening Times*'s lurid announcement on the billboards.

*   *   *

Crippen's letters to Ethel are liberally sprinkled with references to God, invoking His blessing and protection. 'Let us hope God will be good to us and bring me safely through in spite of all,' he had written before his appeal had been turned down. After his appeal had been rejected, Crippen, with all hope gone, turned more and more to his religion for consolation. In particular, he seemed to derive comfort from his belief in a hereafter, assuring Ethel 'we *shall* meet again in another life.' 'We have been always so entirely one in heart and soul, thought and deed, even in flesh and spirit, I cannot believe otherwise but that we shall be together in that other life I am going to soon.'

Crippen also found time towards the last to celebrate his love for Ethel in verse. Unfortunately, only one example of his poetry has escaped destruction. It is not necessary to pass judgment on the poem's merits; the surprising thing, as Dr Johnson remarked of women preachers, is that it was done at all — that the man in the death cell could so order his thoughts as to find words that rhymed.

> When the heart is breaking, and the way is long
> In seeking rest, with no accompanying song,
> Scorn of the world, by cruel Fate undone,
> Friendless, yet not alone — for there is one —
>
> Who truly loves this soon admitted clay,
> Who truly dreads the sure and awful day
> When mortal soul shall fly to realms aloft,
> In life — in death — she still shall speak me soft.[11]

'How can I find the strength and heart to struggle through this last letter?' he writes to Ethel on Monday, November 21st. 'God, indeed, must hear our cry to Him for Divine help in this last fare-well.' Crippen broke down and wept when at midnight Tuesday night Major Mytton-Davies brought him Ethel's farewell tele-gram. Pulling himself together, Crippen then took leave of the major, asking him to accept his rosary made of plain brown beads and a ring made in the form of a crucifix as tokens of appreciation for the kindness the prison governor had shown him.* From accounts of this last interview it sounds as though Crippen were trying to comfort the prison governor rather than the reverse. 'It took father at least a week to get over it every time there was an execution,' Cynric Mytton-Davies tells me. 'Mother used to get theatre tickets for the night of the hanging in order to distract

* The rosary and ring are now the possessions of crime writer Richard Whittington-Egan.

father's mind.' Major Mytton-Davies asked Crippen if he had any last request to make, and it was then that the latter asked that Ethel's letters and her photograph be buried with him, a request which was granted.

Crippen had one last trump card, which he now proceeded to play. William Willis, who assisted Hangman J. Ellis in carrying out Crippen's execution, recorded the story in his diary, excerpts from which were published many years later. 'He [Crippen] asked to use the washroom, and was allowed to go there,' Willis noted. 'While he was in there the permanent warder heard a cracking sound, and when he came out again he noticed that half the steel part of his glasses was missing. The warder said, "Where is the other part of your glasses, Crippen?" He replied, "I do not know." So the warder said, "Get out of bed and let me search you." He let them search him, but they could not find the missing piece . . . Eventually they found it in the inside seam at the bottom of his trousers leg . . . Crippen's idea was to puncture some artery and bleed slowly to death as he was sleeping.'[12]

Hawley Harvey Crippen was hanged at Pentonville at nine o'clock Wednesday morning, November 23rd. Out of consideration for three other condemned men who were awaiting execution inside the prison, no bell was tolled. The first intimation the large crowd outside the prison had that the sentence had been carried out was when the official notice signed by the under-sheriff, the prison governor, and a Roman Catholic chaplain, was posted. At the inquest held immediately after the execution, as required by law, it was stated by the prison surgeon that Crippen had died without a struggle, death being instantaneous from a fracture of the neck vertebrae.

At about the exact hour the execution was carried out, a woman, dressed in black and with a black veil over her face, boarded at Southampton the White Star liner *Majestic*, due to sail at noon for New York. The ship's manifest carried her as 'Miss Allen', but her real name was Ethel Clara LeNeve.

VII

THAT

CURSE AGAIN

COMPANY (Finale)
  'In the year nineteen-ten
  We showed the world again
  That you can't beat a British crime,
    Thank you Crippen,
  You can't beat a British crime,
    Here's to Crippen,
  You can't beat a British crime,
    Goodbye Crippen,
  It's been a jolly time.
SOMEONE (shouting)
  'He was a Yankee!
COMPERE
  'Criminally speaking, sir, he was
  as English as you are.'

—from 'Belle or the Ballad
of Doctor Crippen'[1]

[14]

Crippen's neighbours, if they were to return to life today, would scarcely recognise The Brecknock, which is just round the corner from Hilldrop Crescent. There is very little of its Edwardian grandeur left. Its walls whose tiles owed their floral designs to Pompeii have been covered with a nasty wallpaper of a dark green colour. The frosted bowls of its chandeliers have orange bulbs, which increase the murkiness of the interior. Juke box, fruit machines, and colour television have been installed, along with beer of a gaseous quality.

All that is left of the original pub are old theatrical playbills high on the wall heralding the appearances of Dan Leno, George Robey, the Ethiopian Serenaders, and Ada Reeve. Nowadays in place of the Ethiopian Serenaders pop groups with names like The Scarecrow and The Bone Idol entertain on Friday nights in the saloon bar, the night being made hideous by their amplified electric guitars.

Despite the din, conversation still flourishes in the public bar, where the remnants of an older generation sit hunched over their pints of bitter. With a little encouragement, the conversation can be diverted to Dr Crippen, who, when all is said and done, is as close as the area can boast of having a local hero. 'The Curse of Hilldrop Crescent', one learns, is not just a matter of ghostly laughter, trowels scraping on bricks, and things that go bump in the night. No, it has to do with the misfortunes which dogged those who had anything to do with Crippen, and most particularly with bringing Crippen to justice. (As an example of how persistently the Crippen legend has followed each of its actors, when Paul Martinetti was discovered dead at the Hotel Mustapha in Algiers in December 1924 *The Times* headed its obituary notice: 'Death of Mr Paul Martinetti: Crippen Case Recalled'.)

If ever there was a victim of the Crippen curse surely it was Captain Henry Kendall, the skipper of the *Montrose*, who had wirelessed Crippen's presence aboard his vessel. On May 29, 1914, the *Empress of Ireland*, which Captain Kendall commanded, sank with a loss of 1,062 lives at Father's Point off Quebec, the very same spot where Crippen was arrested and taken ashore in a pilot boat. Captain Kendall himself was among those rescued, but that same year the *Montrose*, aboard which Crippen and Ethel LeNeve had fled in a desperate bid for freedom, foundered on the Goodwin Sands.* Some of the habituées of the Brecknock whom the author talked to felt that there was a certain poetic justice in Captain Kendall's career coming unstuck, for they regarded him frankly as Judas Iscariot, who had wormed his way into Crippen's confidence, the better to betray him. They described the £250 reward which Kendall received from the Home Office as 'blood money'. For the record, the *Montrose*'s one-time skipper died in a London nursing home in November, 1965, at the ripe age of ninety-one.

As the man who actually caught Crippen, Chief Inspector Walter Dew cannot be said to have wholly escaped 'The Curse of Hilldrop Crescent'. Dew resigned from Scotland Yard on November 5, 1910, the day Crippen's appeal against sentence was turned down by the higher court; and while there is no reason to believe that there was any connection between the two events, the inspector was certainly deeply affected by the ultimate fate of the condemned man whom he had befriended. (As evidence of the affectionate regard in which Dew held Crippen he refers to him constantly in his autobiography as 'the little man', 'the little fellow', and more warmly still, 'my little prisoner'). But then temperamentally Dew was never cut out to be a detective, the seamy side of his work in particular being distasteful to him. Indicative of his attitude is his boast, 'So far as I know my wife never entered a police station in her life, and I am sure that with one exception my children have not.' As far as courtroom dramas such as Crippen's were concerned, he writes, 'Personally, I detested the atmosphere and surroundings of criminal courts, and always made a point of getting away at the first possible moment.'[2] Having retired on pension at the early age of forty-seven, Dew grew roses in the

---

* The *Montrose*'s end in December, 1914 was an ignominious one, for earlier she had been sold to the British Admiralty, which filled her holds with cement preparatory to sinking her as a block ship off Dover harbour. Before the work was completed, however, a gale sprang up, and the *Montrose* broke loose from her moorings and drifted onto the Goodwin Sands.

garden of his cottage, The Wee Hoose, in Worthing where on December 16, 1947, he died at the age of eighty-four.

*   *   *

The word ghoul is defined in the Shorter O.E.D. as 'an evil spirit supposed . . . to rob graves and prey on human corpses'. The description would seem to fit Arthur Newton who, by means of forged documents, continued, as has been seen, to batten on his client Crippen even after the latter had paid for his crime on the gallows. How Newton was suspended from practice for twelve months for unprofessional conduct in connection with the Crippen case has already been related. It was not until July, 1913, however, that Newton received his come-uppance, being sentenced to three years' imprisonment for an £18,500 fraud involving the sale of Canadian timberlands. On this occasion the Law Society ordered him to be struck from the rolls as a solicitor. Released from Parkhurst prison early for good behaviour, Newton became a private eye, developed a lucrative side line as a marriage broker in arranging matches between those who had titles and were penniless and those who were titleless but had plenty of ready cash. On October 3, 1930, Newton died at the age of seventy at No. 71A Ebury Street, Chelsea, not far from Tite Street, where his friend Oscar Wilde had lived.

It seems a pity that Newton while in Parkhurst could not have enjoyed the companionship of that other ghoul involved in the Crippen case, but Horatio Bottomley was to remain at large until March, 1922, when he was gaoled for seven years for fraudulent conversion. Bottomley's peculiar gifts were given full play during the First World War when, as one of Kitchener's recruiting agents, he was said to have been a bigger draw at recruiting rallies than any Cabinet minister save Lloyd George, and to have netted £27,000 for his pains. (Bottomley made an extra charge for invoking the name of the Supreme Being in his appeal to young men to fight for King and country, according to his critics.)

Bottomley's most ambitious swindle was his Victory Bond Scheme, in which he offered readers of *John Bull* who subscribed one pound a fifth share in a £5 government Victory Bond, the bonds thus purchased to be handed over to trustees, and prizes to be paid out of the accruing interest. More than £650,000 was subscribed, most of which found its way into Bottomley's bottomless pockets before the law finally caught up with him.

*   *   *

How about Miss LeNeve—was she too a victim of 'The Curse of Hilldrop Crescent'? Was the rest of her life overshadowed by some malign spell? Curiously, Ethel almost alone of the principals appears to have escaped the curse, and to have led a tranquil, if not completely happy life, up to the time of her death at an advanced age.

When last seen Ethel, in widow's weeds, was boarding the *Majestic* at Southampton en route to a new life in the New World. Thereafter, Ethel seemingly vanished from the face of the earth, so far as press and public were concerned, though she was eagerly sought by reporters on both sides of the Atlantic.* The fact that journalists were unable to discover Ethel's whereabouts did not prevent them from reporting on 'unimpeachable authority' that she had been sighted in various parts of the world. She was said to have emigrated to one or another of the Commonwealth countries, to have opened a hat shop in Eastbourne, to be living 'somewhere in Kent'. Fleet Street editors liked to boast that they had Ethel's current address and the alias she was using written down in the little black book in which they kept unlisted telephone numbers, but that 'out of consideration for this little lady who has suffered so much' they were keeping the information secret.

Typical of the journalistic effusions Ethel inspired is the story published in the London *Daily Express* of June 28, 1932, by a reporter who claimed that he had found her in Perth, Western Australia, 'looking out over the Indian Ocean, across which she

---

* In February, 1911 Ethel *in absentia* was granted probate of Crippen's will, his estate being valued at £268. A similar application by Ethel's counsel for probate of the estate of 'Cunigunda (otherwise Cora) Crippen, Deceased' was turned down by the High Court of Justice. At the court hearing the case of Florence Maybrick, who in 1889 poisoned her husband, was cited as authority 'that a person who commits murder should not be allowed to benefit by his or her criminal act'. (The insurance Mrs Maybrick had taken out on her husband was withheld from her on these grounds.) Belle's sister Mrs Theresa Hunn was granted letters of administration of Belle's estate.

fled many years ago to escape the public glare.' 'Ethel LeNeve is living in the direst poverty, under an assumed name—and her alias will remain a secret with me,' the *Daily Express* man writes. He then quotes her as musing, 'Little did I realise on those nights when I visited Dr Crippen in his London flat that under the basement floor was the body of his wife'.

For the record the real Ethel, her secret secure, was living when this interview appeared at No. 110 Parkview Road, Addiscombe, Croydon. Far from looking out over the waves of any Indian Ocean, Ethel looked out of windows onto a modest, tree-lined street, where she could see her children playing.

*   *   *

Disembarking from the *Majestic* in New York on the last day of November, 1910, Ethel had not tarried in the Empire City long, but had made straight for Toronto, about which Crippen, remembering his days there as Munyon's representative, had spoken to her in glowing terms. But Ethel, who got a job in Toronto as a typist, did not find it the paradise that Crippen had painted. For one thing, she was lonely, and found it hard to make friends. For another, the Crippen case was still discussed in lurid terms by the typists with whom she worked, and in conversations overheard in the tea shops where she took her meals. The fact that the little doctor had been arrested on Canadian soil had created an interest that was slow to die out. In those early days Ethel lived in constant fear that someone would recognise her, though she had changed her hair style and made other efforts to alter the way she had appeared in press photos at the time of the trial.

Ethel stuck it out until 1916, when she returned to England to nurse her beloved younger sister Nina, who was dying. She appears to have been using the name of 'Ethel Nelson' at this time, an association perhaps with Britain's naval hero who, like Ethel, was a native of Norfolk. Ethel had no difficulty in getting a job as a typist at Hampton's furniture store in Trafalgar Square. It was here that she met her future husband, Stanley Smith, who was an accountant there. After they married the couple went to live in East Croydon, where in time two children, a son and a daughter, were born to them. The children in turn grew up, married, and Ethel became a grandmother. Then one night Stanley died of a heart attack on his way home from work. Stanley, who was deaf in one ear, and wore a hearing aid, was said to have borne a strong resemblance to Crippen. Crippen, it will be recalled, was hard of hearing too.

Ethel continued to lead a rather humdrum existence, broken only by visits from her grandchildren, and the occasional outing to the seaside with other old age pensioners, until 1954. In that year Ethel celebrated her seventy-first birthday, and her real identity, after being kept secret for nearly half a century, was at last discovered — not by any Fleet Street muckraker, but by a woman novelist, Ursula Bloom.

Miss Bloom (in real life Mrs Charles Gordon Robinson) is no ordinary woman novelist. For one thing, she has 430 full-length works to her credit, not counting her first novel, which she wrote at the age of seven. This should entitle her to a niche in the *Guinness Book of Records*. For another, today at the age of eighty-three Miss Bloom is still going strong. Her vitality is what impresses the visitor who calls at her Chelsea flat behind Sloane Square. Miss Bloom was wearing diamond earrings when I came to tea; these and turquoise eye-shadow were set off by a pink dress of the variety known as a cocktail frock. Altogether the effect was stunning, and made Miss Bloom appear at least twenty years younger than her age.

In 1954 Miss Bloom wrote a fictionalised account of the Crippen case entitled *The Girl Who Loved Crippen*, which was serialised in the *Sunday Dispatch*. No sooner had the first instalment appeared than Ethel's brother Sidney got in touch with the novelist complaining about the way she had portrayed Ethel. 'Up to that point I wasn't even sure that Ethel was alive,' Miss Bloom confessed as she poured the Lapsong-Suchong.

Sidney Neave, who was then employed as a night watchman at the Baker Street Underground Station, was less interested in vindicating his sister's honour than he was in extracting thirty pounds from Miss Bloom, it transpired. Miss Bloom, who gladly paid the gratuity, in turn persuaded the brother to carry a letter to Ethel.

'I exchanged several letters with Ethel through the intermediary of the brother before Ethel, by then confident that I would not betray her true identity, agreed to see me,' Miss Bloom relates. Thus it was that in June, 1954, the encounter between these two women, coming from such different stations in life, took place.

'Ethel was much smaller than I anticipated,' Miss Bloom recalls, 'but at seventy-one she was still pretty, with grey hair gathered in a knot, and intelligent grey eyes.'

Not surprisingly, Ethel turned out to be a human oyster, judging by the amount of information Miss Bloom was able to prise from her. Perhaps it was that the habit of secrecy, of dissimulating even to her nearest and dearest, had become so engrained with Ethel that, even had she wanted to, she could not have unburdened herself to the other woman. One thing was quickly established: neither her late husband nor her children knew that Ethel Smith was the once notorious Ethel LeNeve. Moreover the human oyster was dropping no pearls, only bits of inconsequential grit which Miss Bloom dutifully jotted down and later reproduced in a newspaper article. 'She [Ethel] said that she still loved Crippen,' the novelist recorded. 'Hyoscine traces were found. But LeNeve said "We seldom used hyoscine, it was new and he never liked it." Then summed up: "He did not die for any of these things. It was just that he loved me." Her face was very white.'

Finally, Miss Bloom noted, 'I looked at her. My eyes asked the question I could not put into words. "He doesn't know," she whispered. Neither did her son or the daughter . . . In my notebook I wrote: I asked her if Crippen could have come back again, would she marry him now. Her eyes almost pierced me. "Yes, I would," she said.'[3]

And that was all. It was the sum total of information that Miss Bloom was able to extract from this bivalve at that or at any of the subsequent interviews she had with her, though the two women became good friends, indeed Ethel grew quite fond of the novelist, according to the latter's admission. A hundred questions spring to mind that a trained journalist would have asked Ethel. What was Crippen really like? What did Ethel find so fascinating about him? What did he tell her to convince her to cut off her hair and to flee with him disguised as a boy? Alas, Ethel took the answers with her to the grave.

One result of Miss Bloom's enterprise was that until Ethel's death thirteen years later Ethel was the novelist's 'exclusive': that is, only Miss Bloom and her editors knew about the house at No. 110 Parkview Road, Addiscombe, and its newsworthy occupant (Miss Bloom was careful in her articles never to pinpoint that address, writing that Ethel lived 'in a middle-class district in the

Home Counties'). The rest of Fleet Street was left baying at the moon. Over the next thirteen years Miss Bloom was able to parlay her tiny hoard of knowledge concerning Ethel into a profitable cottage industry, with contributions from her pen appearing regularly in the popular Sunday press.

*   *   *

Starting with 'Trapped by Wireless', a melodrama by actress-authoress Eva Elwes, which played in small halls ('booths' they were called in those days) before the First World War, Crippen has inspired a considerable outpouring of plays, novels, films and television documentaries. The Crippen story has exercised writing talents as diverse as those of Paul Dornhurst, Jeanne de Casalis and Ernest Raymond, whose novel *We the Condemned* is considered by many to be his best. As for television, hardly a year passes but that there is a reconstruction of the Belle Elmore murder on the small screen.

Of all the productions the little doctor from Coldwater, Michigan has given rise to, none is stranger than the musical 'Belle or the Ballad of Doctor Crippen', which opened at the Strand Theatre, London on May 4, 1961. The work of Wolf Mankowitz and Monty Norman, fresh from triumphs with the musicals 'Make Me an Offer' and 'Expresso Bongo', 'Belle' would seem to have had everything going for it. Its thirty-odd musical numbers were clever pastiches of songs made famous and/or written by Leslie Stuart, Harry Champion and Albert Chevalier. Its sets by Loudon Sainthill beautifully captured the loucheness and the lushness of Edwardian London. Its cast included comics Jerry Desmonde, 'straight man' to Sid Field, Norman Wisdom and many others; and diminutive Davy Kaye, whose one-man Salvation Army band turn to the tune of 'The Devil's Bandsman' stopped the show.

And yet 'Belle' met with howls of protest from the press. Among other scenes which drama critics objected to was the actual murder, with Crippen (played by George Benson) injecting hyoscine into various items of a gargantuan meat tea which he serves his wife. The reviewers also took exception to the scene where Crippen, about to saw up his wife, thinks better of it, uses the saw as a musical instrument. 'A Sick Joke with Music' is the way the review of 'Belle' was headlined in the *Daily Mail*, while Bernard

Levin's criticism in the *Daily Express* was so vitriolic that Wolf Mankowitz sent some of the cast dressed as pall bearers and bearing a coffin to Levin's office in Fleet Street.

'Clearly the British public were not ready for a musical based on a murder,' Monty Norman, who wrote the music and lyrics, commented when I talked with him. 'If "Belle" were put on now no one would bat an eyelid.' After all a musical based on Jack the Ripper has only recently finished a very successful London run.

'The Curse of Hilldrop Crescent?' More likely it was 'The Curse of Ursula Bloom' which put the kibosh on 'Belle', according to Wolf Mankowitz, who wrote the book for the musical. 'Miss Bloom reminded the public that Ethel LeNeve was still alive, and that she might be pained to find herself the heroine of a musical which poked fun at the Crippen tragedy,' Mankowitz recalls. 'As a result, there was a rush of sympathy for Ethel, and people stayed away from the theatre in droves.'

No sooner had plans for the musical been announced than Miss Bloom held one of her tête-a-têtes with Ethel in Croydon. 'We have talked about it (the musical), she and I, sitting at tea in her room, with the cloth she embroidered herself and the cake she made with her own hands,' declares Miss Bloom in an interview in the *Sunday Dispatch*.* 'No musical performance would coax her out of the quiet she has chosen,' the novelist adds. 'She asks only to stay as a shadow. For this poor woman does not forget. . . . Ethel LeNeve has her own music about him, and it is the grand opera of very deep emotions.'[4]

*   *   *

Wednesday, August 9, 1967 . . . Headlines are about equally divided between the United States Senate hearings on the effectiveness of the bombing of North Vietnam, and the Biafran struggle for independence, which has entered a crucial phase. Of deaths reported in the London press this date that of actor Anton Walbrook (he played the leading roles in 'Design for Living' and

---

* Miss Bloom appears to have been almost as interested in Ethel's skill as a needlewoman as she was in Ethel as a person. Thus, 'Tea was spread on a cloth that she herself had embroidered' (the *Sunday Dispatch*, June 27, 1954); 'Well, we had tea on a charming cloth that she had embroidered herself' (the *Sunday Citizen*, March 28, 1965).

'Watch on the Rhine') gets an obituary in *The Times*, while the popular dailies reserve their boldest type for the murder of playwright Joe Orton (real name John Kingsley), whose battered body was found in a North London bed-sitting room. Orton, the author of 'Loot' and 'Entertaining Mr Sloane', had been attacked with a hammer by his male flatmate, who had then committed suicide by taking an overdose of sleeping pills.

One may search the press in vain for any mention of the death in Dulwich of a gaunt, grey-haired woman aged eighty-four, whose name had once been in big headlines. 'Cardiac failure' and 'mitral incompetence' are the causes of death given by the attendant physician at the Dulwich Hospital. Expressed more simply, Ethel Clara Smith's tired heart had given out. Her neighbours say that in her latter years she had scarcely been ill a day, though she did suffer from eye cataracts. Ethel had been to see a Harley Street eye specialist, but he could do nothing for her.

Widowed and living alone at the time of her death, Ethel had managed despite her failing eyesight to remain cheerful up to the end, according to her neighbours. She was always ready for a gossip over a cup of tea, took a lively interest in what went on around her, though she was inclined to be close-mouthed when the conversation touched upon her past.

Did Ethel leave this life in the happy expectation of meeting her loved ones in another? Ethel had never been a religious person (the curate of St Martin's Church, Addiscombe, could not remember her ever having attended services, nor had she permitted a church visitor to call). But it may have been that at the last she was reconciled to the possibility of an after-life, the hope that had sustained Crippen at the very end. 'I cannot believe otherwise but that we shall be together in that other life I am going to soon,' Crippen had written to Ethel after his appeal against the death sentence had been turned down. Again, he writes of being with Ethel in spirit 'until we are united where there is no more separation.'

It is nice to picture Ethel meeting Hawley and Stanley, those two men who so strongly resembled one another, in some after life, and strolling with them hand in hand in elysian fields. Or perhaps even now they are listening to some celestial palm court orchestra from the vantage point of a table just below the pearly stairs.

APPENDIX

The twelve letters that follow, with one exception,
were written by Crippen to Ethel LeNeve from a
condemned cell at Pentonville Prison during the
period October 28-November 22, 1910. Ethel's
letters to Crippen for this same period were, at
his request, buried with him following his execution. The passages omitted for the most part concern business details that are of no general interest;
the omissions are indicated by dots. The exception mentioned is Crippen's 'Farewell Letter to
the World', which was printed in *Lloyd's Weekly
News* on November 20, 1910. This was intended
as a vindication of Ethel's innocence, and has been
abridged with this original intention in mind.

My heart has been bursting . . .

Pentonville Prison
Friday, October 28, 1910

You can imagine what my feelings are to have before me your dear handwriting again. I have longed so passionately for a letter from you to sustain me through the long and weary separation, and, although I have been able to subdue my nerves and preserve my outward control, my heart has been bursting and throbbing with the pain of longing for you and even for a few written words from my ever-loving darling. I knew my darling's heart and love for me would never waver in the slightest, and hope sustained me, and that our union has not only been for life but for all eternity.

But, dear wifie, do not yet despair. There is yet the appeal, and friends are coming forward to help. One here in England tells my solicitor he does not consider I had a fair trial, and offers to pay all expenses,* and, just think, Munyon has awakened to his old friendship for me and cabled he will spend £12,000 for me if necessary. I had also a letter from Lady Henry Somerset telling me you were to come to live with her to-day, but for fear that was not certain I am sending this care of Horace to be forwarded to you.†

I do not of course know if you are keeping your own name where you are staying, but I strongly advise you not to do so, and, wifie dear, it would please me so much if you would take my first name or my second Christian name, which you prefer — probably you prefer Hawley — and add 'Mrs' to it, as you will wear my (or our) ring as before. So tell me in your next how and where to address you, which will save delay.

My good things all came at once to-day. Your visit was a surprise. I have just returned from it, and sat down to my letter again.

* The 'friend' referred to is obviously Horatio Bottomley, who paid for Crippen's appeal; though whether Crippen was aware of the 'friend's' identity is not clear.

† Horace Brock, married to Ethel's sister Nina.

I nearly broke down, but struggled to be composed and not upset you. My own dear heart, how I longed even to touch your hand. To hold you in my arms would have been paradise, but we must look forward to that.

To return to what was taken from my pockets at Quebec, be sure you get the prescription for 'Sans Peine'. I have written to my solicitor to see that it is returned; but this will be your authority to demand it from him, and I want you to keep it safely until I tell you, darling, what to do with it. It may be of great value to us.*

Write me fully, wifie dear, and tell me everything, but don't arrange anything finally until my appeal is over, because I shall want you with me *at once* to comfort me and help me to regain my nerve, which is beginning to break down. If all goes well, as please God, I hope you will come to me at once, won't you, darling? After this I shall try and write often, and hope to have good letters from you. Dear wifie, greatest love of my heart and soul, God protect you and keep you safe.

*   *   *

Let us hope God will be good . . .

Pentonville Prison
Sunday, October 30, 1910

I had a letter from my solicitor saying the appeal might be heard on Thursday, and let us hope God will be good to us and bring me safely through in spite of all.

My solicitor writes me he gave you £5, and says he will make great efforts with regard to what I want from him to you. I have replied to remind him of his promise and insisted as plainly as possible in his allowing you 30s. a week as an advance until the Charing Cross Bank affairs are settled. I told him he ought to do it, as such a small weekly sum would not amount to much against the dividend that the bank is sure to pay out of £600, after some months. I write all this so you will know how to talk to him.

---

* Press reports state that a phial of liquid and a packet of white powder were taken from Crippen at the time of his arrest. These were the ingredients of the patent pain-killer which he had invented called 'Sans Peine', and which he was hoping to market in America.

I have also told him I decidedly object to anything on the stage for you, darling.*

My dinner is just waiting, and I must eat it while it is hot. Have just had a nice dinner — roast mutton, vegetables, soup, and fruit — and now back to my wifie again.

I have also told him that perhaps the friend who has come forward to pay the expenses of my appeal would be willing to advance the 30s. per week I want for you (if my solicitor will not do it).

Do not forget though, my own wifie, your promise to me to keep your money for yourself. If God helps us through safely, I myself, with you at my side to help me, will then help Horace to clear off all their debts as a little return for their great kindness.†
Please always when I write give my greatest love to them as I shall now only write to you for the present.

I am glad you arranged the newspaper matter as you did. Remember, you owe my solicitor nothing, as *I myself* arranged to pay all the expenses of the trial for you from the first. I am coming to the end of my letter, darling, and have not said half I want with regard to business, but must say this, there was £100 advanced by Mr Harvey (Mr Hamilton, he says), £114 odd realised from the sale of our furniture, and £500 for my memoirs.‡

*   *   *

So little time and space . . .

Pentonville Prison
Monday, October 31, 1910

My solicitor distinctly told me a friend had come forward and guaranteed payment of the expenses of the appeal with the understanding I would, in return, do certain things that were not to be

---

* Shortly after her arrest an American vaudeville circuit had offered Ethel £200 a week to appear in a sketch entitled 'Caught by Wireless'.

† Apparently Nina and her husband Horace were having financial difficulties. They had stood by Ethel in her troubles, and for that, if for no other reason, Crippen was genuinely fond of the Brocks.

‡ The 'Mr Harvey' referred to is Eddie Marr, Crippen's backer in the Aural Remedies Company, who operated under many aliases. The £114 realised from the sale of Crippen's household effects went to Arthur Newton, who had a first lien on it. The offer for Crippen's memoirs was from the *New York American*, a Hearst publication.

unreasonable, among which I might be asked to open business in America. Of course that would suit both of us, would it not, darling wifie? So you see, as the matter stands now, so far as I know — and my solicitor has not written me otherwise — the expenses of the appeal are provided for, and, besides, he has Munyon's offer.

I saw the two letters you enclosed about 'Lady S'.* I did not intend to write her again, but to-day I had a letter from her asking about you and saying she thought of publishing something which she thought would help my appeal, so I had to get permission to write and *forbid* her to do any such thing.

Oh! darling, there is so much I want to tell you and so little time and space. I told my solicitor to notify Scotland Yard that all property outside your own was to be sent to his office, and that no one has a claim on it but myself. This is to keep off those 'harpies' you mention. Legally, no matter what happens, *all* comes to me, and then I have instructed my solicitor you *must* be allowed to select what you want, and the balance is to be sold for you.

As to Char. X Bank, they must pay some dividend, and if only 1/4, that would mean a good sum. My greatest grief has been the disappointment in not being able to put *all* in your hands *at once* without all this trouble and make you independent of *all*.

One thing more on business, dearest. While at Brixton I wrote an account (12 foolscap pages finely written) of my experiences of seven weeks, and my solicitor has this, *yet unpublished*. I am going to ask him to give it to you to be rewritten, as, with your experiences, you can enlarge on it, and then sell it as a help to my own dear wifie.

Do not forget to insist on having at once the trunk of silver, and sell it to best advantage for present needs, and get the Brixton MSS. I have written, but get a good sum for it.

*   *   *

Not even death can come between us . . .

Pentonville Prison
Tuesday, November 1, 1910

Your visit last evening was precious indeed to me, but I am afraid I did all the talking, darling, and you had no time to explain

* Lady Somerset.

much. Probably you did not have time to write to me last night, as I have had no letter yet. Perhaps it may come later when the Governor comes in to see me.

In the meantime, wifie, I must content myself with those you have sent me up to now—four of them, and all treasured more than diamonds. I read them over and over again, and get great comfort from your loving words and the thought that, though we are separated, your love is all mine for always, as my love is yours to eternity. It is so precious a thought to me to tell you are always and ever my wifie, and that not even death can come between us. My heart rejoices in the promise that you will always bear the name you have taken, no matter what comes.

I suppose I am down-hearted to-day, because I have a letter from my solicitor saying the chance of anything from the Char. X Bank is most remote. I had looked forward to being able to provide wifie dearest the means of *my own* to keep you in comfort for a long time, and the bitterness of this terrible disappointment would be worse to me than death itself.

Pray God to help us in the appeal, that I may be spared to protect you again and keep you, darling, as I have always hoped. My only thoughts now are that you shall be kept from all harm in life, as I would keep you. We have been so long one in heart, soul, thought, and deed that, wifie darling, nothing can separate our inward consciousness and spirit.

I had notice also this morning that the appeal will be heard Thursday. Well, the sooner the better, if only my counsel and solicitor are prepared to fight.

*　　*　　*

There are many who can understand . . .

Pentonville Prison
Wednesday, November 2, 1910

You will find at Whitefriars Street safely to-day, I hope, the letter I wrote you yesterday. As I write I jot down the facts that come into my mind which I want you to know.

Do not forget the prescription for 'Sans peine' . . . You see, hub's darling, I am trying my best to see that you may be independent and not be led into any false step through obligation to anyone. I want my wifie's life to be a happy and comfortable one. That is the greatest desire of my heart. I had indeed hoped there would be enough left to let you establish yourself in some business, when you could order your life as you wished it, without being put into a position where another's will might force you to submit to anything opposed to your wishes.

I quite understand what people say, and even at the trial the prosecution deliberately misrepresented our relations to each other for their own ends. But I know there are many who can understand what we are to each other, truly husband and wife, sacredly so; no more sacred relations to each other such as ours could ever exist.

May God bless us again and restore us to each other, darling, and may God protect you and always keep you safe from harm. Every time I write you I find there is more to be said before I finish, and oh! how I long for our hopes to be realised that letters soon may no longer be necessary.

* * *

I dare not even hope . . .

Pentonville Prison
Friday, November 4, 1910

I hope you will find no trouble with my MS. As soon as you have it look it over, and during one of your visits tell me anything you do not understand. I expect they will want to make a copy of the plans of the buildings I have drawn, as they serve to illustrate. I hope you can obtain a good price for it, to add to what your clever little business has secured for your own work.

Yes, it is a comfort to me to know you have secured for yourself sufficient to carry you over 2 years, and if you do well with my MSS and in the sale of the furs, etc., I shall feel satisfied you will be well cared for.

I have had so many disappointments, I dare not even hope tomorrow will bring release, but oh! how I pray to be spared to take care of my own wifie and make her happy again.

* * *

Hub's heart is broken . . .

Pentonville Prison
Saturday, November 5, 1910

The Appeal has decided against us. Hope has completely gone, and your hub's heart is broken. No more can he hold his wifie in his arms, and the life he planned to devote to making your life comfortable is rapidly drawing to its end.

Death has no terror for me. I fear not at all the passing from this life, but, oh! wifie, my love, my own, the bitterness of the thought that I must leave you alone, without me in the world, to those who can never, I am sure, love you, cherish you, and protect you as I would have done hereafter as in the past.

These years past that we have been all in all to each other I was always looking forward to our happy life, to years together in a paradise of our own, like that we have always enjoyed since we have been everything to each other. I did not intend to write so mournfully, but my heart overflows in spite of all my efforts and opens itself to wifie, all I have in the world and all I ever wanted.

Your letter came after I had gone this morning, but I had it to-night, also another one, and one from Nina. Please tell Nina and Horace, although I cannot repay their great kindness to me, I shall pray God to help them through their troubles and make their life smoother and easier than in the past, and give them all my kindest love.

Your letters are such a comfort to me, my own wifie. I just feel your love surrounding me, and those dear, sweet words of your love shall lie on my heart at the last.

I hope you will have no trouble, now the appeal is finished, in getting everything from Scotland Yard through my solicitor. A new date will be fixed in place of Nov. 8th,* so I hope I shall be here long enough to know that you have everything all right. You see, I want you to have all my personal property, my watch, chain, plain-band ring, clothes, etc., as *my* gift to you now . . .

About the diamonds, I want you to have them to wear as long as you can afford to keep them and to sell to help you anytime you need money. I shall on Monday write my solicitor to hand all those things over to you.

To-day the Governor has written to the Home Office for permission for me to make a new will, explaining that I wish to cancel the one signed at Brixton, and also asking permission for the prison authorities to be witnesses . . .

I shall feel bereft of everything indeed if I cannot give you at

---

* Nov. 8th had been the date originally fixed for the execution. After the appeal had failed November 23rd was fixed as execution day.

least one good-bye kiss, but oh! wifie dear, I am fearful it may not be permitted. Still, when I know what day our last farewell must be, I shall beg the Home Office to grant us that favour.

It is comfort to my anguished heart to know you will always keep my image in your heart, and believe, my darling, we *shall* meet again in another life. We have been always so entirely one in heart and soul, thought and deed, even in flesh and spirit, I cannot believe otherwise but that we shall be together in that other life I am going to soon.

I am not so selfish, darling, as wish you not to marry again, but inasmuch as you have been the one woman who has had all my heart, so do I believe you will ever keep me in your heart.

If only I could have left you well provided for I would have wished our little one had lived that you might have had what would have been part of both of us. But, like other things, it was not to be . . .

If you can I should like to know your plans for the future before I am gone; it would be a comfort to me indeed to know how wifie, my own darling, is to be provided for . . .

I have not been able to keep the tears back to-night, the bitter news of the disappointment has been so terrible, and my longings for my wifie have been so intense. But I shall soon be brave again and keep up to the end.

Were it possible I would wish to be *cremated*, and wish wifie then *to dispose of my ashes as she desires*. Please, darling, when you think of something to suggest or ask me, put it down on a memo. to write me about or to ask me when you see me. The time is short, and we must try and think of everything for wifie's benefit and get all settled for you that I can accomplish.

To-day at the appeal I realised more and more that the medical evidence for my defence was so mismanaged that it told against me rather than for me. This I saw at the Old Bailey in the judge's summing up and again to-day in the summing up of the Appeal. I am powerless now, and can do nothing more, but bow to the inevitable.

*   *   *

Pictures of ourselves together . . .

Pentonville Prison
Sunday, November 6, 1910

All day I sit here by a table with my eyes on a book, and I suppose the guards believe me to be reading, but over and over again the words are only a blank before my eyes, and the book with pictures of ourselves together.

I see ourselves in those days of courtship, having our dinner together after our day of work together was done, or sitting sometimes in our favourite corner in Frascati's by the stairway, all the evening listening to the music. The dinner too with Nina with us, in anticipation of her marriage; and ah! how even in those early days we began to realise how near and dear we were to become to each other.

One Sunday, how early I came for you — six years ago last summer it was — and we had a whole day together, which meant so much to us then. A rainy day indeed, but how happy we were together, with all sunshine in our hearts. It is good to think, darling wifie, that even in those early days before our wedding came that we were always in perfect harmony with each other. Even without being wedded.

Then came those days when hub felt, and wifie too so earnestly felt, it was impossible to live on and not be all in all to each other, and from our wedding day all has been a perfect honeymoon of four years to Dec. 6 next.

*   *   *

Whatever God wills it to be . . .

Pentonville Prison
Undated, but circa November 13, 1910

What a nice long letter from you this morning, and what comfort do I indeed derive from wifie's loving words. I was anxious to read what you had written in my defence, and you have my wifie dear, most ably set forth important facts that must tell with great weight in the minds of the unprejudiced.* Well, we must wait patiently the end, whatever God wills it to be.

* Crippen is probably referring to the first instalment of Ethel's short autobiographical sketch which appeared in *Lloyd's Weekly News* on November 6th.

Should it be that I must die, I have no fear of that, sure of my wifie's comfort to the end and of being with her in spirit after, until we are united where there is no more separation. Should I be spared, we must look forward to time to prove my conviction unjust, with your help, to drag out the evidence that some day must be found.

I have never intended to wound you, wifie dear, with suggesting I might become a burden to you, but I know my wifie understands I could not bear to think my love might be so selfish as to ask of you an unreasonable sacrifice. Darling, my own wifie dear, you can see, I am sure, that my love for you has become so great, so absorbing that I was afraid I should ask of you, in my longings to be all in all to you, what would be unreasonable. But no, dearest, I shall only think now that as I would have been ready any time and at all times to lay down my life and soul to make you happy, so you too are mine for ever.

*   *   *

I first kissed your face . . .

Pentonville Prison
Monday, November 21, 1910

How can I find the strength and heart to struggle through this last letter? God, indeed, must hear our cry to Him for Divine help in this last farewell.

How to control myself to write I hardly know, but pray God help us to be brave to face the end now so near.

The thoughts rush to my mind quicker than I can put them down. Time is so short now, and there is so much that I would say.

There are less than two days left to us, only one more letter after this can I write you, and only two more visits, one to-night before you read this letter and one to-morrow.

When I wrote to you on Saturday, I had not heard any news of the petition, and though I never at any time dared hope, yet deep down in my heart was just a glimmer of trust that God might give us yet a chance to put me right before the world and let me have the passionate longing of my soul.

Your letter written early Saturday came to me late Saturday

evening, and soon after the Governor brought me the dreadful news, about ten o'clock.*

He was so kind and considerate in telling me, in breaking the shock as gently as he could. He was most kind and left me at last with, 'God bless you; good-night', that I know you will remember him most kindly.

When he had gone I first kissed your face in the photo, my faithful devoted companion in all this sorrow.

Oh! how glad I was I had the photo. It was some consolation, although, in spite of all my greatest efforts, it was impossible to keep down a great sob and my heart's agonised cry.

How am I to endure to take my last look at your dear face; what agony must I go through at the last when you disappear for ever from my eyes! God help us to be brave then.

*   *   *

Never have I passed one unkind word . . .

Pentonville Prison
Tuesday, November 22, 1910

When I received your letter on Sunday eve I saw that you did not then know the bad news, and I prayed God to help you in the morning when you did learn it.

I know what your agony will be, for I know your heart, like mine, will be broken. God help us indeed to be brave.

That is my constant prayer, now that the last refuge to which we had looked with some hope has fled.

I am comforted at least in thinking that throughout all the years of our friendship never have I passed one unkind word or given one reproachful look to her whom I have loved best in life, to whom I have given myself heart and soul, wholly and entirely, for ever . . .

---

* News that Winston Churchill, then Home Secretary, had refused to intervene with a stay of execution was given to Crippen on Saturday night, although it did not appear in the press until Monday morning, November 21st. Churchill's action came after petitions had been presented to him bearing 15,000 signatures and urging that Crippen's sentence be commuted to life imprisonment.

*   *   *

Farewell letter to the world . . .

Pentonville Prison
November 19, 1910

This is my farewell letter to the world. After many days of anxious expectation that my innocence might be proved, after enduring the agony of a long trial and the suspense of an appeal, and after the final endeavour of my friends to obtain a reprieve, I see that at last my doom is sealed and that in this life I have no more hope.

With all the courage I have I face another world and another Judge — from Whom I am sure of justice greater than that of this world and of mercy greater than that of men.

I have no dread of death, no fear of the hereafter, only the dread and agony that one whom I love best may suffer when I have gone . . .

About my unhappy relations with Belle Elmore I will say nothing. We drifted apart in sympathy; she had her own friends and pleasures, and I was a rather lonely man and rather miserable. Then I obtained the affection and sympathy of Miss Ethel LeNeve.

I confess that according to the moral laws of Church and State we were guilty, and I do not defend our position in that respect. But what I do say is that this love was not of a debased and degraded character.

It was, if I may say so to people who will not, perhaps, understand or believe, a good love. She comforted me in my melancholy condition. Her mind was beautiful to me. Her loyalty and courage and self-sacrifice were of a high character. Whatever sin there was — and we broke the law — it was my sin, not hers.

In this farewell letter to the world, written as I face eternity, I say that Ethel LeNeve has loved me as few women love men, and that her innocence of any crime, save that of yielding to the dictates of the heart, is absolute.

To her I pay this last tribute. It is of her that my last thoughts have been. My last prayer will be that God may protect her and keep her safe from harm and allow her to join me in eternity . . .

I make this defence and this acknowledgment — that the love of Ethel LeNeve has been the best thing in my life — my only happiness — and that in return for that great gift I have been inspired with a greater kindness towards my fellow-beings, and with a greater desire to do good.

We were as man and wife together, with an absolute communion of spirit. Perhaps God will pardon us because we were like two children in the great unkind world, who clung to one another and gave each other courage . . .

I myself have endeavoured to be equally courageous, yet there have been times during her visits to me when an agony of intense longing has taken possession of me, when my very soul has cried out to clasp her hand and speak those things which are sacred between a man and woman who have loved.

Alas! We have been divided by the iron discipline of prison rules, and warders have been the witnesses of our grief.

Why do I tell these things to the world? Not to gain anything for myself — not even compassion. But because I desire the world to have pity on a woman who, however weak she may have seemed in their eyes, has been loyal in the midst of misery, and to the very end of tragedy, and whose love has been self-sacrificing and strong.

These are my last words.

I belong no more to the world.

In the silence of my cell I pray that God may pity all weak hearts, all the poor children of life, and His poor servant,

H H Crippen

NOTES ON SOURCES

[1]

1 Book by Wolf Mankowitz, music and lyrics by Monty Norman.
2 Seymour Hicks. *Not Guilty, M'Lord*. London: Cassell and Company 1939.
3 *Daily Express* July 15, 1910.
4 *Evening News* July 15, 1910.
5 Walter Dew. *I Caught Crippen*. London: Blackie and Son, 1938.
6 Sir Melville Macnaghten. *Days of My Years*. London: Edward Arnold, 1914.
7 *The Times* October 26, 1910.
8 *Daily Telegraph*, July 15, 1910.
9 *Pall Mall Gazette*, July 15, 1910.
10 Don Ross in a letter to author.
11 *The People*, April 23, 1933.
12 Douglas G. Browne. *Sir Travers Humphreys*. London: Harrap, 1960.
13 Raymond Chandler. *Raymond Chandler Speaking* (Dorothy Gardiner and Katherine Walker, editors). London: Hamish Hamilton, 1962.
14 Max Constantine-Quinn. *Doctor Crippen*. London: Duckworth, 1935.
15 Filson Young. *The Trial of Hawley Harvey Crippen*. London: William Hodge and Company, Ltd, 1920.
16 *Ibid*.

[2]

1 Book by Wolf Mankowitz, music and lyrics by Monty Norman.
2 John Van Druten. *The Widening Circle*. London: Heinemann, 1951.
3 *Ibid*.
4 Young, *op. cit*.
5 Crippen's testimony at the Old Bailey, October 20, 1910.
6 *Daily Express*, July 15, 1910.
7 *New York American*, July 15, 1910.
8 *New York American*, August 1, 1910.
9 *John Bull*, December 10, 1910.

[3]

1 Clarkson Rose. *Red Plush and Greasepaint*. London: Museum Press Ltd, 1964.

2 *John Bull*, December 10, 1910.

3 *Los Angeles Examiner*, December 15, 1910.

4 Crippen's statement to Inspector Dew, July 8, 1910.

5 Crippen testifying at the Old Bailey, October 28, 1910.

6 Young, *op. cit.*

7 *Daily Express*, July 18, 1910.

8 Richard von Krafft-Ebing. *Psychopathia Sexualis*, 12th Edition. London: Heinemann, 1914.

9 Miller testifying at the Old Bailey, October 18, 1910.

10 Samuel Hopkins Adams. 'Preying on the Incurables'. *Colliers*, January 13, 1906.

11 Testimony given before the House of Commons Select Committee on Patent Medicines, July 11, 1912.

12 Evan Yellon. *Surdus in Search of His Hearing*. London: The Celtic Press, 1906.

13 Ethel LeNeve. *Ethel LeNeve: Her Life Story*. Manchester: The Daisy Bank Printing Company, 1910.

14 *Answers*, August 27, 1910.

15 *Weekly Dispatch*, August 7, 1910.

16 LeNeve, *op. cit.*

17 *Lloyd's Weekly News*, July 17, 1910.

18 *Lloyd's Weekly News*, November 6, 1910.

[4]

1 Harold Scott. *The Early Doors: Origins of the Music Hall*. London, 1946.

2 Naomi Jacob. *Our Marie*. London: Hutchinson and Company, 1937.

3 Young, *op. cit.*

4 Lord Birkenhead. *Frederick Edwin Earl of Birkenhead*. London: Thornton Butterworth Ltd, 1933.

5 LeNeve, *op. cit.*

6 *Answers*, September 3 and 10, 1910.

7 *Answers*, August 27, 1910.

8 *Truth*, July 20, 1910.

9 *New York Tribune*, July 17, 1910.

10 *Lloyd's Weekly News*, November 20, 1910.

11 *Daily Express*, July 15, 1910.

12 Crippen's statement to Inspector Dew, July 8, 1910.

[5]

1 Browne, *op. cit.*

2 Macnaghten, *op. cit.*

3 Dew, *op. cit.*
4 *Ibid.*
5 *Ibid.*

[6]

1 Dew, *op. cit.*
2 Young, *op. cit.*
3 Edgar Lustgarten. *Verdict in Dispute.* London: Allan Wingate, 1949.
4 *Ibid.*
6 *Le Petit Parisien*, August 7, 1910.
5 *Lloyd's Weekly News*, November 20, 1910.
7 Priestley, *op. cit.*
8 Crippen's statement to Inspector Dew, July 8, 1910.
9 Mrs Jackson's testimony at Belle Elmore inquest, September 9, 1910.

[7]

1 The letter is reprinted in the *New York American*, July 15, 1910.
2 Young, *op. cit.*
3 Hicks, *op. cit.*
4 *John Bull*, December 10, 1910.
5 *Pall Mall Gazette*, July 15, 1910.
6 *Answers*, September 10, 1910.
7 *Lloyd's Weekly News*, July 17, 1910.
8 Young, *op. cit.*
9 *John Bull*, December 10, 1910.
10 Michael Gilbert. *Dr Crippen.* London: Odhams Press, 1953.
11 *Daily Mail*, September 22, 1910.
12 LeNeve, *op. cit.*

[8]

1 Chandler, *op. cit.*
2 LeNeve, *op. cit.*
3 *Daily Mail*, July 18, 1910.
4 *Daily Mail*, September 20, 1910.
5 *Daily Mail*, July 18, 1910.
6 *Daily Mail*, September 20, 1910.
7 *Daily Mail*, July 18, 1910.
8 *Lloyd's Weekly News*, July 17, 1910.
9 *Ibid.*
10 *Daily Express*, July 16, 1910.
11 LeNeve, *op. cit.*

[9]

1 *Lloyd's Weekly News*, July 17, 1910.
2 *Los Angeles Examiner*, July 15, 1910.
3 *Daily Mail*, July 18, 1910.
4 *The Performer*, July 21, 1910.
5 Macnaghten, *op. cit.*
6 Dew, *op. cit.*
7 Macnaghten, *op. cit.*
8 Dew, *op. cit.*

[10]

1 MacDonald Hastings. *The Other Churchill.* London: Harrap, 1963.
2 Clarkson Rose, *op. cit.*
3 *Sunday Express*, October 6, 1933.
4 Marshall Hall's introduction to *The Trial of the Wainwrights*, edited by H. B. Irving. London: William Hodge and Company, 1920.
5 Macnaghten, *op. cit.*
6 LeNeve, *op. cit.*
7 *Daily Mail*, July 27, 1910.
8 LeNeve, *op. cit.*
9 Dew, *op. cit.*
10 *Daily Mail*, July 26, 1910.
11 Priestley, *op. cit.*
12 LeNeve, *op. cit.*
13 *Daily Mail*, August 2, 1910.
14 *Daily Mail*, August 1, 1910.
15 Edgar Wallace. *The Four Just Men.* London: Tallis Press, 1905.
16 Dew, *op. cit.*
17 *Daily Mail*, August 2, 1910.

[11]

1 Mrs Jackson testifying at inquest, September 19, 1910.
2 Dew, *op. cit.*
3 *The People*, April 23, 1933.
4 Marshall Hall, *op. cit.*
5 Chandler, *op. cit.*
6 Michael Gilbert. *Dr Crippen.* London: Odhams Press Ltd, 1953.
7 *The Times*, July 13, 1911.
8 *The People*, May 14, 1933.
9 *Daily Mail*, August 4, 1910.
10 *The People*, April 23, 1933.
11 A. E. Bowker. *A Lifetime with the Law.* London: W. H. Allen, 1961.

12 Edward Marjoribanks. *The Life of Sir Edward Marshall Hall.* London: Gollancz, 1931.
13 Bowker, *op. cit.*
14 Marjoribanks, *op. cit.*
15 Travers Humphreys. *Criminal Days.* London: Hodder and Stoughton, 1946.
16 *The People.* April 23, 1933.
17 *Ibid.*
18 *Daily Mail*, October 19, 1910.
19 Viscount Alverstone. *Recollections of Bar and Bench.* London: Edward Arnold, 1914.
20 *The Times*, October 24, 1910.
21 *The People*, April 23, 1933.
22 Lustgarten, *op. cit.*
23 S. Ingleby Oddie. *Inquest.* London: Hutchinson and Co., Ltd, 1941.
24 Douglas G. Browne and E. V. Tullett. *Bernard Spilsbury.* London: Harrap, 1951.
25 *Ibid.*
26 Humphreys, *op. cit.*
27 Crippen letter to Ethel LeNeve dated November 5, 1910.
28 Sidney T. Felstead. *Sir Richard Muir.* London: The Bodley Head, 1927.
29 Felstead, *op. cit.*

[12]

1 Felstead, *op. cit.*
2 Young, *op. cit.*
3 *Ibid.*
4 Marjoribanks, *op. cit.*
5 Young, *op. cit.*
6 Marjoribanks, *op. cit.*
7 *Ibid.*
8 Oddie, *op. cit.*
9 *Daily Mail*, September 13, 1910.
10 A. W. Blyth. *Poisons: Their Effects and Detection.* London: Charles Griffin and Company, 1884.
11 *Ibid.*
12 Louis Goodman and Alfred Gilman. *The Pharmacological Basis of Therapeutics.* New York: Macmillan and Company, 1941.
13 Oddie, *op. cit.*
14 *Evening News*, July 15, 1910.
15 *Daily Mail*, July 16, 1910.
16 François Truffaut. *Hitchcock.* London: Secker and Warburg, 1967.

17 Colin Wilson and Pat Pitman. *Encyclopaedia of Murder*. London: Arthur Barker Ltd, 1961.
18 Macnaghten, *op. cit.*

[13]

1 The Earl of Birkenhead. *'F.E.'*. London: Eyre and Spottiswoode, 1959.
2 *Ibid.*
3 Oddie, *op. cit.*
4 Young, *op. cit.*
5 J. C. Ellis. *Blackmailers & Co.* London: Selwyn and Blount, Ltd, 1928.
6 *Lloyd's Weekly News*, November 27, 1910.
7 *Sunday Dispatch*, December 10, 1939.
8 *Los Angeles Examiner*, August 1, 1910.
9 Margaret Lane. *Edgar Wallace: The Biography of a Phenomenon*. London: William Heinemann, Ltd, 1938.
10 Edgar Wallace. *A Short Autobiography*. London: Hodder and Stoughton, Ltd, 1923.
11 The poem is printed in Herbert Arthur's *All the Sinners*, published by John Long in 1931.
12 *Sunday Dispatch*, February 26, 1956.

— [14]

1 Book by Wolf Mankowitz, music and lyrics by Monty Norman.
2 Dew, *op. cit.*
3 *Sunday Citizen*, March 28, 1965.
4 *Sunday Dispatch*, January 29, 1961.